On Language

Other Avon Books Coming Soon by

William Safire

WHAT'S THE GOOD WORD?

William Safire On Language

AVON
PUBLISHERS OF BARD, CAMELOT, DISCUS AND FLARE BOOKS

AVON BOOKS
A division of
The Hearst Corporation
959 Eighth Avenue
New York, New York 10019

First Avon Printing, December, 1981

The Times Books edition contains the following Library of Congress
Cataloging in Publication Data:

Safire, William L.
  On language.

  Includes index.
  1. English language—Idioms, corrections, errors.
  2. English language—Usage I. Title.
PE1460.S16 1980 428′.00973

Printed in the U.S.A.

DON 10 9 8 7 6 5 4 3

To "Peter Porcupine"

Contents

Usage

Style

Contents

Slang

Origins

Pronunciation

Neologisms

Jargon

Dialect

The Great Permitter

They were sitting around in the executive editor's office on the third floor of *The New York Times,* breaking their heads over a new column in the Sunday magazine. A political column was not a good idea; a newsy analysis or informed polemic is best when it runs close to the news, with its closing deadline on the afternoon before the newspaper appears. *The New York Times Magazine,* with its color pages, closes a week ahead.

"Eureka!" shouted A. M. Rosenthal, the Executive Editor. To his colleagues, some of whom had not studied Greek, he added, "That means 'I've found it!' Safire will do a language column."

I had already written a 400,000 word political dictionary, which was a lexicographic success and a financial flop, and every year contributed a "Vogue Word Watch" column to the *Times Magazine.* ("Watch out for 'feisty' this year; it is even hotter than last year's 'perceived.' ") But I had no other linguistic credentials, not even a college degree. When the idea was presented to me by Editor Ed Klein—"Guess what, you'll do a language column—great idea, huh? How soon can you start?"—the thought crossed my mind that perhaps I was not yet equipped to become a Language Maven, Word Wizard, Pronunciation Arbiter, or Usage Dictator.

Moreover, I am the sort who worries about whether "breaking their heads," as used in the opening sentence of this introduction, is too slangy for literary style, or if *whether* should not be *if,* earlier in this sentence. Since *scratching their heads* is permissible to signify puzzlement, and since *breaking their heads* is in current use, but is more vivid and not such a cliché, I say to go ahead and use it. As to if/whether: When an alternative is implied, *whether* is preferred. Thus, "whether 'breaking their heads' . . . is too slangy" is correct, because the writer is obviously wondering whether *or not.* Later in that sentence, I wrote ". . . or if *whether* should not be *if,*" which is wrong—it should be "or whether *whether* should not be *if,*" because I am still talking about a choice. Rule: Use *whether* to signify a choice, *if* to indicate a general possibility or doubt.

Where do I come off, tossing about such terms as "permissible," "correct," and "wrong" in the previous paragraph? Who is to say what is "permissible" and what is not? Russell Baker wrote of the Great Mentioner, the secret source responsible for candidates being "mentioned for President"—on that analogy, where is the Great Permitter who prefers "if" for the conditional, "whether" for the alternative?

As Casey Stengel used to say: "You could look it up." That's what I did, in a half-dozen usage books. The authorities did not completely agree— Great Permitters display degrees of permissiveness—and so I had to think it over. My imperative, authoritative ruling, "Use 'whether' for choice, etc.," is based on what the other usage writers say, as amended by what I think.

Now to the question I asked myself before undertaking this enterprise, and which has been posed by hundreds of readers since. What, other than sheer chutzpah, gives authority to any language "authority"—or, as my correspondents put it, "Who the hell are you to say?"

I'm a working writer, that's who. (That's *whom*? No. Who is correct.) I write because I enjoy expressing myself, and writing forces me to think more coherently than I do when just shooting off my mouth. Because I both write to live and live to write, I have taken an interest in the implements of my craft. (Why *implements*? Why not the shorter and more understandable *tools*? Because that would draw me into "tools of my trade," a cliché. But isn't it better to use a convenient cliché than to seem to labor to get away from it? Yes; I should have written "tools of my trade.")

In this essay, I have been writing like a character out of Eugene O'Neill's *Strange Interlude,* spouting soliloquies in parentheses to show rather than to say how a writer about language writes. Such asides, when overused, are annoying to the reader; he does not like being constantly jerked back into a previous paragraph. But the writer, and the careful speaker, is constantly catching himself and correcting himself, if he cares.

There is a big difference between being conscious of your language and being self-conscious about the way you write and speak. To be conscious of language is to be proud of the magnificent and subtle instrument in your hands; to be self-conscious about the possibility of error, or fearful of the derision of your listener at your experiments with the instrument, is to be a nerd, a schnook, and a wimp.

Who are the Great Permitters? We are the people who care about clarity and precision, who detest fuzziness of expression that reveals sloppiness or laziness of thought. Henry Fowler was one; Ted Bernstein was one; Bergen Evans was one; Jacques Barzun is one; I'm one. If you've read this far and are prepared to go further, you're one. We live the life of the mindful, and we intend each utterance to say a mouthful. We are not fuddy-duddies: If we want to carefully and deliberately split an infinitive, we do so with zest, knowing that the most fun in breaking a rule is in knowing what rule you're breaking. (That's why I can get away with all these parentheses.)

Rules? Who the hell are you and I, then, to arrogate the right to make or defend rules, to assume responsibility for deciding what is "correct," to dictate what is to be embraced as good, preferred, or "standard" usage—and what is to be ridiculed and reviled as vulgar, barbaric, or confusing?

We are the people who care; we've registered for the linguistic primary. Our interest is our power.

Otto Jespersen, the Danish linguistic philosopher, defended his right to resist those who insisted that "usage is king." Esaias Tegner, who popularized linguistic research in Sweden, wrote in 1874: "The greatest absurdities in the world become correct, as soon as they have got Usage fully on their side, just as the worst usurper becomes legitimate, as soon as he is completely established on his throne."

Jespersen replied in 1925: "I am not one of those who recognize the worst usurper as legitimate as soon as he is firmly established on his throne . . . there is a higher linguistic morality than that of recognizing the greatest absurdities when they once have usage on their side." Then he set forth the Code of the Great Permitters. He granted the point of lexicographers who insist that the task of investigators of language is to describe the actual language in use, and not to lay down rules for a more orderly language they wish existed. "But at the same time," Jespersen wrote, "the investigator as a user of the language has the same right as others to influence the language where he can, and he ought to be able by virtue of his greater knowledge to do this with greater insight and greater effect than those who have no linguistic training."

Now we have come to the bone of contention that has been gnawed by everyone who works in the world of words: Do we "go with the flow," as the laid-back set advises, or do we try to direct the flow? Are we to be good scientists, clinically descriptive, or are we to be activists for clarity, prescribing the usage that helps a string of words make more sense?

I choose activism. I do not "opt for" activism, because "opt" connotes decision made on impulse, and what I do in this case is to chew it over before making a choice.

That choice of activism forces the next choice. Try an analogy: In politics, I chose conservatism. But that choice immediately forced another choice: Would I become a traditionalist, preserving the values of society, or a libertarian crawling out on that other branch of conservatism which rejects the force of organized society in determining individual moral decisions? For example, should prostitution, which is immoral, be legalized? Traditional conservatives, defending society's values, say no; libertarian conservatives say yes—it is the responsibility of the individual, not the government, to make moral decisions. I'm a libertarian conservative: Let thinking people decide for themselves.

In the same way, the linguistic activist—who is willing to struggle to conserve the clarity and color in the language—has to decide whether to be traditionalist or libertarian. (See? The "whether" is fine.) The traditional activist derides and often sensibly resists change in the language—why use "rip-off" when "theft" will do? Why concoct "contact" as a verb instead of "get in touch with"? The libertarian activist counters that "rip-off" graphically describes an act of theft, and by virtue of vividness as well as widespread acceptance deserves its place in the dictionary; "contact" may be a verb overused by businessmen, but has the same etymological root as "get in touch with" and is shorter.

A libertarian language activist is not one of those relax-and-enjoy-it purely descriptive types. He wants to cheer on "parameter," borrowed from mathematics and now used to mean scope, or limits; at the same time, he wants to hoot at such nonce expressions as "What am I looking at?" now used to mean "What are the consequences?" or "How deeply am I likely to become involved?" Similarly, he will welcome "full court press" from basketball lingo to replace the tiring "all-out effort," but will ridicule the vogue verb "defense against" from football, preferring the more direct "defend." It's a matter of taste.

English is a stretch language; one size fits all. That does not mean anything goes; in most instances, anything does not go. But the language, as it changes, conforms itself to special groups and occasions: There is a time for dialect, a place for slang, an occasion for literary form. What is correct on the sports page is out of place on the op-ed page; what is with-it on the street may well be without it in the classroom. The spoken language does not have the same standards as the written language—the tune you whistle is not the orchestra's score. Even profanity's acceptance changes: In the 30's, Clark Gable's line in "Gone With the Wind"—"Frankly, my dear, I don't give a damn"—was passed by the Hays Office provided the actor placed the emphasis on "give" rather than "damn." Today, traditionalists would be happy to settle for an emphatic "damn" rather than an earthier expletive.

The Great Permitters—both the demanding traditionalists and the selective libertarians—want to give this change a shove in the direction of freshness and precision. When we see "the embattled Secretary of Defense" in print, and we know the writer meant the significantly different "besieged," we feel beleaguered (besieged by encirclement). Adjective salad is delicious, with each element contributing its individual and unique flavor; but a puree of adjective soup tastes yecchy.

This urge to fight the good fight—"good" in the sense of "righteous," as in "the good Book"—explains the resurgence of interest in usage and jargon. Let's not go overboard—people who care about language are book-buyers and letter-writers, and the noise of our outcry makes us appear more numerous than we are—but the popularity of language books and dictionaries, and the torrent of mail that pours in whenever I misuse "who" for "whom," suggests a growing lust for standards in speech and writing.

My "Shame on You!" file is bulging, despite the establishment of a separate file under "Y" for letters that begin "You, of all people. . . ." The correct spelling of the town called "Chumly" is Cholmondeley. Protests about puns are ignored (let a simile be your umbrella), but nit-picking about tired or mixed metaphors is respected and acted upon. I once wrote a speech for Everett Dirksen hailing "a firm hand on the rudder of the Ship of State," and a letter-writer set me straight with, "If that's true, somebody is drowning, and nobody has a hand on the tiller."

These letters of constructive criticism and warmly apoplectic chastisement make up the best part of this book. The constituency of English-lovers is also responsive to queries, as columns on "mondegreens," shibboleths, and "fumblerules" have illustrated. The Lexicographic Irregulars who have taken it upon themselves to set me straight or help me out (I should do a piece on the proliferation of "out"—in teenage argot, "out" is "in") make clear that the language activists have never been more active.

Some of the interest in the world of words comes from people who like to put less-educated people down—Language Snobs, who give good usage a bad name. Others enjoy letting off steam in a form of mock-anger, treating their peeves as pets. But most of the interest, I think, comes from a search for standards and values. We resent fogginess; we resist manipulation by spokesmen who use loaded words and catch phrases; we wonder if, in language, we can find a few of the old moorings. We are not groping for the bygone, we are reaching for a firm foothold in fundamentals. And we are pushing for the personally possible: Since we cannot get our hands on macroeconomics and defeat inflation, or single-handedly sweep back the Soviet tide, we seek some other area where personal action has effect—we can stand fast against the tide of solecisms that enshrines ignorance and fight the inflation of modifiers that demeans meaning.

The old moorings are in the process of moving out to sea, as they have always been in the English language, but a decent respect for the usage ukases of the Great Permitters offers this generation some sense of orderliness in discourse. To paraphrase Emerson on being well-dressed, the knowledge of speaking correctly gives the speaker a feeling of inner tranquillity that religion is powerless to bestow.

The sense of powerlessness that has been bothering so many intellectuals—anomie-tooism—should stop at the edge of language. There, in classroom and home, some personal muscle can be flexed: "Different from" is preferable to "different than," because "from" separates more strongly than "than." Oldsters may find it hard to discuss the old spine of self-reliance, or to adapt to the tieless-in-Gaza dress codes, or to hear children call their teachers by their first names, but when it comes to the basic tool of human communication, some guidance bottomed on the unchanging values of clarity and grace can be provided. A start can be made by denouncing mushy meanings and high living in syntax.

People who care about good writing, whether readers or writers, have the power to set the criteria for good usage higher than that level acquiesced in by Norma Loquendi. The common denominator—another term for "usage"—need not be a standard to which those hooked on elegance or grace, or zonked out on vividness or precision, can repair. Common usage excuses; good usage demands.

The phrase "movers and shakers" has come to mean "big shots," or "power elite." Its origin in Arthur O'Shaughnessy's poem suggests that all of us in the legion of language lovers may have more linguistic influence and cultural potency than we realize:

> *We are the music makers,*
> *And we are the dreamers of dreams . . .*
> *Yet we are the movers and shakers of the*
> *world forever, it seems.*

On Language

abbreviations, *see* **ZIP codes**

Abscam, *see* **stings and scams**

accordingly, *see* **clearly in vogue**

ace

"Ace," from the Latin word for single unit, means a Number One achievement, the work of an expert: In cards, an ace counts as higher than a king; in golf, an ace is a hole in one, and in tennis, an unreturnable serve; in aviation combat, it is a pilot who has shot down at least five enemy planes. As a noun, it rests securely in the dictionaries.

As an adjective, however, this necessary descriptive word has never been regarded as more than a colloquialism, and is in decline. It occasionally is played in crisp, informal newspaper copy; columnists Evans and Novak wrote recently of "ace Soviet diplomat Vladimir Vinogradov."

The columnists could have chosen the trite "highly regarded" or "top-ranking," or the pompous "distinguished" or "esteemed"; their selection of "ace" carried a connotation of derring-do, of the lone expert, of the high card being played. As an adjective, it has a snappy, sassily informal air; "ace" is to an individual what "crack" is to "troops."

I think of Ace Parker, Brooklyn Dodger professional-football quarterback, tossing one of his unique jump passes, just as radio reports interrupted the game with news of the raid on Pearl Harbor. Come back, "ace," as an adjective, from your linguistic limbo—we need a word that takes "first-rate" and "premier" and adds a little of the loneliness of the long-distance winner.

Dear Mr. Safire:

The language of the deaf, sign language, or more specifically, Amslan, puts each English word, group of words or concept in its most basic form, one word, which is then translated into one sign.

An example from your recent column comes to mind—"ACE" becomes #1 and the sign for #1 is used for the ace in cards, ace in golf, tennis ace, and that lone, brave pilot. Whether the person is distinguished, top-ranking or other, s/he is #1!

Conversation is less fraught with complications in American Sign Language. If you want to tell your friend with whom you have just attended a movie that it was, in your opinion, really terrible, that you couldn't stand it, etc., the one gesture which means "vomit" is signed, graphically, and tells it all! ...

> *Sincerely,*
> *(Mrs.) Fran Blakeney*
> *Concord, New Hampshire*

Dear Mr. Safire,

Your affection for the word "ace" would be tempered if you talked to Sid Zelinka, an old comedy writer who has worked for the Marx Brothers, Jackie Gleason, Carol Burnett and many others.

Sid once told me that whenever he wanted something to sound slightly shady, he called it the Ace ———. Thus the Ace Detective Agency had a boob for a boss. The Ace Laundry always tore the sheets. The Ace Auto Repair Agency was to be avoided like, how shall I say, The Plague.

> *Sincerely,*
> *Philip Cohen*
> *New York, New York*

---

adverbial lapel-grabber

Julie Williamson, a native of Texas now studying New Yorkese, writes: "Lately I have been particularly aware of a certain mode of expression which—in my experience—is peculiar to this area: to 'see visually' (or 'visually see'), to 'verbally tell,' to 'physically pull' (or 'put, place'), to 'manually place' ('put, pull') to 'search physically,' to 'see personally,' and others which—at this moment—I cannot mentally recall. Am I alone in thinking such constructions to be redundant?"

No, Miss Williamson, you are not solitarily alone. You are among the multitudinous many who wince at being subjected to the adverbial lapel-grabber or weakening reinforcer pressed upon us by speakers who worry about being considered too unimportant to be listened to—or who think their listeners are too preoccupied to understand.

David B. Guralnik, at Webster's New World Dictionary, calls this "the redundancy of the colloquial" and cites such familiar tautologies as "enormous giant," "brilliant genius," and "penniless pauper." The adverbial lapel-grabber, he says, is no longer used merely to reinforce the speaker's point: "Today, I suspect, the speaker is trying to make sure that he will not be misunderstood. It's all of a piece with 'Ya unnerstan?' 'Know what I mean?' "

"Such expressions are now particularly characteristic of young business types, who are often not sure that they are getting across," this lexicographer personally writes. "And no wonder. It is probably also a symptom of the verbal avalanche used these days in snowing others. Or do I have my metaphors logically transposed?"

Guralnik has, indeed, put the fall before the snow, but he has an insight lurking in his inundation. Because so much of today's discourse is vague and insubstantial, a need has arisen to break through and make an impression. For example, "to see" has come to mean "to perceive" to such an extent that when the speaker means *to see with your eyes,* his temptation is to say "to visually see," and even to add, "I mean, with your eyeballs and the optic nerves reporting reality directly to the brain."

Same with "physically," which once meant merely "bodily," but has come to mean "with your own hands, actually, none of this metaphoric stuff or promises about the future, but really, no-foolin', made to happen in a way that produces discernible results." That is the meaning of "I want you to physically make sure he gets this." (The lapel-grabbing "physical" has recently come to mean "a football team adept at inflicting pain on opponents without incurring penalties.")

Thus, when "I personally feel" anything, I am saying that my feeling is mine, all mine, and not gleaned from advertisements or the result of Lazarsfeld's Theory of the Two-Step Flow of Communication from source through opinion leader to me. No opposite exists: A person is no more likely to say "I impersonally feel" than a football announcer is likely to say "The reason they're flat is that they are a very mental team."

Advertising: Belt the kids!

Bank advertising has begun to give me withdrawal symptoms.

"Free Gifts Galore and a Whole Lot More From Citibank" offers the outfit that used to call itself The First National City Bank of New York before its imageers went on a diet of short'nin' bread.

"Free" gifts? What other kind of gifts are there?* Like lions, gifts are etymologically born free. When it offers "a dazzling array of free gifts," Citibank is either hinting that the competition is offering gifts that are sneakily unfree, or is making a redundant deposit in its word account. It is possible for gifts to be described as "costly," but never from the point of view of the receiver. It's either free, or it is a gift; it is never a free gift.

Citibank—the name evokes Ian Fleming's car, *Chitty-Chitty-Bang-Bang*—is to be commended, however, for its new slogan, "The Citi Never Sleeps." This is derived from "The Eye That Never Sleeps," the slogan of the Pinkerton's detective agency which appeared under a picture of an open eye and was the origin of the phrase "private eye."

Over at what used to be called The Chase Manhattan Bank (when The Chase National Bank merged with the Bank of The Manhattan Company) the name-chopping has resulted in calling the place "the Chase," which was evidently preferred to "Chabank."

In a curious Chase advertisement, a woman in a doctor's smock is saying "Once my future became clear I put the Chase behind me." This was obviously intended as an extension of the bank's slogan, "You have the Chase behind you," but as I understand the language, the phrase "to put something behind you" is to forget about it. Writes Richard Philips of Matawan, N.J.: "When I first read the headline to this advertisement, I thought the next words from the doctor would be, 'Thank goodness, I never have to bank there again!' "

In Washington, D.C., banks bank on radio spots, and the enumeration of "free gifts" often starts with "plus." For some reason, the name of this mathematical symbol for addition has been snatched from the center of equations and placed smack at the head of sentences, as if to mean, "Not only that, folks, but—"

The "plus" phenomenon was observed by the poet Karl Shapiro in 1971: "There had come into the debased speech of a certain breed of American college student the word *plus—at the beginning of a sentence!*" He quoted one student as saying "Plus I really love it when the school is so quiet," and wondered, "If they use *plus* as *also* or *alors* or *allora* or the beautiful *and yet* or *still*—if they use *plus* to start a period, then why not *minus?* 'Minus I don't like to go home.' Or *equal:* 'Equal he isn't exactly my type.' "

Moreover (a word the plusniks never deign to use), the use of "plus" as a sentence-starter goes far beyond bank advertising. The Strand Book Store in New York, my favorite haunt, headlines its catalogue: "*Plus* Reviewers [sic] Copies of New Books at Half Price." And that's where I buy my dictionaries.

Credit the people at Citibank and Chase with getting the word "savings"

See "Redundancy redounds" for apology.—W. S.

right. What you put in a savings account is your savings. However, when you save money by finding a bargain, you drop the "s." Advertisers who urge you to hustle to their emporia "for a fantastic savings on your winter wardrobe" mean "fantastic saving." Watch out for such "saving"; the only good play on the word is in Panasonic's advertisement for its electric beard chopper: "shaving grace."

In this week's harangue, I seem to be taking apart the work of the advertising copywriter; the target is inviting, but some of the most careful English is used in advertising copy. Many copywriters are unnecessarily self-conscious about their commercial craft—indeed, they should be prouder of their contribution to vivid and persuasive language.

Consider the Maine Highway Safety Committee, concerned about the number of children maimed in auto accidents because seat belts were not fastened. The committee's adman adopted a zingy slogan that has been going the rounds in the safety dodge: "Have you belted your kids today?"

Then, on second thought, not wanting to offend the child-abuse crowd, the committee withdrew the advertisement. How pusillanimous! That copy line was a grabber, an unforgettable caution—why throw it away because some humorless types may take a play on words seriously?

I have pasted a card on my dashboard: "Belt the kids!" It's a livesaving reminder to the driver, and keeps some passengers in line, too.

Dear Mr. Safire;
   You wrote:

> *For some reason, the name of this mathematical symbol for addition has been snatched from the center of equations and placed smack at the head of sentences, as if to mean, Not only that, folks, but—*

I believe that "plus" as a mathematical symbol is not found at the center of an equation, but that the equal symbol is. Indeed, the very word "equation" would bear me out. Picas aside, the only center of an equation would be that symbol for which this mathematical form is named.

Very truly yours,
Dennis Purcell
New York, New York

Dear Mr. Safire:
   "Free gifts? What other kind of gifts are there?"
   *When you yourself said, in another context in the same article, "Let's try to keep the singular and plural meanings separate...."**
   Your style of word patterns are very unfortunate. Plus you have a brilliant mind, but lousy grammar.

Grammatically,
Alice E. Coleman
Brooklyn, New York

Afghanistanism, *see* crisis crisis

---

airline-ese

Why is a stewardess (excuse the sexism—"flight attendant") trained to say "Mint?" when she offers you what most other people would call a Life Saver? Not because the airlines want to avoid plugging a commercial product. The reason "Life Saver" is taboo is the same as the reason "safety belts" are now called "seat belts": Airline-ese is the language of reassurance, and they don't want anyone reaching for a piece of candy to get the notion that the pilot is preparing to ditch.

   The studiously lazy drawl of the pilot (soon to be designated Supreme Commander of the Flight Deck) is part of the orchestration of careful unconcern. Writer Tom Wolfe, in a recent *Esquire* article on pilot Chuck Yeager, described "a particular folksiness, a particular down-home calmness that is so exaggerated that it begins to parody itself ... the voice that tells you, as the airliner is caught in thunderheads and goes bolting up and down a thousand feet at a single gulp, to check your seat belts because 'it might get a little choppy.'"

* See *"ethnic and other slurs."*—W.S.

This drawl, affected by most pilots, originates in Appalachia: "in the mountains of West Virginia, in the coal country, in Lincoln County so far up in the hollows that, as the saying went, 'they had to pipe in daylight.' In the late 1940's and early 1950's, this up-hollow voice drifted down ... down, down from the upper reaches of the flying fraternity to all phases of American aviation. ... It was 'Pygmalion' in reverse ... pilots from Maine and Massachusetts and the Dakotas and everywhere else began to talk in that poker-hollow West Virginia drawl, or as close to it as they could bend their native accents."

This aw-shucks, flyin'-is-jes'-a-piece-a-cake tone mingles with certain familiar phrases to soothe the overly wary. One such phrase, part of every airline announcement made by every airline employee, with each word bitten off, Brinkley-style, is "at ... this ... time." Everett Briggs of the U.S. Embassy in Columbia* is bothered by "Passengers are requested *at this time* to observe [*sic*] the no-smoking sign." (You don't observe a sign, you observe the rule.) "Flight 907 is ready for boarding *at this time.*" Never "now"; give an airline employee a microphone, and he becomes a throwback to the train announcer for Jack Benny, reciting with glazed tonsils the schedule for "Anaheim, Azusa and Cucamonga."

This formal informality is designed to soothe by boring. It takes off in fuzziness: "Welcome to the New York *area,*" and "At this time, we are beginning the boarding *process.*" And it cruises on euphemism: Ask a flight attendant for a barf bag and see what a look you get—not for being nauseated, but for being so uncouth as not to request a motion-discomfort container. On the cruise, however, a pretentious new term has been upchucked: The airline-industry verb *to deplane.* "Passengers will deplane by the rear door." Never "Please leave by the rear door." The fine old verb "debark" has been put over the side.

Have to go now; my pet, Peeve, is debarking.

Dear Mr. Safire,

Your thoughts on stewardess-ese were fascinating. (I have, by the way, once heard the phrase "now at this time": and English stewardesses still allow you to "disembark"—note, not "debark," which has something to do with trees.)

But the most chilling phrase, for an Englishman, uses the word "momentarily." English usage has the meaning "for a moment": American usage "in a moment." Every time an American stewardess tells me that my plane will take off momentarily, I have visions of kangaroo-hopping across the countryside to wherever I am going.

Your comments on airline euphemisms reminded me of an early Xerox story.

* See p. 250 for the tirades on my misspelling of Colombia.—W.S.

Some government agency requested early machines to be fitted with a fire extinguisher. A fire extinguisher implies fire, and the thought terrified management. After a lot of creative thought, machines were sent out with a small green cylinder inside (not red) prominently labeled "Smoke Eliminator." Which, after all, is what a fire extinguisher ultimately does. . . .

> *Yours sincerely,*
> *Nicholas Lane*
> *Pittsburgh, Pennsylvania*

In your airline-ese be sure to add the word "off-load." I.e., passengers on the Logan Airport shuttle bus "wishing to off-load" at the Airport Hilton must notify the driver.

> *Bon voyage,*
> *Lisa Schwarzbaum*
> *Cambridge, Massachusetts*

alphabet soup

Alf Landon's Republican Presidential campaign of 1936 was notable for three slogans: "Land a Job With Landon"; "A New Frontier" (picked up later and used more effectively by another nominee); and "Up With Alf—Down With the Alphabet," an aspersion cast at the proliferation of "alphabet agencies" set up by President Roosevelt.

How fares the alphabet agency today? Triumphing, the way that the word "proliferate" is defeating "spread." Rarely do Supreme Court Justices allow their exasperation to show through in their opinions, but recently one of the brethren had to plow through an outburst of initialese:

"O.F.C.C.P. regulations require that Chrysler make available to this agency written affirmative action programs (A.A.P.'s) and annually submit Employer Information Reports, known as EEO-1 Reports . . . which culminate in Compliance Review Reports (C.R.R.'s) and Complaint Investigation Reports (C.I.R.'s) respectively."

This form of writing was too much for Justice William H. Rehnquist, who added this footnote to the opinion he wrote on behalf of the Court, where it now stands as a kind of terminological *obiter dictum*: "The term 'alphabet soup' gained currency in the early days of the New Deal as a description of the proliferation of new agencies such as W.P.A. and P.W.A. The terminology required to describe the present controversy suggests that the 'alphabet soup' of the New Deal era was, by comparison, a clear broth."

alternate/alternative

In telling the world not to use "centers around" when it meant "centers on," I wrote: "The confusion stems from the alternate phrase 'revolves around.' "

The point was right, but the use of the adjective "alternate" was wrong. A reader in England makes this correction: "To use 'alternate' as a synonym for 'alternative' is considered to be a sign of semiliteracy outside the U.S.A. Unfortunately, Webster's Third Unabridged allows this [misuse]. The two words really do have quite separate and distinct meanings: 'alternate' implies the taking of turns, and 'alternative' implies a choice."

If you are one of those who believe that usage determines "correctness," then Webster's III is right—"alternate" can be used as a synonym for "alternative," and the nice distinction that our English reader makes can be ignored. What's more, history will be on your side: A century ago, "alternative" meant "by turns," and was even then synonymous with "alternate."

But if you like to use words that split hairs and make meaning more precise, then you will tell common usage it is befogging a useful difference by merging "alternate" with "alternative." Sometimes it is worth putting up a scrap.

Start with the verb "to alternate" (pronounced *AL-ter-nate*) and carry its meaning over to the adjective "alternate" (pronounced *AL-ter-nit*). You have a useful modifier that says, in a word, "First this one, then that one," or, "Now me, then you, then me again, and so on." Don't corrupt "alternate" with any other confusing meaning.

Then take "alternative," which means the choosing of one out of two courses; as a noun, it means such a choice (or "option"), and as an adjective, it is a synonym for "substitute." Limit it to that.

You have now struck a blow for precision. Lexicographers will call you elitist—"a self-appointed 'protector' of the language"—but a worthy distinction deserves all the protection it can get. Let's not blow alternately hot and cold on this: the alternative to holding the line is fuzziness.

anachronism

A phrase that has come into use since the Soviet invasion of Afghanistan is "the second cold war," or "cold war II," and was probably coined in the mid-70's by Richard J. Whalen, now a key Reagan defense adviser. (An aide or adviser who isn't "key" is locked out.)

This brings to mind the best intentional anachronism I ever saw, useful in illustrating the meaning of that word. Comedian Sid Caesar, in a skit about the doughboys in 1918, came onstage in an Army uniform and shouted happily, "World War I is over!"

Dear Mr. Safire:

You tell us that you think the best intentional anachronism was Sid Caesar, dressed as a doughboy, shouting "World War I is over!"

My favorite comes from D. H. Fischer's Historians' *Fallacies (*Harper & Row, 1970*): "Dear Diary, The Hundred Years' War started today."*

Chacun à son goût.

> Sincerely,
> Frank J. Stech, Ph.D.
> Senior Psychologist, Mathtech
> Bethesda, Maryland

---

androlepsy, *see* crisis crisis

---

anxious or eager?

An item pointing to the distinction between "anxious" (worried, apprehensive, anticipating* with dread) and "eager" (ardent, impatient, anticipating with joy) touched a chord in more readers than any other subject except "who-whom." (The whomniks are an organized lobby, from who we can soon expect a single-issue-candidate, with headquarters in Qom.)

"Up-tight and anxious" was the way Billy Carter's personal physician, Dr. Paul Broun, described his patient, using "anxious" correctly, from its roots in *"Angst"* and the Latin word for "pain." Billy was anxious about an F.B.I. investigation, and certainly not eager to testify.

Yet "anxious to" is often used to express anticipation with enthusiasm,

---

* *Warren W. Smith, of the Columbus, Ohio, Academy of Medicine, informs me I misused "anticipate" in the above: That word should contain the element of foreseeing with the possibility of forestalling. What I should have written was "expecting with dread" and "expecting with joy." —W.S.*

and without the fear of pain. Does this common usage make it right? Sir Ernest Gowers, in his revision of Fowler's *Modern English Usage,* thinks so: He calls the use of "anxious" to mean "eager" a "natural development" and the difference now negligible. On the other hand, William and Mary Morris in the Harper Dictionary of Contemporary Usage hold that "careful speakers use *anxious* when some doubt or worry exists ('She is *anxious* because the plane is long overdue') and *eager* when the mood is one of joyous anticipation ('I am *eager* to hear the awards announced')."

We cannot say that the use of "anxious" minus its *Angst* is incorrect—in the end, usage calls the tune—but we can say that people who know the difference and use the word precisely are more expressive of their meaning. I am anxious about my misuse of "who" a few paragraphs back; a whomnik would be eager to correct me.

A little group of willful men, representing no opinion but their own and anxious about the fuzzying-up of English, are eager to make an issue out of "anxious-eager." Hats off to them; the fight may be a loser, but it is the good fight to call attention to the beauty of precision in speech.

---

any more/anymore

"Time was," I wrote in a column about the sudden exodus of talent from the National Security Council, "an N.S.C. job was the most coveted in Washington; not anymore."

You can write anything anytime, anyplace, anywhere, about anybody, but you have to be careful about "any more," which is sometimes two words and other times one.

When you're talking about something additional—as "I don't have any more . . ."—it is two words; when you are using it as an adverb, as "I don't want to work for the N.S.C. under Brzezinski anymore," it is one—"anymore" modifies the verb "want."

So all the people who wrote "shame on you" letters will kindly get off my back. One astute critic, however, brought out an interesting point: the tendency toward word implosion. "I'm seeing 'anymore,'" writes Emerson Stone of CBS News, Radio, "'golfball,' 'awhile,' 'someday,' 'lifework,' 'everyday' (as an adverb), the doubly opprobrious 'alright,' and even, from Senator McGovern, the title of his book, *Grassroots.*" Where will it all end? Are we headed toward collapsing all the 600,000-odd English words into one long word? Imnotsurethatsalltothegood.

Anyway (in any event), you can't just use "anymore" in any way.

WILLIAM SAFIRE

Dear Mr. Safire:

I suggest there's more to be said about "any more" vs. "anymore" than you say in your column. Memory tells me that "any more," whether used as adverb or adjective or noun, was invariably spelled that way (except maybe by the semi-literate) until some 25 years ago. The only dictionary in which I've found so much as a passing reference to "anymore" is Webster III, which (as I recall—I haven't a copy at hand) remarks that it's sometimes spelled as one word, especially in the countrified-colloquial sense of "now, nowadays," as in "We always drive downtown Saturday nights anymore." Fowler, in a brief article on "any" and its compounds, doesn't mention "anymore." I feel sure that if there had been accepted uses for it in the 20s, Fowler would have discussed them.

Probably the most famous curtain line ever uttered by Ethel Barrymore (in Captain Jinks of the Horse Marines?) was "That's all there is, there isn't any more." Years after that, there was the song "Annie Doesn't Live Here Any More." Still later, though, along came Tennessee Williams with The Milk Train Doesn't Stop Here Anymore. And I believe it was not so long afterwards that even The New Yorker began capitulating, first just in cartoon captions but soon to the extent of fussily placing a hyphen after "any" at the end of a line if the next one started with "more." The New York Times had capitulated much sooner, though it must have been in Theodore Bernstein's heyday. Did he like "anymore" if it was being used as an adverb?

My point is that "any more" isn't analogous to "anyway, anyhow, anything, anybody," etc., each of which is pronounced as one word, with the stress on the first syllable. However used, the "any more" combo is always pronounced as two words. Instead of trying to persuade people to make the fine distinction you make in your article, why not urge them (as I gather some of your readers have urged you) to abide by "any more" in any circumstance? I'm afraid, though, that this is one more lost cause. Everybody, everywhere, will spell it "anymore" in every circumstance, and then we'll all start pronouncing it that way, too, and nobody will remember the nice exact look of "any more" anymore. Thus the language wends its downward way.

Ruefully yours,
Dan Wickenden
Weston, Connecticut

Dear Mr. Safire:

The distinction which you seek to draw between the spellings "anymore" and "any more" (one supposedly adverbial and the other non-adverbial) has no basis whatever in traditional usage. The orthographic barbarism "anymore," currently popular in this country, is not recognized as correct anywhere else in the English-speaking world and was not recognized here until Webster III ushered in the present era of lexicographical permissiveness. The rule governing such combinations is that they must be stressed on the first syllable ("ányway,"

14

"ányhow," "ánywhere," "ányone," etc.); "any more" always has final or level stress and therefore does not qualify for this treatment. It might also be noted that even the most abandoned devotee of "anymore" would not think of writing "nomore" or "somemore." (Observe the parallel adverbial use of these three: "I won't do it any more"; "I'll do it no more"; "I'll do it some more.")

Yours truly,
Louis Jay Herman
New York, New York

Dear Mr. Safire:

I wondered whether you had run into another usage of this term (only oral, in my experience, so the word-separation question is another matter), particularly among Southerners. Its meaning tends to be "these days," or "currently"; for example: "A good man is hard to find anymore," or "What's the world coming to anymore . . ." Without reference to previous action, now discontinued.

Anyone else notice this?

Cordially,
Robert Amerson
Murrow Fellow
Tufts University
Medford, Massachusetts

Dear Mr. Safire,

You are absolutely correct that you can't just use "anymore" in any way, but you are apparently naive as to the degree to which it is being abused these days.

Here in the Philadelphia area (I am a native New Yorker—accustomed to waiting on line) they do very strange things with "anymore." My understanding of "anymore" indicates that it is used only with a negative statement—as "He doesn't live here anymore." However, around here folks make statements like "I didn't have a car then, but anymore I do," or "We never used to go there, but anymore we do." It is used in a positive sense, synonymous with "now." Further, it is misplaced in a curious Germanic (Pennsylvania Dutch?) construction, and this is true even when it is used in the negative sense, as in "Anymore we can't get gas for the car."

When I try to point out the oddness of this use of the word, people look puzzled. Is this a local disease, or has it spread? Please advise.

Sincerely yours,
Dorothy Harrison, Ph.D.
(Psychology, not English)
Rosemore, Pennsylvania

apostrophe

As the decade of the 80's approaches, we can be sure that pundits and panjandrums will pen such pieces as "Whither America in the 80s?" and "Through the 80's and Beyond." The big question that faces all of us in these end-of-the-decade thumbsuckers is: Does the plural of a number take an apostrophe?

The answer is yes. (If you prefer: The answer is "yes.") We are not leaving the 1970s, we are leaving the 1970's—or if you like to abbreviate, as in the "spirit of '76," we are leaving the 70's. Not the '70s. (The apostrophe goes only before a single year, not a decade.)

Why? Some editors take umbrage at the apostrophe: Lizanne Poppens of *The* (Springfield, Ill.) *State Journal-Register* objects: "It is NOT 80's. . . . In no way is '80s any kind of possessive (as 80's implies). Secondly, the only difference between the 1980's and '80s is the apostrophe, which correctly takes the place of the absent 19th century." (We're in the 20th century, but you get her meaning.)

I disagree. An apostrophe—from the Greek word meaning "turn away"—is a mark inserted when you turn away from using a letter, as in "spit 'n' image." Or it is a doohickey that makes a word possessive, as in "Copley's." Or it is used to form the plurals of numbers and letters, like "mind your p's and q's" (in learning to print, the "p" is often confused with the "q," its mirror image) and "dressed to the nine's" (possibly a reference to the nine Muses, or a corruption of "to the eyes"). Separate uses, different reasons—the use of an apostrophe does not imply a possessive outside its specific use as a possessor.

Dictionaries differ on decade endings, but most prefer the apostrophe—"How well I remember the 40's"—with the exception of decades that are parts of phrases, like "Gay Nineties" and "Roaring Twenties."

While on this subject, let me answer Karen Drew of Paducah, Ky., who has a son named Charles and wonders if she is "Charles' mother" or "Charles's mother." Dear Charley's Mother: You're "Charles's mother," because almost all names and words ending with *s* take an apostrophe as well as another *s* to form the possessive. When this rule causes you to trip over your tongue, for goodness' sake, break the rule.

Apostrophes have always been my Achilles' heel. Why not "Achilles's heel," like "Charles's mother"? Because classical names traditionally take an apostrophe only, without an *s*. That's an idiom. An idiom is language's way of telling logic: "Sorry, Charley, that's the way life is in the 80's."

p's and q's

In a recent item about the apostrophe, there was a small catastrophe: the derivation of "to mind your p's and q's" was ascribed, probably mistakenly, to printers who often confused the two similar letters.

Several readers and a bartender contend that the phrase comes from "mind your pints and quarts," a British customer's warning to a barkeep not to charge for a quart when only a pint was served. To such hawk-eyed drinkers, "p and q" meant "good measure"; such a citation, dated 1612, can be found in *Slang and Its Analogues* by Farmer and Henley: "Bring in a quart of Maligo, right true: and looke, you Rogue, that it be Pee and Kew."

Though the origin is still uncertain—"prime quality" is another possibility—that 1612 use seems solid enough to accept. I enjoy barroom linguistics. Here's a New Year's Eve example, from a drinker who prefers inebriation to surgery: "I'd rather have a bottle in front o' me than frontal lobotomy."

Dear Mr. Safire:

You wrote of the derivation of "p's and q's" in a way with which I differ. Is it not the case that the usage came from minding one's pints and quarts in English taverns, from keeping a careful tab on one's account, or being careful not to go beyond one's limits, financial or otherwise?

Sincerely,
William J. McKeough
Glen Cove, New York

Dear Mr. Safire:

Your argument regarding the use of the apostrophe is shaky at best. You needn't go as far as Springfield, Illinois, to find those who oppose your position and exclude the apostrophe from plural numbers. To begin with, the Modern Language Association (MLA), located right here in NYC, does not use the apostrophe as can be witnessed on page 873 of the most recent issue of PMLA *(94:5). To offer just one more example, such superfluous use of punctuation is considered anathema by Prof. David V. Erdman, Blake scholar and Editor of the* Bulletin of Research in the Humanities (*formerly* Bulletin of the New York Public Library). *As former Editorial Intern of the* Bulletin, *I deleted a fair number of these interlopers, though I estimate more than half the manuscripts received had already omitted them.*

Finally, your possible explanations for the saying "dressed to the nine's" are pretty far-fetched. I'm quite sure this is an Americanization of the British expression that "it takes nine tailors to make the man," referring to one's hatter, glove-maker, etc.

Of course I enter into this debate with the same sense of sport with which I believe you conduct it. But tell me, is it fun to be so constantly under fire? Keep ducking. All best wishes,

> *Sincerely,*
> *John Tessitore*
> *Brooklyn, New York*

Dear Mr. Safire:

I'm pleased to see you setting your readers straight on forming the possessive for words ending in "s," but for the life of me I can't find mention in any reference books of your rule that classical names ending in "s" are exempt from the rule.

I opened Robert Graves's I, Claudius *at random and found: "Thasyllus's knee"; "Augustus's religious reforms"; "Germanicus's men"; "Varus's defeat," and numerous other examples.*

It is my understanding that the rule for forming the possessive of all s-ending words is that if an additional "s" is sounded, it is written; otherwise, the apostrophe alone is called for.

If this rule about classical allusions is a new one, let's start a campaign against it.

> *Sincerely,*
> *Otto Janssen*
> *Hopewell, New Jersey*

appropriate, *see* **inappropriate**

-arama, *see* **mogulese**

arts, *see* **Experience counts**

ASAP's fables

When this column stumbled on the stage, eyes blinking at the bright lights of Sunday, a question was posed to readers: When you want somebody to call you back in a hurry, but you do not want to alarm them with fears of a medical emergency, what word do you use?

"Urgent" is too strong a word; besides, its overuse leaves nothing available in case of a genuine emergency. For example, the French Embassy in Washington sends out all its press releases marked "urgent"—even to pass on the dreary information that "government will spur growth," as if growth were a horse. The French Ambassador should ponder Talleyrand's advice to diplomats: "Above all, not too much zeal."

"Pressing" is the word suggested by one reader, presumably a tailor. Another claims that "mini-emergency" works without striking fear, and an airline executive suggests "without fail." A gentle soul suggests "When he has a chance, please have him call me back," which never works for me. A former government official offers "Please expedite response," and a puckish attorney gets results with "with all deliberate speed."

One Penelope K. Amabile, who describes herself as a "barnstormer, balloonist and adventurer," uses "or else" on her phone messages—return her call "or else."

Since many phone messages are now left on a recording following a beep, some readers report they use a bit of vigorish in their tone of voice. "Very important," normally banal, can be delivered on a recorded message-taker with weight, sexiness, and mystery. Sondra Langford of Chatham, N.J., has this dramatic technique: "I can move my friends to return a call quickly by stating my name and phone number, and no more, in a weak voice." The implicit message: Call before it is too late.

The word, or acronym, that was suggested most frequently was "ASAP"—"as soon as possible." "Soonest," a term from telegraphese, was another favorite.

Max Frankel, editor of *The New York Times* editorial page (which appears regularly opposite the Op-Ed page), adds a note of poignancy: "In emergencies, I say I am anxious. Otherwise, I say I am eager. Preserving the distinction is one of my personal, losing causes."

Dear Mr. Safire:

The press releases which you mentioned as originating from the French Embassy in Washington are in fact sent out by this office in New York.

May I point out however that the press releases and other documents we are happy to send you are not marked "urgent": it is the envelopes they are sent in which bear the word you scorn. Our purpose is not to inflate the importance of the texts we send you, but to be sure that they reach your desk as soon as possible (ASAP, if you will).

You will probably reply that such an injunction to the letter carrier is super-fluous, or that it goes without saying. May I therefore quote another bit of advice from our favorite foreign minister, the Prince de Talleyrand: "Things that go without saying go even better if they are said."

> Sincerely,
> André Baeyens
> Le Ministre Plenipotentiaire
> Ambassade de France
> New York, New York

As I was saying

Unaccustomed as I am to grammatical prescription, let me register an objection to the overuse of "as."

"The New York Times Company named Walter Mattson as president," wrote *The Wall Street Journal,* "succeeding Arthur Ochs Sulzberger, who remains as chairman." Neither "as" is needed (though both men are needed, desperately). Later in the same story, the "as" is dropped: "He also was named chief operating officer." We do not need "as" following designating verbs—"appointed," "anointed," "designated," "named"—any more than we need "to be" following choice verbs—"picked," "chosen," "elected," "selected." Cross 'em out, they clutter up sentences.

Silly as it sounds, the sloppy "as" is stealing a march on "though." Though it has a long tradition of usage in phrases like "much as I hate to do this to you," the growth of the use of "as" as a concession weakens our sentences. Example: "As ordinary-looking as he was, he was unique" is not nearly as concise or emphatic as "Though ordinary-looking, he was unique." Though the concessive use of "as" is legitimate, it is not as strong a concession as "though."

Another construction reaching for our throats is "equally as." Why should something which is "equally valid" be expanded to "equally as valid"? Such an "as" creates an unnecessary complication. "He is equally as infatuated with Jane as with Barbara" is more awkward than "He is equally infatuated with two women." (Such a person should at least drop his infatuation with "as.")

Dear Mr. Safire,

In your column "As I was saying," you have the sentence "Cross 'em out, they clutter up sentences." I see where you're comin' from, but I was always taught that principal clauses not joined by "if," "and" or "but" should be connected by semicolons, not commas.

I like what you're doing; keep up the good work!

> Constructively,
> John Harris
> Toronto, Ontario

Dear Bill,

You of all people surely know that the first member, when a negative precedes, is not any longer "as" but, instead, "so": E.g., "His explanation of whom he'd been with was not so clear as she had hoped it might be." Incorrect usage would be: "His explanation of whom he'd been with was not as clear as, etc."

> Best,
> James C. G. Conniff
> Upper Montclair, New Jersey

Dear Mr. Safire:

As you entered into your attack on the overuse of "as," I was aquiver with anticipation. But you failed me.

As reprehensible as all your other "ases" put together is the word's use in place of "since" or "because": "I can't have dinner with you tomorrow, as I will be in Washington."

Some dictionaries accept this usage. I don't. I hope you don't.

> All the best,
> Samuel Rovner
> New Hyde Park, New York

I do.—W.S.

---

ate-haters

Some Thistlebottom, whose marbles are all puries, is taking leaky pen in hand at this moment to write a complaint about "commentate," a clip used here to mean "making analytical noises like a commentator."

The complainant is the same type who comes out of an orientation course and likes to say he finds it difficult to "orientate" himself, and wanders off to the school administrator to see if that worthy can "administrate" some cold comfort.

Let's get back to verbal basics: If you want to orient yourself, or get the administrator to administer intelligently, we can stop commentating and start commenting.

Dear Mr. Saffire,

... Not only are the purists snobs who want to make the language of the masses conform to their standard, but they use the full force of their power to enforce changes which they desire but which I believe are not fully thought out.

The affix ate *is a good example of this type of action. To simply state that words such as* orientate *and* administrate *are acceptable but* commentate *is unacceptable is not enough. Making such changes in a linguistic vacuum leads to the fragmentation observable in our society as more and more people do not learn how to deal with their own language. Over these past twenty years I have learned to see language as a totality, one which has evolved to its present state having a magnificent underlying structural regularity. The affix* ate *is perhaps the most commonly used structure in the system. Every word ending in the letter sequence* ation *is in reality a combination of two more basic structures—*ate *and* ion. *As with all such combinings, the* e *in* ate *is sublimated in favor of the following vowel (*i*) in the structure* ion. *Such an action does not occur when the structure to be added begins with a consonant, as in* appropriately *or* ultimately *or* articulately.

One frequently hears the affix ate *added to words by non-English-speaking people seeking to find an appropriate word. Recently I heard a French-speaking woman create two such words to fit her meanings—*reformate *(reformation) and* confrontate *(confrontation). Grammatically they were absolutely correct for she used them as verbs, a function incidentally which is the norm for the structure* ate *when it is affixed to root structures. A purist might laugh or feel superior to such usage, but it is my belief that such structural formations were once the rule and it is only usage which has forced the elimination of* ate *in some cases. And we pay a price for we have lost the unconscious signaling function which the visual appearance* ate *played in decoding such words.* Comment *must now appear in a contextual setting if we are to recognize it as a noun or a verb, whereas* commentate *could only signal the verb function of the word.*

I believe the best rule of thumb to use in developing an awareness of the correctness of a word ending in ate *is to go one step further and ask if there is a more complex structure in which the affix* ate *is retained. I personally see no reason to look askance at someone who says, "I don't know how to multiplicate," since what he is doing is multiplication, especially when I don't require him to use the word "duply" when I want him to duplicate some papers for me.*

We all learn or inherit a sense of language and its order at birth since the entire experience occurs in a language milieu. A child is being perfectly logical when he says, "I sleeped all night long last night." The inflection ed *fits all other such real experiences in his life, why not sleep? He will learn as we all do that there is an order to the deviations, or apparent deviations, in his language and he will eventually learn the entire category of such change, as in weep-wept, keep-kept, sleep-slept, creep-crept, etc. . . .*

Sincerely,
Raymond E. Laurita
Director, The Learning Center
Yorktown Heights, New York

Dear Mr. Safire:
You insult me. I am a reader and I take your comments personally. I am not a Thistlebottom. My ballpoint pen does not leak. My marbles were not all puries. Indeed I suspect that the proportion of members of the Times *editorial staff whose marbles were all puries is far greater than the proportion of* Times *readers who had no common marbles.*

If we analyze the possible consequences of your definition, To commentate—"make analytical noises—emulate a commentator," we must consider the fellow who actually comments. Is he a commentor engaged in the process of commention? I might, being weakened by having just been subjected to Parents Orientation at the university my son will enter this fall, agree that the result of sitting through an institutional orientation is to become "orientated." But, what about the fellow in the wilds who is trying to align his map with prominent, recognizable features of his environment? Is his process oriention? Or the chap who actually administers his department, is his process administion? Also if swimming is natation, is making motions in the appearance of swimming to be natatation?

Sir, maintain certain values. Neither change nor resistance to change are intrinsically good. To commentate, or orientate, to administrate . . . this is the language of the White House. Do we wish such a lexicon to propagate, to proliferate? I promise you, if you no longer commentate I will remain oriented as I wander through the linguistic jungle.

Very truly yours,
Richard F. Pavley
Stamford, Connecticut

---

aw-ri-i-ight!

The sound most often made by happy discocrats is "Aw-ri-i-ight!"

Black athletes may have originated the locution, which is often spoken while a hand slap is substituted for a handshake, first up, then down. The

combination of word and gesture seems to mean, "That's cool," or, "Nice goin'," or, "Look-a-me, I'm on top of the world."

The word sounds like "awry," as in "What has gone awry?" The origin, presumably, is "all right," but the "ll" is silent, the "i" is drawn out, and sometimes the "t" is clipped. Oldsters who try to pick up on ("pick up on" is upbeat-music slang) teen-agers' lingo often err in pronouncing the "ll" sound, a sure sign of cultural ignorance. I tried it, and my daughter sympathized with "That's aw-wrong!"

Dear Mr. Safire,

While I hate to leave myself open to the charge of being a klauznik*, I'd like to call your attention to your description of a handshake, first up, then down. Try it. What you'll get is the sound of one hand clapping, four times.

Regards to your daughter.

Sincerely,
Cory R. Greenspan
New York, New York

banana

To most Americans, the word "depression" has come to mean a psychological funk rather than an economic slump. Memories of the "Great Depression" have faded, and most of us shy away from the term in its economic sense.

* *See "pettifogging."—W. S.*

Politicians thought F.D.R. had killed the word for good in the 30's, just after a Republican suggested that New Deal policies might cause a depression. Said President Roosevelt: "There is an old and somewhat lugubrious adage that says: 'Never speak of rope in the house of a man who has been hanged.' In the same way, if I were a Republican leader speaking to a mixed audience, the last word in the whole dictionary that I think I would use is that word 'depression.'"

Although thus buried at a crossroads with a stake through its heart, the word has risen, Draculalike, again. Alfred Kahn, chairman of the Council on Wage and Price Stability (who is described briskly as "the nation's chief inflation fighter" or "anti-inflation czar") partook of the forbidden word recently: "If the inflation accelerates, is permitted to accelerate, sooner or later we will have such a tightening, such a total breakdown of the organization and morale of our economy that we will have a deep, deep depression."

The Administration's chief word-fighters promptly called in the innocent czar and read him the Riot Act (an English law, passed in 1715, which could be read to disperse a crowd of 12 or more). Not only was "depression" taboo, but "recession" was frowned upon as a word for economists of good will.

Mr. Kahn got the message. He announced he had never predicted any, uh, "that word," and, being a man of puckish humor, added that whenever he felt the urge to reflect on the possibilities of recession, he would substitute the word "banana." He has since been heard to mutter, "The worst banana you ever saw."

"Banana" is a funny word, as Mr. Kahn—who resembles a young Jimmy Durante or an old Woody Allen—well knows. A "banana republic" is ridic-

ulous; a "banana boat" is slow; the word is often used in a get-away line by political speakers who say: "I'm like the little girl who said she knew how to spell 'banana' but never knew when to stop."

Calling a recession a banana is better than calling it a "rolling readjustment," a "crabwise movement of the economy," or—borrowing a phrase from moonshot pioneering days—"a soft landing." The problem is that editorialists across the country have already begun to characterize every knee-jerk, cheery Administration statement in the face of bad news as "Yes, We Have No Banana."

In a related gaffe, Mr. Kahn (husband of Czarina Kahn) warned labor leaders that he "does not want to give the impression that there's flexibility around the corner." ("Fred, baby, we want you to forget that phrase 'around the corner.' And there'll be no 'chicken in every pot' either. . . .")

Bananaville, *see* ethnic and other slurs

---

bent out of shape, *see* White House-ese

---

between a rock and a hard place

Embarrassed at having publicly released secrets that helped *The Progressive* magazine explain how to make an H-bomb, a Department of Energy official in Washington, D.C., insisted: "We are not involved in a cover-up. We got caught between a rock and a hard place. . . ."

On that same day, in Boise, Idaho, the head of the Farm Bureau—who had arranged grain sales with Libya, a nation pressuring Idaho's Senator Frank Church into approving the sale of troop-transport planes—was quoted as saying: "Church is in between a rock and a hard place."

Where is this rhetorical tight spot? As a metaphor for a difficult decision, it has wrestled "the horns of a dilemma" to the ground and inundated "the devil and the deep blue sea."

Thanks to lexicographer Anne Soukhanov, formerly of Merriam-Webster and now with the American Heritage Dictionary, we have a clue to the origin in a 1921 issue of *Dialect Notes.* "To be between a rock and a hard

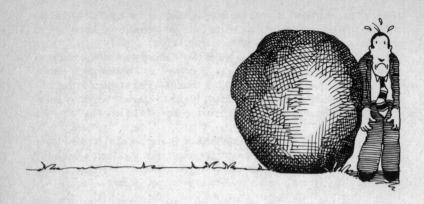

place," wrote Professor B. H. Lehman, was "to be bankrupt," and he reported that the Western phrase was "common in Arizona in recent panics, sporadic in California."

Originally applied to a person who is "tightly pressed" for money to the point of bankruptcy—as if between a rock and a substance even harder than a rock—the expression became generalized as it moved eastward and was applied to anyone in trouble (or, as a vogue phrase would have it, in Big Trouble).

The Arizona phrase has established itself so securely in the American language that it rates wordplay; when Washington editorialists were discussing a headline for a piece on Iran, a nation with borders on Iraq and the Soviet Union, one wag suggested "Between Iraq and a Hard Place."

We may assume with confidence that the metaphor will be turned around one day to apply to its opposite: "Sitting pretty" or "in the catbird seat" will have as a jocular synonym "between a marshmallow and a soft place."

Dear Mr. Safire,

You can go back a little further, Mr. Safire, about 2,000 years back to the Roman writer Titus Maccius Plautus. Plautus wrote comedies in Latin. Usually a slave was involved in helping his master getting into and out of predicaments. At Brooklyn College in 1938, I took Prof. Joseph Pearl's course in Plautus. Prof. Pearl made the Latin come to life as we translated some of Plautus' works. In one play, the slave was in a real predicament and said, in Latin, "Inter aram saxumque sto." Translated, this means "I am standing between the altar and a rock." The audience did not need much imagination to picture the slave on his knees, acting out this situation: the slave has his head on the altar and a priest is holding a stone, ready to bring it down on the slave's head. When he says, "In between the rock and the altar," he's in a tough spot because he is very close to being killed.

Enough about Plautus. Just thought you would like to have this epexegesis.
>*Cordially,*
>*Allen Sher*
>*Professor of Education*
>*College of St. Joseph the Provider*
>*Rutland, Vermont*

Dear Mr. Safire:

Mirabile dictu, you and your lexicographers have goofed again. It's hard to believe that no New York Times Magazine staffer was able to tell you that the origin of the phrase "between a rock and a hard place" was classical mythology.

According to Webster's Second College Edition, the phrase is a descendant of "between Scylla and Charybdis"—a rock and a whirlpool in the Straits of Messina—"neither of which can be evaded without risking the other."
>*Yours,*
>*Larry Sherman*
>*Bronx, New York*

Dear Mr. Safire,

When I was a young girl, back in 1918 or thereabouts, and was studying ancient history, our teacher explained a similar expression "Between Scylla and Charybdis."

Is it possible that the "rock" and the "hard place" came into being because the names in the classical phrase were hard to recall, hard to spell, or forgotten entirely?
>*Sincerely,*
>*Marjorie D. Wetzel*
>*Danvers, Massachusetts*

---

bi the bi

Bi means "two." A *bicycle* has two wheels. *Bilateral* talks are between two nations, as against multilateral talks, when everybody chimes in. *Bipartisan* means "two-party" and is different from *nonpartisan*, meaning "no-party." *Bicentennial* means "every two centuries," *biennial* means "every two years," *bimonthly* means "every two months."

Here comes the trouble: some people use *biweekly* to mean "twice a week," and many people use *biannual* to mean "twice a year." They've been doing that ever since the locution began more than a century ago, and the dictionaries dutifully define *biweekly* as meaning both twice a week and every two weeks.

The time has come to end the confusion. *Bi* should mean "two" and not "twice." No more pussyfooting, no more stylebook admonitions to avoid the troublesome prefix by writing "twice a year" and "every two years." I don't want to get prescriptive or anything, but the people who use *bi* for "twice" should cut it out. If you mean "half," and don't want to say "half," use *semi;* if you want a good old word for half a month, try "fortnight," which comes from "fourteen nights."

Language offers many blessings, and the greatest of these is clarity. Get a bumper sticker: "Bye-bye, bi! (meaning 'twice')." Use *bi* only to mean "two"; glare at others. Maybe we'll win. This plea will be repeated biannually. (For tickler file: Repeat in two years. Or in six months.)

---

bloviation, *see* rhetoric

---

boggling the mind

Believe it or not, the vocabulary of disbelief has come into its own. Years ago, the standard response to a startling statement was "You've got to be kidding," which replaced the ancient "G'wan" and "Pshaw!" Now, the most popular phrase in teen-agers' patois—picked up and amplified by television sitcoms—is "I don't believe it," usually pronounced, "I don't buh-LEEV it," and its variant, "I don't buh-LEEV this."

The meaning of the phrase goes well beyond "I give no credence to what you say"; rather, it connotes "I don't believe I'm standing here, rooted as I am in reality, and listening to this incomprehensible blather," or "Why must I have to suffer the presence of nincompoops?"

Advertisers have quickly moved to capture the spirit of the expression of open-mouthed wonderment. Drawing on the "credibility gap" of the 60's, the Ford Motor Company has built a campaign for its 80's models on the word "incredible." One of its television models, thunderstruck by the innovation in the new cars, asks, "Is there such a word as 'incredible-er'?"

No, but there is a word in the hottest vogue for that next stage after "in-

credible": the favored locution is "mind-boggling." "Boggle" is a jowl-shaker of a verb, in the same league with "stagger" and "stupefy."

The original "bogle," one "g," was the name of a ghost, specter, apparition, or goblin. When horses shied with fright, they were said "to boggle"—as if they had seen a ghost. In humans, this alarm can be false: "You boggle shrewdly," says a character in Shakespeare's *All's Well That Ends Well,* "every feather starts you." The sense of alarm—of stepping back in sudden fright—has been replaced by a meaning of "to perplex, astound, shock, overwhelm with complexity or vastness." Because the phrase conjures spirits from the vasty deep, "to boggle the mind" has a built-in exaggeration that pleases those who delight in irony.

Perhaps this hype of hyperskepticism will soon pass into disuse: Would you believe what happened to "would you believe"?

---

bogus titling

"Fugitive financier Robert Vesco . . ."

Mr. Vesco, accused of many manipulations and currently on the lam, is invariably described as a "fugitive financier." Maybe it's the alliteration that does it, but the title has fused with his name in all newspaper accounts. He owns that title, just as Howard Hughes retired the title of "reclusive billionaire," and Ralph Nader has laid claim to "consumer advocate."

Similarly, certain adjectives have affixed themselves to institutions. The Ways and Means Committee is always "the powerful Ways and Means Committee," and the Chrysler Corporation is now "the ailing Chrysler Corporation." (For a time, "financially troubled Chrysler Corporation" had a fling, but the brisk "ailing" won out.) Children reared on TV and radio news think one auto manufacturer is named "Ayling-Chrysler."

Time for a change of bogus titles. "Renegade richie Robert Vesco ..."

---

bomfog, *see* rhetoric

---

bouquet of flowers, *see* Redundancy redounds

---

cannot help but, *see* Help! but

---

census-ese

The 1980 census will be the first to have pretested its words. ("Pretested" is silly, as is "prerecorded"; kill the redundant "pre.") The phrasing of the questionnaire was tested four years ago in a National Content Test on 28,000 households to discover what would be most understandable and inoffensive.

"Head of household," that mainstay of previous national nose counts, has been beheaded. "The unfortunate assumption in the 1970 census," says Arthur Norton, chief of the Census Bureau's branch of Marriage and the Family, "was that the 'head of household' was male." Instead, the former h-of-h is now referred to as "Person in Column One," defined cautiously in the questionnaire as the household member "in whose name the home is owned or rented." If the lease or title is signed jointly, the Census Bureau caves in quickly to avoid a fight, pleading with "any adult household member" to pose as the Person in Column One (let's call the boss PICO). The Person in Column Two, which is what domineering women will be calling their henpecked spouses from now on, is asked about his/her relationship to PICO. "Husband/wife" or "son/daughter" offer easy choices, but one cate-

gory is sensitive: the person with whom PICO is sharing bed and board in an unmarried state. Walter Cronkite, reporting on the Lee Marvin case, called such paramouring "a live-in relationship"; writer Jane Otten reviewed many of the possibilities in a *Newsweek* piece titled "Living in Syntax": cohabitor, friend, fiancé, lover, consort, companion, swain, suitor, and mate.

The official United States Government name for one who lives with another without benefit of clergy is now "partner/roommate." Mr. Norton rejected "living together as consensual partners" as too complex for his questionnaire, and turned aside "bio-companion" because "it implied a relationship of a physiological nature and is therefore too restrictive." He chose "partner/roommate" because he wanted to play down the sex angle—as he puts it, "It said the least about personal relationships."

"Sex" is forthrightly listed as one of the categories (choices are limited to "male" and "female") as is "marital status"; however, one category, which used to be called "race," goes nameless. The Census Bureau, nibbling its nails in fear of the word that is the root of "racism," simply asks, "Is this person ———," and then lists "White," "Black or Negro," "Japanese," and 12 other racial or ethnic groups.

"The Census Bureau eliminated the word 'race,' " explains David Silver, a statistician familiar with the National Content Test that determined the present questionnaire, "because to include it with the 15 categories would not have been scientifically sound. Is Guamian really a race? We didn't want people to stop and ponder these kinds of questions."

At the urging of some black leaders, the word "Black" was placed before "Negro," a reversal of the 1970 form; however, "White" is not accompanied by "Caucasian." "There was no pressure to do so," explains statistician Silver, "and the addition might have added confusion."

In a question about schools, the time-tested "parochial" was dropped this

33

year, and the compound adjective "church-related" was substituted. The test in 1976 showed "parochial" to be less understood than "church-related." The Census Bureau, groping for the lowest common denominator, tossed out "parochial" (from "of the parish," and originally rooted in the Greek for "stranger in a foreign land") and replaced it with the compound adjective, a favored snippet of bureaucratese.

American Demographics magazine noticed that the housing category included a question on condominiums (the plural is "ums," as in "Tums") for the first time. In the 1976 test, the Census Bureau used the noun "cooperative" and was surprised by an inflated figure—many PICO's checked that word if they lived in public housing, or belonged to a food cooperative or neighborhood association. The more specific word for an individualized form of cooperative ownership, "condominium," drew a more accurate response.

A hopeful note: In the 1980 question about water supply, PICO is asked: "Do you get water from ( ) a public system? ( ) an individual drilled well? ( ) an individual dug well? ( ) some other source (a spring, creek, river, cistern, etc.)?" The 1970 questionnaire did not differentiate between a drilled well, which is deeper and has been drilled by machine, and a dug well, which is shallow and has been dug by shovel or scratched out by diggers with sharp fingernails. Query to the census man: Since PICO's are too sensitive to be afflicted with the word "race," and too stupid to know what a "parochial" school is, aren't you guys getting pretty technical on the water supply? The answer is as refreshing as a cool dipperful of artesian well water: "People who have wells know what kind of wells they have."

Dear Mr. Safire:

Since you're obviously a good fellow you won't mind my suspicion that you're "stupid" by your own definition: "PICO's . . . too stupid to know what a 'parochial' school is." What would you say if your daughter attended Friends Central? "Parochial"? Or "church-related"? Or neither? Seeing as Friends have neither parishes, nor (strictly speaking) churches, but rather "meetings."

In the same paragraph I'm afraid you betray your egregiously city-slicker orientation. Anyone who has ever lived in the country knows the difference between a drilled well and a dug well, as well as they know that between an outhouse and indoor plumbing. The distinction is by no means "pretty technical." A dug well is essentially an old-oaken-bucket type, even if it's in somebody's cellar: easily polluted by ground water, surface drainage, etc. A drilled well, by implication, has penetrated the rock or hardpan beneath the soil, and reached a naturally filtered source that is relatively invulnerable to surface pollution.

"Artesian well water" is not necessarily any more refreshing than any other kind. It may in fact contain heavy doses of sulphur or crude oil, not conducive to refreshment.

Glenn Bernard
Willow Grove, Pennsylvania

center on

"The controversy," I wrote, "centers around . . ." And then I went into what people were arguing about. A reader circled "centers around" and wrote "neat trick."

When you stop to think about it, nothing can center "around" anything. The center is the middle, the focal point, the place around which all else circles. If the metaphor is to mean anything, it should be expressed "centers *on.*"

The confusion stems from the alternate phrase, "revolves around." Wrote a *Time* magazine movie reviewer recently: (that verb-before-the-subject-before-the-colon usage is *Time*-ese) "The plot is raveled. It revolves around the U.S. Attorney General's office, which employs the Mafia to find a cool freelance hit man to abduct a Robert Vesco-like tycoon. . . ." In that current use, all that revolving is done "around" the office, which is the center; it could also be said to "center on" the office. "Centered around" is as meaningless as "revolved on."

Dear Mr. Safire:

I disagree with your statement "'Centered around' is as meaningless as 're-volved on.'"

A wheel revolves "on" an axle, the earth revolves "on" an orbit, etc. The wheel does not revolve "around" an axle, nor does the earth revolve "around" an orbit. Even the moon revolves "on" an orbit while revolving "around" the earth.

Doesn't this make sense?

Sincerely,
Virginia Lee Ziagos
Brooklyn, New York

center will not hold

I went out to buy a new pair of eyeglasses the other day and almost missed the optician's shop because he had changed the name of his store to *Vision Center.*

The naming of many new enterprises is afflicted with centrism. The *shopping center* probably started it; then the local pool hall started calling itself a *recreation center;* the local soup kitchen, a *welfare center,* and now there is hardly anybody left on any periphery.

The Washington, D.C., phone book lists 68 "Centers for," from the "Center for Applied Linguistics" (you guys should know better) to the "Center for Women and Work," followed by the "Center of Concern," which is presumably the focal point of worry in America.

What is at the heart, or nerve center, of this nominal centralization in what is said to be an era of decentralization? To be a center, I suppose, is to be more than a piddling little enterprise, a one-issue campaign, a last, lonely gas station before the speedway of modern life. To be a center is to be diversified and complex, and at the same time to be the cynosure of all eyes.

About a mile west of Hartford on Interstate 84, reports Steven Delano of Marlborough, Conn., the State of Connecticut has erected a large green and white sign that declares "UNIVERSITY OF CONNECTICUT HEALTH CENTER." Beneath that sign hangs a smaller, explanatory sign which reflects the failure of "center" to communicate meaning: "Hospital."

This rush toward trendy center nomenclature will be stopped only when an owner of a cemetery drops all euphemism of *final resting place* or *mortuary* to call his establishment *Dead Center.*

Dear Mr. Safire:

In your column today "center will not hold" you use the expression "cynosure of all eyes."

May I refer you (timidly) to the Dictionary of Contemporary Usage by Wil-

liam and Mary Morris, page 163. They suggest that this is a cliché which is also
a redundancy, and go on to explain why.

> Respectfully yours,
> Clarence Snyder
> Chadds Ford, Pennsylvania

Dear Mr. Safire:
  Your column on "centers" which struck the target right in the er, middle, has
caused us fans and fellow language lovers to change the name of our William
Safire Fan Center to Fan Centre. However there was nothing we could do
about our Corporate name which is now the William Safire Fan Centre Center.

> Centrally,
> R. C. Brown
> Jackson Heights, New York

---

chivy, *see* Kissingerese

---

clearly in vogue

Now that "hopefully"—replacing "it is to be hoped"—has won the usage
battle, another adverb is making its bid. "Clearly"—to replace "it is clear
that"—is certainly the favored term among public speakers.

But "hopefully" had a reason for being: There is no "hopably" or "ho-
pedly," and the alternative—"one hopes" or "it is to be hoped"—is hifalu-
tin. The word has few defenders (my "shame on you" file is bulging after the
defense in this space) but it surely has a multitude of users.

"Clearly," however, is a transparent cop-out: It is the equivalent of the
Soviet propagandist's "as is well known." If the speaker means "this is for
sure," he should say "surely" or "certainly"; if he means "the evidence
points to," he might try "evidently"; if he means "it cannot be argued or
disputed," there is "indisputably"; if he wants to say "any dope knows," he
should try "any dope knows."

The vogue use of "clearly" spreads the word over all these meanings, de-
basing the precision of "it is clear to me." The irony is in the fire: Of all the
words used to befog our discourse and undermine clarity, the last should be
"clearly."

Your objection to using "clearly" instead of "it is clear that" seems to me clearly *a case of pedantry! You allow "certainly" for "it is certain that" and "evidently" for "the evidence points to—it is evident that"—and "presumably" would permit "one presumes that"; so why on earth do you boggle at "clearly"?*

With so many targets to aim at, this one seems to me ill chosen! I propose instead you attack the phrase frequently used in reporting on the status of negotiations:

"Both sides are still very far apart." (I try to imagine what would be the case if only one *side was still far apart. . . .)*

Yours,
Helen M. Franc
New York, New York

Dear Mr. Safire:

An even more transparent (nauseating) cop-out than "clearly" is "accordingly." This word is used by writers (or speakers) to suggest (imply or aver) that the statement they are about to make follows logically or inevitably from what they have just said whereas, in fact, it may do no such thing.

Is there any way we can protect ourselves from the corruption of "accordingly"?

Sincerely,
Nancy Allen
New York, New York

Dear Mr. Safire:

Do not abandon "clearly" too quickly. "Clearly . . ." means "I invite you to accept my unsupported assertion that . . ." and thus is (not the only but) the most reliable tag identifying argumentative weak links.

Faithfully,
Homer D. Schaaf
New York, New York

Dear Mr. Safire:

Your attack on "clearly" baffles, and bothers, me.

The old Webster International warrants "obviously" right behind "clearly" under a discussion of "distinctly," to which the reader is referred when he turns to "clearly." Evan Webster's Unspeakable defines "clearly" as "without doubt." American Heritage, Random House merely treat it as an adverb form of "clear," which, however, is defined as "plain, evident."

Your grudge against clearly is quite unclear to me. With best wishes,

Sincerely yours,
George Kelley
Editorial writer
The Youngstown Vindicator

closings

In the labor movement, letters between union officials are customarily signed "Fraternally yours." This is going to cause a problem when women become high officials in organized labor; meanwhile, in less organized fashion, the rest of us will be examining our own closings.

Some writers, tired of salutations and automatic sign-offs, drop the *Dear* at the beginning and the *Yours truly* or *Sincerely* at the end: President Carter often takes the personalized memo route and writes in longhand, "To——" and ends his communication abruptly.

Most of us, like onstage performers, struggle for a graceful way to get offstage. *Regards* is pedestrian; *With warm regards* may be more than you want to say; *Warmly* is not cool. *Cordially,* almost as popular as *Sincerely,* has a slightly patronizing air—better to write "patronizingly."

We have come a long way from *Obediently yours,* breathed into a microphone by the young Orson Welles, or the standard closing of a French business letter: *Veuillez agréer, cher Monsieur, l'expression de mes sentiments les plus distingués* (when you are writing to a bigshot, *distingués* becomes *respectueux*).

Instead, Americans now scribble the unchangingly noncommittal *As ever,* the meaningless *Yours,* the insipid *All the best,* the dangling *Best* (probably clipped from *Best wishes*). *Personal regards* is a weak effort to add humanity to a business communication.

Hastily is frantically apologetic, as is *Yrs,* both written illegibly to conceal the lack of thought and time given the recipient; nobody ever signs a letter *Laboriously.*

Your friend is a politician's favorite, written only to people the friendly signer does not know. *In friendship* is better, if that is the actual relationship between sender and receiver.

Which brings us to *Love.* That's a troublesome one, which is why so many people write *Affectionately,* which falls short of love; "affectionately" is proper in addressing a small child, and it may be safer in a lawsuit, but what it says is "I have this feeling for you that I am not prepared to call anything profound." To avoid the sloppiness of stark emotion, some love-signers write a breezy *Much love* or change the spelling to *Luv.*

"My wife says it is wrong to sign family letters, 'Affectionately,' " writes Arthur B. Hooker of New York. "She says, 'Write, "Love." ' This can create difficulties if you are an inexpert typist. I once signed a letter to my future mother-in-law 'Lover to all.' " He adds: "My aunt used to sign checks, 'Affectionately, Mary,' when hurried. After a brief struggle, the bank ceased to resist."

I don't see why a writer has to characterize himself, or attribute a tone to his letter, with an adverbial bow. If the tone is cheerful, no *Cheerfully yours* is needed; if the purpose is to end a love affair, a *Regretfully* is insufficient and a *Painfully* a bit much—a direct *Goodbye forever* makes the point (never *Have a nice life*).

"I like the simple 'Thank you for the help,' or action, advice, recommendation or whatever," suggests Michael G. Mattis of *The Sacramento Bee.* "Or, 'I hope this advice or information is helpful.' Often a simple 'Thank you' is most effective."

I hope the advice has been helpful. Thank you.

Dear Mr. Safire,
In the 20's to 40's era, my father guided (fishing and hunting) a gentleman from Philadelphia, who, when he wrote, always ended his letters as follows:

> *"Says,*
> *Jos. S. Potsdamer"*

In reflection, it seems to have covered a multitude of situations.
> *Says,*
> *Lauchlan Fulton*
> *St. John, New Brunswick*

---

closing the loop, *see* White House-ese

---

code word

Early this year, in his speech to a joint session of Congress (it's a joint "session" whenever a President speaks, a joint "meeting" at most other times), President Carter used a word that has taken the place of another in the intelligence field: "encryption" is in and "encoding" is out.

Aware that he was adopting the C.I.A. patois which had been immortalized in the treaty text, Mr. Carter used both the old word and the new in explaining SALT verification: He claimed that the treaty "forbids the encryption of the encoding of crucial missile-test information."

Follow the tricky trail of the name of this deception game: "To put into code" was the early verb use, but the verb "to codify" could not be used since that already had a meaning—"to arrange a system of laws." The word chosen for the verb was "encode," coined about 30 years after "decode," its direct opposite.

At the same time, "cipher" was being used—from the word for "zero"—and from "decipher" came its opposite, "encipher." One noun used in this dirty business ("Gentlemen do not read each other's mail," said Henry Stimson, but not until after World War II) was "cryptogram," from the Greek word meaning "to conceal," and so in the early 1940's a new verb sprang up on the analogy of "encode" and "encipher": "to encrypt."

At first, I intended to make a fuss about the needless substitution of "encrypt" for "encode," to the point where it even involved a Presidential speech, but now I see what's going on. This constant switching of the verb that means "to hide the meaning" is all a brilliant plot: *They're constantly changing their code.*

New York Times Memo to Irv Horowitz
Re Joint session-joint meeting Safire is wrong, no?
                                                    Al Siegal

New York Times Memo to Al Siegal
According to Bill Brown, the Parliamentarian of the House, a Joint Session of Congress is an occasion at which the two Houses convene to do business, as to hear the State of the Union Message or count electoral votes. A joint meeting transacts no business, but occurs during a recess for the purpose of hearing a speaker, such as astronauts. Brown could recall no occasion at which a President addressed a joint meeting. So Safire is technically wrong but, in practical terms, correct.

                                                    Horowitz

Dear Mr. Safire,
It is my impression that you were simply wrong concerning "code" and "cipher" last week. Properly, "code" should be used for word for word substitutions, while "cipher" should be used when dealing with letter for letter substitutions. These are quite different in principle and in practice. Basically, there are a lot more words than there are letters. A code book is a dictionary but a cipher key can be a scrap of paper. It thus seems worth while trying to maintain the distinction even though the two words are often confused in common speech. You should sympathize with that feeling.

As I understand your attitude toward such matters, you regard the words you understand as the soul of civilization and the words you do not understand as elitist jargon. This attitude is frequently charming. We often enjoy your column.

                                                    yours,
                                                    John M. Greene
                                                    Princeton, New Jersey

Dear Mr. Safire:

Your criticism of President Carter for using the term "encrypt" in describing the process by which missile-test data would be rendered unintelligible to the opposing side is entirely misplaced. Instead you should have protested his use of the word "encode," for while the data are encrypted, they are not encoded.

The words "encrypt," "encode," and "encipher" have very distinct meanings to a cryptographer. Encrypt means to render communications between two points unintelligible to unauthorized parties. This is also the colloquial, but technically inaccurate, definition of encode. If you want to encrypt a message, you have two ways to do it: encode it or encipher it.

Generally, in a code, "code groups" of 4 or 5 letters or numbers are substituted for words, phrases, letters, or syllables of plaintext. For example, in the Acme Commercial Cable Code "barhy" means "anchored" and "winum" means "where and when are you sending fuel." Ciphers, on the other hand, perform a letter-by-letter transposition or substitution of ciphertext for plaintext. Remember your Magic Decoder Ring? It was really a Magic Deciphering Ring.

The instruments in a test-missile sense data in analog form, i.e., as a continuously variable voltage in an electronic circuit. The information is then digitized (another word I would defend), i.e., converted from that continuously variable voltage into the discrete bits (binary digits, not little pieces) used by computers. The data would then be encrypted by an onboard dedicated computer (N.B. Just as a high-fidelity stereo is no more loyal than a monaural player, a dedicated computer isn't particularly assiduous. It's the opposite of a general-purpose computer). Although English-language words are not involved at any stage in the process, you can see that the encryption method does more nearly resemble enciphering, rather than encoding.

By the way, the ciphers generated by modern cryptosystems are considered holocryptic, i.e., utterly, eternally, unbreakable, which is why such a stink is being raised about all this in the first place.

> *Yours for clearer communications,*
> *Thomas Wrona*
> *Yonkers, New York*

---

coffee nerves

Order "regular coffee" and what do you get?

"In the United States," reports Phil Shea, public relations director of Sheraton hotels, "with only one exception, an order for 'regular coffee' would produce plain coffee with sugar and cream on the side.

"The exception is Boston. An order for 'regular coffee' in the coffee shop would produce coffee with cream already added, and sugar on the side. In the hotel restaurant, the waiter would question the guest to clarify the order."

Since Americans drink about 460 million cups of java on a winter's day, it may be helpful to examine other regional language distinctions in the ordering of coffee. I put the question to the president of the National Coffee Association, who started talking about a study of "preferences for creaming agents." I could tell he was not my man; to me, a "creaming agent" is a hit man.

Vann E. Hettinger, a reader from Redding, Conn., supplied a useful variation: "Coffee, light," in the North, is coffee that is light-colored because of the great amount of cream, half-and-half, milk, nondairy creamer, or other, uh, creaming agent, it contains. However, in the Southeast, "coffee, light," means coffee with a small amount of white stuff—the "light" refers to going lightly on the cream, or not pouring with a heavy hand.

Perhaps because of this confusion about "light," or perhaps a spillover from British usage about tea, the word "white" is sometimes used to differentiate an order from "black" coffee. When used in the United States, "coffee, white" means "not black" and leaves to the pourer's discretion the amount of cream to agent.

The man from DARE—Professor F. G. Cassidy, editor of the Dictionary of American Regional English—saw this query as a perfect example of our language's variety.

"Get down into Tennessee and such parts," reports Cassidy, "and they'll know what *egg coffee* is—you throw eggshells in the pot so the last of the egg white will *settle* the grounds and *clear* the coffee. Coffee is serious stuff, but jocular types may call it *barefoot* (black) and *with socks on* (white). Get down into New Orleans and a different distinction comes up: coffee will be either *chicory* or *pure* (no chicory). Get out West and you may be lucky enough to find *range* or *cowboy* coffee, which when properly made is *boilt.* The wagon cook's recipe, or *receipt,* for making cowboy coffee went something like this: 'Take two pounds of Arbuckle's, put in 'nough water to wet it down, boil for two hours, and throw in a hoss shoe. If the hoss shoe sinks, she ain't ready.' "

How is weak coffee characterized? Americans are united on *dishwater,* though *bilge water* is heard up North, *stump water* down South, and *scared water* out West. In Virginia, it's *driddle water.*

Strong coffee is equated in the American language with good coffee: Words of praise include *Norwegian, creekbank, sawmill, shanty,* and *sheepherder's* coffee. However, Professor Cassidy reports that, on occasion, strength and viscosity go too far, and in rural Wisconsin farmers complain: "It's too thick to drink, and too wet to plow."

The best put-down is "If this is coffee, bring me tea, and if it's tea, bring me coffee." At my local greasy spoon, after the confusion of "coffee, light" and arguments over what constitutes "regular," I always sing out, "Coffee, with a side of soybean creamer and a packet of saccharin," which gets me coffee, regular, along with a black look.

Dear Mr. Safire:

More coffee: While eating my first required dinner at London's Middle Temple I was startled by a waitress who asked for my car key while she poured coffee. After at least five minutes of total confusion I realized that coffee with a small amount of "creaming agent" often is called khaki (cocky, not cacky) in Britain.

> *Yours sincerely,*
> *Frederick Arnold*
> *New Haven, Connecticut*

Dear Mr. Saffire:

I don't know how many million New Yorkers order "regular" coffee every day at Chock Full O' Nuts restaurants, but when they do, they mean coffee with cream(er)—one spurt from the automatic dispensers that enable the waiters and waitresses to add cream without setting down the cup. You remember, they put the cup under the lever and lift up. If you ask for light coffee, it means two lifts of the lever. And if you ask for coffee with cream, they'll say, "You mean regular." Sugar is always on the side, on the counters.

You've been in the Washington bureau too long!

> *Sincerely,*
> *Diane Wolfe Levy*
> *Silver Spring, Maryland*

Dear Mr. Safire,

In your recent article on coffee nomenclature (caffeineclature?) you omitted my most affectionate term for overboiled re-reheated java: killer mud. *Beware of KILLER MUD! Gets them every time.*

By the way, do Americans really drink 460 million cups a day? Even if half the country consumes coffee that would be four and a half cups per person each day. Does our country seem that awake to you?

Anyhow, keep grinding away,
With great caffinity,
Andy Gyory
Burlington, Vermont

P.S. I think if the third world war begins it will be aptly named, for won't it be fought over the control of the third world?

Irregular Coffee, sir

In Black Lamb and Grey Falcon, *Rebecca West reported a droll Yugoslavian coffee-ordering usage:* Kaffee mit ohne *(literally, coffee with without) for coffee with cream.*

Kaffee mit ohne *evolved in pre-World War II Yugoslavia when the Serbs and Croats heard the ubiquitous (and usually unwelcome) German and Austrian tourists ordering* Kaffee mit *(meaning* mit schlag, *i.e., with the traditional Viennese whipped cream). The Yugoslavs began calling black coffee* Kaffee ohne *(coffee without). After* Kaffee ohne *became standard from Zagreb to Dubrovnik and Split, the Yugoslavs invented that ridiculous* Kaffee mit ohne.

For stronger stuff, incidentally (i.e., coffee with only a dash of the—ulp— "creaming agent") the coffee-wagon man in the Time Life Building used to dispense "dark coffee." Is that common only in N.Y.C.?

Bon appétit,
Jean Bergerud
Harrington Park, New Jersey

Sir—

Not "receipt" but ruh-seep. In Louisiana and East Texas, chicory-coffee, boiled black and strong, is commonly called "coon-ass" coffee, no racial derogation implied. Weak coffee I've heard equated with "Love in a canoe," i.e.: "fuckin' near water."

> *Yours, and truly,*
> *John Phillip Palmer*
> *Balboa, California*

Dear Mr. Safire,

In regard to "coffee nerves":

You might have commented on what we tell the folks in Westwood when they say "this coffee tastes like mud." We reply "well it should, it was ground yesterday."

> *Very truly yours*
> *Charles Kuhner*
> *Westwood, New Jersey*

Dear Mr. Safire:

Your piece on light coffee and black looks reminded me of an incident that happened many years ago while I was a graduate student at Brown University. A number of us ate dinner together most nights at a small neighborhood restaurant in East Providence. The waitresses, knowing our preference, would bring coffee in cups to the table with the main course. On this occasion we had a visitor, a young lecturer from Australia. When the waitress put a cup of coffee in front of him, he said, "I'll have my coffee later," but being Australian, it came out, "I'll have my coffee lighter." No one noticed this in the din of conversation, until the waitress returned with his cup with more cream added. Once again he said, "No, I want my coffee lighter." By now we natives at the table realized what was going on, but wicked imps that we were, no one interfered. The waitress returned with darkened visage, put the cup of ivory-colored liquid in front of the Australian with considerable force and said, "If you want it any lighter than this, buster, you'd best buy a cow!"

> *Sincerely,*
> *Thos. P. Mulhern*
> *Stamford, Connecticut*

coming on

"I'm getting an image of coming on tough," candidate John Connally told a group of Republican governors, according to columnists Evans and Novak. "I'm not going on tough. I'm only coming on candid."

This marks an important evolution in the locution "to come on." The phrase originated in the 1940's, as "to come on like *Gangbusters,*" which was a radio program that crashed through the airways accompanied by a howling siren and the rat-a-tat of machine-gun fire. Slightly toned down to "come on strong," a title of a play by Garson Kanin, the phrase was used through the 70's as a mild derogation of someone whose self-confidence or stridency was excessive.

Now, however, the phrase has been clipped to "come on" and means "to make an entrance" (to come onstage, to enter the scene)—in any way that the following modifier describes. It is possible to come on soft, to come on uptight, to come on flaky, to come on sincere. Instead of saying "he has the smarts," we now say "he comes on smart."

Note that the correct usage of this idiom forbids the adverbial form: The verb is not being modified. Just as one never came on strongly, one does not come on weakly, or smartly, or flakily. This is because "in a manner" is understood, and an adjective describes that manner: He comes on (in a) strong (manner). Use the adjectival form, and do not feel bad or act guiltily about it.

. Why did Governor Connally object to the characterization of "coming on tough"? There was a nuance observable: He could not object to "coming on strong," because "strong" is a leadership quality; on the other hand, "tough"—except in "tough-minded"—has the connotation of mock-strong, or bellicose, and can be sharply denied. ("Tough-minded" will soon lose its hyphen because I am tenderhearted.)

That's why he picked "coming on candid," certainly a proper coming-on for a candidate, the word rooted in the virgin-white toga worn by those who sought office in ancient Rome.

Curious, though, that Connally should pick a show-business phrase to describe his entry. Though show-biz lingo plays a role in political discourse, and Big Jawn has a need to upstage the rest of the cast of characters, will the ex-actor he's playing opposite find him a tough act to follow?

We'll see; some voters are coming on skeptical.

Dear Mr. Safire:

I feel the need to write to you again because of your piece on "coming on." You stated that "the correct usage of this idiom forbids the adverbial form: the verb is not being modified." So far, you are correct. But the reason you give is wrong. It is not "because 'in a manner' is understood, and an adjective describes that manner"; it is because "to come on" is a verb of "being, becoming, appearing, feeling, seeming or tasting" (as my seventh-grade English teacher used to drill us) and is thus followed by the adjective (or sometimes noun) which is in the nominative case, or would be if one declined English. Thus, "he looks old," "this tastes good," "he seems a fool," "she comes on sexy." It is comforting to have a rule to explain why we should say things the way we intuit that we should.

> *Cordially,*
> *Amy B. Unfried*
> *Bronxville, New York*

Dear Mr. Safire:

Many thanks for your column; I enjoy reading it, and look forward to it— However . . .

In your discussion of the verb "come on," you neglected its use (with "to") as a substitute for the phrase "make a pass at." To come on to someone is to approach someone flirtatiously or seductively, as in the following sentence: "When her boss started coming on to her, the secretary requested a transfer."

> *Seasonal greetings,*
> *Patricia E. Nealon*
> *Bronx, New York*

And

Then there is "come-on": lure, deceiving enticement, scam (!).
And "Aw, come on*": don't kid me.*
And "come on": make advances to, flirt, make a pass at.
What an economic language! Like Latin (in a way, that is.)

> *D.B.S.*
> *(Diana Bonnor Lewis)*
> *New York, New York*

Dear William Safire,

A qualification, theatrical, on the phrase "come on." It more accurately means "appear (on the stage)" than "to make an entrance." Only characters, strictly speaking, make an entrance, and then they may only "come on" since making an entrance implies a minimal impact; actors on the other hand come on (the stage) in the first and third acts, or only in the second act, etc. For instance in Hamlet, *the King and Queen enter and the courtiers come on.*

The distinction undoubtedly goes back to the time when dramatic literature was routinely more elaborate, and most actors expected to play several characters in the course of the action. "Mr. X appears as Bertram in the first two acts and the last, and comes on as a priest in Act Three, and an executioner in Act Four."

Thus one comes on like Gangbusters, like a lion, as a wandering minstrel, nice and easy, or candid. In every case the word means "appear" (like, as, to be). In popular usage, someone present may begin to "come on" in a particular fashion; since no entrance is involved, but only a change in manner, the meaning is demonstrably to begin to "appear." In this context, the element of deliberate pretense is noted.

> Sincerely,
> John Boyt
> New York, New York

Commencement Address

Classmates:

I entered Syracuse University with the Class of '51, dropped out after two years, and am finally receiving my degree with the Class of '78. There is hope for slow learners.

My subject today is "The Decline of the Written Word." If the speech I have written is disjointed and confusing, you will get my point the hard way.

We have not heard a really eloquent speech out of the White House in a long time. Why? When you ask the speechwriters of Mr. Ford and Mr. Carter, they give you this explanation: They say that "high-flown rhetoric" is not their man's style.

But that is not responsive. A flowery speech is a bad speech. Simple, straight English prose can be used to build a great speech. There has to be a more profound reason for the reluctance of the Presidents of the 70's to write out their thoughts plainly and deliver them in words we can all understand.

If you press the President's aides—and that's my job, to press them hard—they'll admit that their man much prefers to "ad-lib" answers to questions. He's not good at what they call a "set" speech.

What do they really mean by that? They mean a speech—a written speech, developing an idea—is not what people want to hear. People prefer short takes, Q. and A.; the attention span of most Americans on serious matters is about 20 seconds, the length of a television clip.

In the same way, people do not want to read articles as they once did; today, if you cannot get your message in a paragraph, forget it.

As a result, we're becoming a short-take society. Our Presidency, which Theodore Roosevelt called a "bully pulpit," has become a forum for 20-second spots. Our food for thought is junk food.

What has brought this about? I don't blame President Carter for this—he reflects the trend, he did not start it. I don't flail out at the usual whipping boy, television.

The reason for the decline of the written word—speeches, written articles—is that we, as a people, are writing less and talking more. Because it takes longer to prepare our thoughts on paper, that means we are ad-libbing more, and it also means we are thinking more superficially. An ad lib has its place, but not ad nauseam.

That's one of those sweeping statements that pundits are permitted to make. But let me turn reporter for a minute and prove to you that we're talking more and writing less.

Most people are not writing personal letters anymore. Oh, the volume of first-class mail has doubled since 1950, but here's the way the mail breaks down. Over 80 percent is business-related; over 10 percent is greeting-card and Christmas-card; and only 3 percent is from one person to another to chew the fat.

More and more, we're relying on commercial poets and cartoonists to express our thoughts for us. Tomorrow is Mother's Day; how many of us are relying on canned sentiments? I remember my brother once laboriously hand-made a card for my mother: On the front was, "I'll never forget you, Mother," and inside it said, "You gave away my dog." Okay, he was sore, but at least he was original.

The greatest cultural villain of our times has a motherly image: Ma Bell. The telephone company. Instead of writing, people are calling; instead of communicating, they're "staying in touch."

There you are, all about to be holders of college degrees. When was the last time you wrote, or received, a long, thoughtful letter? When was the last time you wrote a passionate love letter? No, that takes time, effort, thought—there's a much easier way, the telephone. The worst insult is when kids call home, collect, for money; when my kids go to college, the only way they'll get a nickel out of me is to write for it.

As the percentage of personal mail has dwindled, the number of telephone installations since 1950 has quadrupled. The average person's need to write has been undermined by simple economics: As the cost of a letter has gone up, the cost of a call has gone down.

During World War I, a first-class letter cost 2 cents an ounce; in a few weeks, it will be 15 cents an ounce. In that same 60 years, a New York-to-San Francisco call has gone from $20 for three minutes down to 53 cents today, if you're willing to call at night or on a weekend. The penny postcard is a dime. Letters up almost 800 percent; phone calls down to one-fortieth the cost to grandpa. No wonder the market share of communication has dropped for letter writers. In the year I was a freshman here, the Postal Ser-

vice had over a third of the communication business; today, it is one-sixth, and falling.

And it's going to get worse: Phonevision is on the way. We have seen what happened to the interpersonal correspondence of love in the past generation. The purple passages of prose, and tear-stained pages of the love letter—that's gone now. It has become the heavy breathing, grunts, and "like, I mean, y'know, wow" of the love call. The next stage, with the visual dimension, will not even require a loud sigh: We can just wave at each other to say hello; wiggle our fingers to express affection; raise our eyebrows to ask "What's new?" get a shrug in reply, and sign off with a smile and a wink.

We need not degenerate further from written English to verbal grunts, and then to sign language. We need to become modern reactionaries; I consider myself a neo-Neanderthal, and my happiest moment of the year comes as daylight saving ends in October, when I can turn back the clock.

How do we save ourselves from the tyranny of the telephone? How do we liberate our language from the addiction to the ad lib?

If this were an off-the-cuff presentation, I would drift off into a fuzzy evasion like, "There are no easy answers." But one thing I have learned in preparing my first commencement address, and the main advice I shall burden you with today, is this: There are plenty of easy answers. The big trick is to think about them and write them down.

There are four steps to the salvation of the English language, and thus to the rejuvenation of clear thinking in your working lives.

First, remember that first drafts are usually stupid. If you shoot off your mouth with your first draft—that is, if you say what you think before you've had a chance to think—your stupidity shines forth for all to hear. But, if you write your first draft—of a letter, a memo, a description of some transcendental experience that comes to you while jogging—then you fall on your face in absolute privacy. You get the chance to change it all around. It is harder to put your foot in your mouth when you have your pen in your hand.

Second, reject the notion that honesty and candor demand that you "let it all hang out." That's not honesty, that's intellectual laziness. Tuck some of it in; edit some of it out. Talking on your feet, spinning thoughts off the top of your head, and just rapping along in a laid-back way have been glorified as "expressing your natural self." But you did not get an education to become natural, you got an education to become civilized. Composition is a discipline; it forces us to think. If you want to "get in touch with your feelings," fine—talk to yourself, we all do. But, if you want to communicate with another thinking human being, get in touch with your thoughts. Put them in order; give them a purpose; use them to persuade, to instruct, to discover, to seduce. The secret way to do this is to write it down and then cut out the confusing parts.

Third, never forget that you own the telephone, the telephone does not own you. Most people cannot bear to listen to a phone ring without answering it. It's easy to not answer a letter, but it's hard to not answer a phone. Let me pass along a solution that has changed my life. When I was in the Nixon Administration, my telephone was tapped—I had been associating with known journalists. So I took an interest in the instrument itself. Turn it upside down; you will notice a lever that says "louder." Turn it away from the direction of louder. That is the direction of emancipation. If somebody needs to see you, he'll come over. If others need to tell you what they think, or even express how they feel, they can write. There are those who will call you a recluse—but it is better to listen to your own different drummer than to go through life with a ringing in your ears.

My fourth point will impress upon you the significance of the written word. Those of you who have been secretly taking notes, out of a four-year habit, will recall that I spoke of "four steps" to the salvation of the English language. Here it is: There is no fourth step. I had the fourth step in mind when I began, but I forgot it.

Now, if I were ad-libbing, I would remember I had promised four points, and I would do what so many stump speakers do—toss in the all-purpose last point, which usually begins, "There are no easy answers." But, in writing down what you think, you can go back and fix it—instead of having to phumph around with a phony fourth point, you can change your introduction to "there are three steps." Perhaps you wonder why I did not do so. Not out of any excess of honesty, or unwillingness to make a simple fix—I just wanted you to see the fourth step take shape before your very eyes.

Is the decline of the written word inevitable? Will the historians of the future deal merely in oral history? I hope not. I hope that oral history will limit itself to the discovery of toothpaste and the invention of mouthwash. I don't want to witness the de-composing of the art of composition, or be present when we get in touch with our feelings and lose contact with our minds.

I'm a conservative in politics, which means I believe that we as a people have to lead our leaders, to show them how we want to be led.

Accordingly, I think we have to send a message to the podium from the audience: We're ready for more than Q. and A. We're ready for five or ten minutes of sustained explication. A "fireside chat" will not turn out our fires. On the contrary—if a speaker will take the time to prepare, we are prepared to pay in the coin of our attention.

That, of course, is contrary to the trend, against the grain. It can come only from people who care enough to compose, who get in the habit of reading rather than listening, of being in communication instead of only in contact.

When Great Britain was fighting World War II alone, an American President did something that would be considered cornball today: F.D.R. sent Churchill a poem, along with a letter, that read:

> Sail on, O Ship of State
> Sail on O Union, strong and great!
> Humanity with all its fears
> With all its hopes of future years
> Is hanging breathless on thy fate!

Churchill took the message—delivered to him by Wendell Willkie, who had just been defeated by F.D.R.—and selected a poem in answer. At that moment, looking East, England faced invasion; looking to the West across the Atlantic, Churchill saw potential help. The poem he sent concluded with the words:

> And not by eastern windows only
> when daylight comes, comes in the light
> In front, the sun climbs slow, how slowly
> But westward, look, the land is bright.

High-flown rhetoric? Perhaps. And perhaps poetry, which had an honored place in a 1961 inauguration, is too rich for some tastes today.

And now I remember the fourth step. I like to think we can demand some sense of an occasion, some uplift, some inspiration from our leaders. Not empty words and phony promises—but words full of meaning, binding thoughts together with purpose, holding promise of understandable progress. If we ask for it, we'll get it—if we fail to ask, we'll get more Q. and A.

I believe we can arrest the decline of the written word, thereby achieving a renaissance of clarity. And not by eastern establishment windows only. The hope is on this side of the Potomac, the Charles, and the Hudson rivers—westward, look, the land is bright.

—Syracuse University, May 13, 1978

committee, *see* working group

community, *see* floutsmanship

condominium, *see* Kissingerese

copacetic

If you're feeling aw-ri-i-ight but do not want to act as if you are in your second childhood, you might try an old slang term that is enjoying a rebirth: "copacetic." It means "fine; no complaints; hunky-dory; cool." There is a touch of restraint in the word: When everything is copacetic, all is sailing smoothly, but it's not "excellent," "fantastic," or "terrific," those ecstasies of yesteryear.

The word's origin is a mystery. The Oxford English Dictionary supplement tracks it to 1919, in a book by Irving Addison Bacheller: " 'As to looks I'd call him, as ye might say, real copasetic.' Mrs. Lukins expressed this opinion solemnly. . . . Its last word stood for nothing more than an indefinite depth of meaning." Go figure that out. In 1926, the word was spelled "kopasetee" in a book about the black middle class by Carl Van Vechten, and defined therein as "an approbatory epithet somewhat stronger than *all right.*" In 1934, that writer with the golden ear, John O'Hara, used it in *Appointment in Samarra,* and in 1937 *American Speech* magazine suggested that the term was "used by Negroes in the South."

Why should the vocabulary of approval, the lexicon of good feeling, be so shrouded? Why can't we find the origin of the words that express our contentment? It's not copacetic; on the contrary, it's aw-wrong.

Copacetic II

Plenty of mail on the origin of "copacetic," the revivified term for "all goes well."

One group holds that it was a gangland term out of Chicago. The origin was speculated upon by Michael MacDougall, as told to J. C. Furnas, in a 1939 book titled *Gamblers Don't Gamble*. A certain hotel detective was the nemesis of the small-time crooks who liked to make his hotel a headquarters. When weary and no longer vigilant, the detective would prop his feet on a settee in the lobby; a lookout would say "The cop is on the settee," which meant "all clear." In time, the sentence ran together as "copasettee," or "copacetic."

"Sounds fishy, doesn't it?" observes Robert C. Stern of Cleveland Heights, Ohio, who sent it in. Sure does, but a handful of phrase detectives is convinced that the cop-on-the-settee story is not the folk etymology it seems to be.

A more likely explanation, offered by many linguistic Javerts, is the Hebrew term *"hakol b'seder,"* a frequently used phrase meaning "all in order." A slight corruption, *"kol b'tzedek,"* means "all with justice."

On an early mission of the astronauts, writes Phyllis Simpson of Philadelphia, her son—watching the moon shot on television—"remarked that, in response to a question from ground control about how things were going, a strange thing had happened: the astronaut had replied in Hebrew. I laughed. . . . He insisted he had clearly heard the reply as *'kol b'tzedek.'* "

But if the origin is in Hebrew, how come the word was popularized by Bill (Bojangles) Robinson, the dancer, and used by black jazzmen? Mrs. Simpson has a theory: "Robinson, Fats Waller and Louis Armstrong grew up in the South at the turn of the century. At that time, there were many Jewish storekeepers in the area, not too long in this country from Europe. I can picture a Negro child in a small store, either as a customer or as an employee, hearing the storekeeper up front calling to his non-English-speaking, Hebrew-oriented father in the rear, to ask if everything was all right, and the father replying, in Hebrew, *'Kol b'tzedek.'*

"To the ears of the Negro child, this sounded like 'copacetic,' the same as, in reverse, 'copacetic' [as used by the astronauts] sounded to my son like *'kol b'tzedek.'* "

A pleasant fancy; perhaps even true. Such speculation helps etymologists cope.

To: *William Safire*
As an etymologist, will you cope ascetically or cope esthetically?
Gerard S. Case
New York, New York

Dear Bill:
Amateur etymologists are people whose imaginations tend to wag the dog. They are fictioneers manqués. It goes against their grain to admit that an ety-

WILLIAM SAFIRE

mology could be not merely uncertain but totally unknown. They believe the vacuum can be filled, if one sets about it uninhibitedly. The two essentials of a good etymology, that the form of the word or phrase, and its meaning, should be fully and accurately derivable from the claimed source, and that the historical and logical circumstances should be truly plausible, are too much for them to accept. Such rules clip the wings of imagination. Far better to invent a whole-cloth story, or to defend a bad but titillating guess, than dully to admit ignorance.

So for copacetic—*the* cop-on-the-settee, *a charming picture of indolent authority—which means "all clear," though* copacetic *would have to be twisted to make it mean that. And that Hebrew* Kol b' zedek, *which means "all with justice," and is supposedly picked up as* copacetic *by some impressionable pickaninny from the local storekeeper, who talks in profundities like Rabbi Ben Ezra when all he means is "everything is all right" or "all OK." The creative imagination in full bloom—yes, but hardly authentic etymology.*

> Frederic Cassidy
> Dictionary of American Regional English
> University of Wisconsin
> Madison, Wisconsin

Dear Mr. Safire:

In reference to your word copacetic, may I suggest it is a corruption of the word co-phasetic, not found in Webster, although Webster does give co-phasal, to be in the same phase.

> Sincerely yours,
> A co-phasetic stringer
> Venice, Florida

Dear Mr. Safire,

. . . *The derivation from* hakol b'seder *or* kol b'tzedek, *suggested by Phyllis Simpson just doesn't hang together. For one thing* hakol b'seder *is a Hebrew phrase that is in use primarily in Israeli Hebrew whose phrases and particular idioms only became known in the U.S.A. in general and among American Jews in particular after 1948 and "Copacetic" is a word I recall hearing in Toronto as far back as the 1930's. Moreover,* hakol b'seder *is not part of the Hebrew vocabulary or idiom which is an organic component of the Yiddish language. This doesn't mean it wouldn't be understood by a reasonably literate user or speaker of Yiddish but it's just not a Hebrew word grouping that rolls off the tongue or is readily used in a Yiddish context such as:* mazel-tov *or* im-irtze hashem (God willing) *or* sholom aleichem. *It was introduced to America by Israelis or Americans returning from Israel as part of their native or acquired Hebrew vocabulary and is most unlikely to be used by Jewish shopkeepers in the South who would have other idioms at their disposal. The Yiddish-English*

56

dictionary of the late Uriel Weinreich published in 1967 which lists hundreds of Hebrew words and phrases that have been integrated into Yiddish makes no mention of hakol b'seder. *It has* kol, hakol, *and* seder, *of course, in other contexts but not the phrase as an entity. The same applies to* kol b'tzedek, *a phrase that I've never heard in six decades of closely listening to Yiddish in all its nuances and dialects. The phrase closest in meaning would be* kosher v'yosher, *meaning "(everything is) proper and just" or "correct and fair" or "fair and square" and there's no likelihood of it being eroded or corrupted into "copacetic."*

A few more relevant points: If kol b'seder *were to be used in the U.S.A. by immigrant Jews from Eastern Europe—and this is possible, if only theoretically—the likely pronunciation would be* b'sayder *to rhyme with "raider" rather than the sound it has in the Sephardi pronunciation of Hebrew prevalent in Israel which is closer to the third vowel in "copacetic."*

I hope I haven't been too longwinded but I did want to scotch this serpentine etymology before it wound itself around the lexicographers.

> *Yours etymologically,*
> *B. G. Kayfetz*
> *Toronto, Ontario*

Dear Mr. Safire:

... You completely missed the only logical explanation for the origin of "copacetic." Enclosed is a copy of my letter dated November 8, 1974, to G. & C. Merriam Company, publishers of Webster's Third New International Dictionary, suggesting an Hebraic source for that word. (Also enclosed is a copy of their pettifogging reply, disputing my suggestion.) ...

> *Very truly yours,*
> *Morton M. Steinberg*
> *Chicago, Illinois*

Mr. Philip Babcock Gove, Ph.D.
Editor-in-chief
Webster Third New International Dictionary
G. & C. Merriam Company, Publishers
Springfield, Massachusetts

Dear Sir:

I was recently informed of the fact that the 1971 edition of Webster's Third New International Dictionary, Unabridged, contains the entry of the word "copacetic" (alternately spelled "copesetic"). The origin of this word is indicated as "unknown." I wish to suggest that the origin for this word is the Hebrew language. In Hebrew, the two words "kol ba-tzedek" (כל בצדק) is a rather common phrase, the literal translation of which is "everything is in fairness," meaning "everything is good" or "satisfactory." The striking similarity between the pronunciation of the English "copacetic" and the Hebrew "kol batzedek" and their virtually identical meaning would indicate that the origin of the English word is indeed Hebrew.

An explanation can be had for the introduction into the English language of the word "copacetic." The great number of European Jews which immigrated to this country in the latter part of the 19th and early part of the 20th century brought with them their Yiddish language with its many colorful and expressive idioms. Many of these words and phrases became transliterated into English and are now part of our language. Webster's Dictionary has numerous examples of this process: "schlemiel," "schlepp," "goy," and "kosher" are but a few English words with Yiddish origins. Of course, many Yiddish words are actually of Hebrew origin (such as "goy" and "kosher" in the above examples). The word "copacetic" is apparently another of these examples.

I would appreciate your research into the derivation of the word "copacetic" and your comments relative thereto.

Very truly yours,
Morton M. Steinberg

Morton M. Steinberg, Esq.
Arnstein, Gluck, Weitzenfeld & Minow
120 South LaSalle Street
Chicago, IL   60603

Dear Mr. Steinberg:
Your letter of November 8, addressed to the late Dr. Gove, has been given to me for reply. The suggestion that copacetic might have a Hebrew origin was first offered to us a few years ago, in 1969, and has been submitted by several correspondents since then. This is certainly a more satisfactory explanation than any other we have heard, but there are difficulties in the way of its acceptance. We cannot explain how a Hebrew phrase of this sort could have become known to, and adopted as a slang expression by, Americans in the southern states as long ago as the 1880's. Almost all English words derived directly from Hebrew are either from the Bible or terms applied to Jewish religion or customs. It is difficult to see how such an expression as this can have become current in America so long before the modern revival of Hebrew as a colloquial language, unless it was taken into Yiddish. But we have found no evidence for the phrase in Yiddish dictionaries. We can do no more than keep this suggestion in our files and hope that time will bring to light more information about the origin of copacetic.

Thank you for taking the trouble to write.

Sincerely yours,
Gretchen Brunk
G. & C. Merriam Company
Boston, Massachusetts

cotton checks

A useful illustration of the way the written word can fail to convey the sound of a word as spoken occurred when *Washington Post* reporter Ted Gup interviewed former warehouseman Jimmy Hayes, who worked with Billy Carter on warehouse receipts for peanuts at the Carter family enterprise.

"That's what I call kitein' money," said Hayes, as reported in a transcript of the recorded interview.

"You call it . . .?"

"Kitein' money."

"Gotten money?" asked the reporter, a Northerner.

"Kitein'—K-I-T-E-I-N-G," the Southerner spelled it out, explaining, "like writing a bad check and beating it to the bank."

The light dawned: "Kiteing" is pronounced to sound like "cotton" or "gotten" in a southern dialect. The word is properly spelled "kiting"; the newspaper was correct in following the spelling directed by the interviewee, but a "[*sic*]" might have been useful.

could care less

Now to a phrase that means the opposite of what it says. Happily, the expression "I could care less"—meaning "I could not care less"—seems to be petering out. The phrase popped up first about 1960, appeared in a letter to columnist Ann Landers in 1966, and in a few years began to cause concern as a barbaric attack on meaning. Acheson Hench, in a 1973 article in *American Speech* magazine, claimed it was a slurred form of "couldn't" resulting from two adjacent dental stops: "dnt." Five years later, linguist James McMillan argued that in familiar sayings "less than the whole may effectively carry the semantic burden (hence such shortenings as syncope, clipping and nicknaming)."

Usage seems to have peaked in 1973, when *The Wall Street Journal* headlined: "More and More Girls Flip for Gymnastics; Boys Could Care Less." A healthy derision set in; Herman Wouk called the inversion of meaning "a breezy vulgarism without tang" in the Harper Dictionary of Contemporary Usage, which called it "an ignorant debasement of the language." Maybe the attacks on the antimeaning helped; eventually, like most vogue phrases, it wore out its welcome.

Farewell, "could care less"! You symbolized the exaltation of slovenliness, the demeaning of meaning, and were used by those who couldn't care less about confusing those who care about the use of words to make sense.

---

courier, *see* Molasses Delivery Systems

---

coverup, *see* hyphenating Americans

---

crash, *see* gorilla

---

creaming agent, *see* coffee nerves

---

crisis crisis

Crises always generate platitudes, but sometimes turn up useful old words or bright coinages.

A reader, Saul Singer of Brooklyn, suggested "androlepsy" to describe the Iranian crisis, driving me to the second edition of Merriam-Webster's New International Dictionary: "The seizure by one nation of the citizens or subjects of another . . . to enforce some right claimed by the former against the latter." The obscure term was dropped in the third edition by lexicographers who evidently presumed the practice and its description had disappeared from civilization.

The Economist, a magazine published in London and always interested in neologisms, coined "ochlotheocracy" to describe Iran's government. "You are no doubt familiar with the word 'ochlocracy,' " writes Robert S. Salomon Jr. of New York, fortunately adding, "meaning 'mob rule.' In coining the word 'ochlotheocracy,' *The Economist* has provided a religious connotation to mob rule."

A powerful, little-used word was discovered in a diplomatic cable leaked by the State Department to embarrass Senator Edward Kennedy after his

attack on the idea of asylum in the United States for the deposed Shah. The cable was from the American Ambassador to Argentina, Raul H. Castro, to his superiors at State, summarizing the reasons given by Argentina for not wanting the Shah; among them was reluctance to expose that nation to attacks from prominent United States politicians, as well as "recrudescence" of terrorism. This was defined as "recurrence" in some newspapers, but that loses the flavor: "to recur" means only "to occur again," but "to recrudesce" means "to break out again," evoking the loathed return of a boil or skin disease that had abated. Either an Argentine foreign official speaks English colorfully or Ambassador Castro is improving the quality of our State Department cables.

Finally, the crisis crisis. When the Korean War needed a name, it was officially dubbed "the Korean Conflict" by a Congress which had never declared it a war. The events in Iran are called "the Iranian crisis." But a crisis—from the Greek "to separate"—is a decisive moment, or turning point requiring quick resolution. A "chronic crisis" is a contradiction in terms. "Affair" is not somber enough, and "matter" is weak; Russell Baker alluded to "situation" by writing of deliberations in the "White House Stalemate Room."

"Stalemate" is a possibility, although it has macabre overtones: "stale" is rooted in the Old French "safe place," where ambushers lie, and "mate" means "death." In chess, a stalemate occurs when any move a player made would place his king in check; the result is a draw. ("Checkmate" comes from the Persian "shah mat," or "the shah is dead.")

Deadlock? Challenge? Standoff? Fresh locutions to resolve the crisis crisis would be welcomed.

Meanwhile, an event in the same area churned up a word long used in the newspaper business: "Afghanistanism," which means "too much interest in foreign affairs." William Ringle, chief correspondent of Gannett News Service, called the term to my attention and sent me on its track. The meaning is always pejorative: "It was used way back—back before World War II," recalls Turner Catledge, former executive editor of *The New York Times,* "as a criticism of the coverage of far-off places at the expense of local news." Murrey Marder of *The Washington Post* gives the reporter's view of the word's meaning: "writing about a place or a subject so offbeat that nobody knows if you're right or wrong."

According to Merriam-Webster's *6,000 Words,* Afghanistan was chosen because it was so remote, where little of interest to Americans happened. Now, after the recent Soviet move across its borders, the country has become a cynosure. Says Catledge: "You can't talk about 'Afghanistanism' anymore."

Dear Mr. Safire:

... I believe its choice had nothing to do with Argentine foreign officials speaking "colorful" English. Ambassador Castro, as millions of other Hispanic Americans, is lucky to have two cultures and two languages at his disposal to improve the quality of memos and a few other things. "Recrudescence" is the English equivalent of "recrudecimiento," a powerful but much-used word in Spanish, especially in a political context. The word of course, is of Latin origin. ...

> Cordialmente,
> Dolores Prida
> Executive Senior Editor
> Nuestro, The Magazine for Latinos
> New York, New York

---

crisp, *see* flat

DARE me

"Ah-choo!" goes the sneezer.

"God bless you," some people respond.

"Gesundheit," say others.

"Scat!" is the expressed wish of millions of Southerners.

In all cases, the response stems from the same superstition: When you sneeze, your soul goes out of your body, and unless you are promptly blessed, you are possessed by demons. (Some of the best political columns are written between a sneeze and a blessing.)

"Gesundheit," the German word for "health," is used five times more often than "Scat!" a direct order to entering demons. In Texas, 19 people say "Gesundheit" to 12 for "Scat!" but in Arkansas, it's "Scat!" 6 to 1.

This useful information about how American English varies from place to place comes from preliminary research done by busy linguists producing the Dictionary of American Regional English. DARE is not a book you can buy, but is a project that has several of the early letters of the alphabet finished, and its director hopes to complete its monumental work by the end of 1983.

Professor Frederic Cassidy of the University of Wisconsin, whose Dictionary of Jamaican English has already put him in the league of James (*Caught in the Web of Words*) Murray of the Oxford English Dictionary, can show computerized proof of the frequency of varying vocables beginning with A to M. "Bell pepper" in the South is "green pepper" in the North, and a "fuss" is a "bother" up North but a "fight" down South. For the standard command "Turn out the light," you will hear "Cut off" in the South, "Shut off" and "Snap off" in the North, and, occasionally, "Outten the light" in Pennsylvania and South Carolina, probably from Scottish influences. My own favorite usage—"Douse the glim"—is, Professor Cassidy smiles, widely remembered.

The raw data churn up great questions. Is "Headache!" used as a warning shout by anyone other than mechanics dropping wrenches from great heights in Oklahoma? Is "hootenkack" used as a verb meaning "to talk someone into doing what he doesn't want to do" in any other state than Colorado? Is "pinkletink" used to describe a tree frog that makes that sort of sound except on Martha's Vineyard, Mass.?

If you don't give a hootenkack for a pinkletink, you're insensitive to the color and excitement in our migrating, changing language. DARE is a valuable study of the real American tongue, showing how richly inventive and widely different we are. The American Dialect Society and the University of Wisconsin should be saluted for their sponsorship, and DARE is among the most useful expenditures being made by Joe Duffey at the National Endowment for the Humanities, the Rockefeller Foundation, and the Mellon Foundation. Bequests are wanted from millionaires about to kick the bucket ("boot the pail" in some areas).

I had lunch with Professor Cassidy recently, and it is good to know that a great scholar is hot on the trail of "pop" versus "soda" versus "tonic"; "milkshake" versus "frappe" versus "cabinet"; and "hoagy" versus "sub" versus "hero." He is scrupulous, but no fussbudget (in New York, he is not a "fusspot," and in South Carolina, he is not a "fussbox").

He questions everything about our spoken language. A waiter asked: "Bibb lettuce salad?" And he said: "Thank you," adding to his companion: "Who do you suppose Bibb was?"

Anybody knows that: Major John Bibb was an American grower of the 19th century who produced a lettuce with a small head.

While I'm helping, a loose brick that can be tossed is called an "alley apple" in Washington. And on the subject of shouts of warning for falling objects, let me tell DARE about the piano-moving specialist for the Weissberger Moving and Storage company in New York who was known as Look-Out-Below Bernstein.

As a youngster guarding the short left-field fence at Joan of Arc Junior High in Manhattan, I would occasionally sneeze and be blessed with "Smattagottacoh" by the third baseman. For years, I thought "Smattagottacoh" was a Spanish alternative to "Gesundheit," until it dawned on me that what he was saying quickly was "What's the matter, you got a cold?"

Dear Mr. Safire,

I was interested in your discussion of the differences in the use of words in various parts of this country.

Some years ago I moved from Oregon to New York City. When I 'phoned the grocer for "butter lettuce," my delivery arrived minus the lettuce. I received the message that there was none to be had. On further inquiry I discovered that what to me was "butter lettuce" is here called "Boston lettuce."

Other differences: In the West it is "green onions." In the East it is "scallions." Western "dried onions" are Eastern "cooking onions." Oregon "limestone lettuce" is New York "Bibb lettuce." Away out there we enjoy "sugar peas," which are here called "pea pods."

And getting away from vegetables to flowers, Eastern "corn flowers" are

*Western "bachelor buttons." Eastern "bachelor buttons" West of the Missis-
sippi are "daisies." Luckily a rose is still a rose and an apple an apple.*

Sincerely yours,
Mrs. Jan de Graaff
New York, New York

Dear Mr. Safire:

  . . . *Though I never played baseball at Joan of Arc, I understood smattagottacoh without the translation. But that may be because a college friend from
Brooklyn taught me that "jeet jet" means "did you eat yet?" and "skweet"
means "let's go eat."*

Sincerly,
Eva Moseley
Medford, Massachusetts

Dear Mr. Safire:

  *Your column touches on not one, but two regional variations of definition
that have long fascinated me; those of milkshake/frappe/cabinet, and
hoagy/sub/hero. It must be difficult for Professor Cassidy, from out there in
Wisconsin, to define with reasonable precision the geographical boundaries of
these expressions.*

  *When I lived in Quincy, Massachusetts, as a young person, one had to con-
sider carefully one's location when using the first set of definitions. Just south of
Boston, ordering a milkshake would get you milk mixed with flavored syrup; no
ice cream was included. "Frappe" was the order if ice cream was also desired.
"Cabinet" occurred further south yet, toward the Rhode Island line. If one ordered a frappe there, the reaction was a blank stare; a cabinet came with both
syrup and ice cream, but so did a milkshake, at least until you got to Providence. Incidentally, the French ending of frappe (assuming it was originally
frappé) was never pronounced; it came out "frap."*

  *The large sandwich known as a hero, or hoagy, must be known by those
names far from New England. I think I've seen such names for it in California.
The interesting thing to me, though, is that the name "sub" or even "subma-
rine" is never, to my knowledge, used for such a sandwich anywhere near New
London/Groton, where many of the Navy's submarines are designed, built, and
stationed. Here, they have always been called grinders.*

Sincerely,
John Hunter
Groton, Connecticut

datum/data, *see* plural of "um"

deaccession, *see* prettifiers

demarche, *see* Kissingerese

deplane, *see* airline-ese

depression, *see* banana

desks who write

Whenever I get a note headed "From the desk of . . ." I am inclined to sizzle back something like this: "Tell your desk, which has written to me recently in your name, that it should clean itself out and stop trying to pass itself off as a source of correspondence." When the pompous "From the desk of . . ." comes from a close friend, however, the best reproof is to begin the reply: "Dear Desk."

Desk Top

A recent harangue in this space was directed at writing desks—those pieces of office furniture which presume to send out memos by themselves headed "From the desk of . . ."

A reply has come in from a distressed desk, belonging to Martin Panzer of New York. It points out that nobody ever buys memo pads saying "From the desk of . . ." but receives them from promotion-minded printers.

In its defense, the desk argues that it gets mail from "offices of . . ." rather than from flesh-and-blood executives. "I heard from the office of the president of General Motors," writes this desk. "I got a letter from the Oval Office, it should live and be well. There was a letter from the Middle East

Desk." The metonymy of nonhuman correspondence continues: "There was a note from the White House and one from the Hill. We also hear sometimes from Editorial Departments."

The memo-writing desk suggests the reason for referring to place, instead of people, as the source of correspondence: "A desk also needs friends. A desk has feelings." Ergo, desks stay in touch with offices, departments, and other desks.

I sit corrected.

My dear Mr. Safire:
I enjoy reading your articles each week in The New York Times Magazine. *My attention was particularly attracted by the discussion about desks which send out messages. It reminded me of an organist and choirmaster of a New York City church who remarked that it bothered him when the minister would say, during the service, "And now the organ will play Bach's 'Prelude' or some other piece." He told me once that he thought that one day he would just sit back and listen to the performance!*

Sincerely,
(Miss) Ruth Fitchett
New York, New York

---

disbeliever's lexicon, *see* boggling the mind

---

disconnecting noun

"This is a final disconnect notice," writes the New York Telephone Company. What's a "disconnect"? As a noun, the word should be "disconnection." When the verb form—"disconnect"—is used as a noun, you have a linguistic wrong number. The ding-a-ling who wrote that should self-destruct.

"If your service is interrupted," the same ominous notice continues, "restoral charge will apply." The recipient of this strange communication from the communications company was Richard Amdur of *Cosmopolitan* magazine, who writes, "If I'm not mistaken, the word 'restoral,' used here by the phone company, does not exist."

Right; the word intended is "restoration." The term concocted by the phone company is a good try, on the analogy of "removal," but rings false because there is no need to create a new word when an old one is doing a fine job. (Who would buy tickets for a Restoral comedy?)

However, *"Vea español en el reverso,"* says the notice. In Spanish on the other side, the threat is rendered as *"Un cargo por reinstalación aplicará."* The translator for the phone company eschewed "restoration," which would have been easy to say in Spanish, and ducked "restoral," whatever that means—choosing instead the easily understood "reinstallation." The translator should be writing the English side, too.

I am responding in this space because when I call Mr. Amdur, all I get is a recording.

Re: disconnecting noun

Dear Mr. Safire:

I would like to add a postscript to the Telephone Company's notice—the use of the word "final." It seems to imply "last notice," as though several notices had been sent previously. In fact, only one notice is sent—the offending one.

The "final disconnect" can also be taken to mean "we have taken several steps to disconnect your service and the ultimate scissoring is imminent."

I do believe Ma Bell has managed a rather unique triple-play: the word "final" is at once improper, redundant and ambiguous.

Yours truly,
Susi Resnick
Bayside, New York

Dear Mr. Safire:

Your comment on the Telephone Company's use of "disconnect" as a noun reminds me that it was in San Francisco I first heard the verb "commute" performing a nounal function. Radio and television people here speak of "the daily commute." It jarred; but as time went by, it jarred less, particularly when I considered the obvious alternative. "Commutation" is what the dictionary prescribes but common sense proscribes it: commuters after all commute, they do not commutate. Long ago we accepted the nouns "repute" and "dispute"; so why not "commute"? Indeed, one day soon we will no doubt go into the connect room for the daily compute.

But I imagine we will still be taking medication.

Yours faithfully,
Gordon Sager
San Francisco, California

Dear Sir:

... *The language of telephoney goes back almost 100 years and some of it has gone through many changes. However, many of the original terms, word forms, and usages have stayed the same, principally due to laziness and the lack of a better term. For example, the term PEG COUNT is still used to describe how the system keeps track of the number of calls even though it is now done in computer memory banks. Originally, the operator moved a peg along a board with holes in it (similar to a cribbage board). We've come a long way, Baby!* ...

In any industry some phrases are traditional, stem from original sins (of ignorance), or for lack of a better word or phrase. A similar example is the present-day use of the phrase "steamer connection" in the Fire Service. We don't have horse-drawn steam pumps anymore but we still use the phrase to describe a certain act.

So in the trade, sometimes a verb form is used in place of the noun form. A typical phrase commonly heard inside a central office is: I have three disconnects, two denys, and one restore to work on today.

The interesting point of your article is this: The telephone man (person) who wrote the words "final disconnect notice" was doing the natural thing. The Spanish translator (non-telephone type) made a natural-to-him correction during the translation process.

To sum it all up—Bell System—all bells and no system.

> *G. W. Bates*
> *Documentation Engineer, I.T.T.*
> *Stratford, Connecticut*

Dear Mr. Safire,

You have opened Pandora's Box by mere mention of The Phone Company (TPC to fans of "The President's Analyst"). Your mailbox will be filled with examples of that institution's demolition of the English language.

One example which comes to mind (I was a service representative for Pacific Tel.) is the use of "abeyance" as a concrete noun. Abeyance referred to a three-shelved metal bin on top of one's desk in which pending paper work was kept. "Look in my abeyance" was a common suggestion when something could not be found. It should be noted that no one laughed on hearing this.

> *Sincerely,*
> *Ellen Chatterjee*
> *Allentown, Pennsylvania*

---

double negatives, *see* not un-

---

downhill

"The meanings of the terms 'uphill' and 'downhill' have always confused me," writes Eleanor Gruber of Ridgewood, N.J. "Although the downhill direction represents ease, one is said to be a failure when he 'goes downhill.' Yet I have heard the phrase 'It's an uphill struggle' meaning a difficult struggle, as well as the phrase 'It's all downhill from now on,' meaning, 'Easy!' "

Mrs. Gruber, you came to the right place. Writing this column has been downhill all the way.

According to Grose's Dictionary of the Vulgar Tongue, "downhills" and "uphills" are gambling terms: "downhills" is when dice are loaded to bring out a low, or down, number, and "uphills" is when the dice are loaded to come out high. This has no bearing whatever on Mrs. Gruber's query, but I hate to waste good research.

More to the point: "uphill" offers no confusion. It means "the hard way." Whether you say "It's an uphill struggle," or "It's going to be uphill from now on," that means you're in for a real character builder. No easy answers—even the questions will be hard. You have a challenge ahead; "nobody ever drowned in his own sweat," and all that.

"Downhill" is a different story. "To go downhill" is to decline, in business or in life. When a relationship goes downhill, it's splitsville. (Does anybody have a good replacement for "relationship"? There's a word going downhill.) When "go" is the verb near "downhill," the news is bad; use Jack 'n' Jill for a mnemonic.

However, "downhill," without the "go"—as in "From here on, it's downhill all the way"—probably means "Now it's going to be easy," and may have its origin in skiing (many skiers find it easier skiing downhill than up). In a nutshell, to "go" downhill is to decline—especially if followed by "all the way"—but to "be" downhill is to be sailing along easily. Understanding the difference is uphill.

Just a darn minute, there, Bill Safire! "Downhills IS WHEN"? . . . and "Uphills IS WHEN"? Master Carol Brown at Westtown used to scold his classes about this. My wife remembers that very well.

Query: Does the Copy Desk write your headings? Ours does, changes mine any time it wants to (usually does). . . . But fine column today. A good column is when . . .

> Sincerely,
> John F. Gummere
> (The Philadelphia Inquirer)
> *Philadelphia, Pennsylvania*

Dear Sir:

In Stings and Scams *I found your definition of "uphills": ". . . 'uphills' is when the dice are loaded to come out high." I saw in this "definition" one of your fiendish booby-traps strewn about to keep your readers on the qui vive. Other such "definitions" would be: a jaguar is when a cat has spots; or a definition is when meaning is given to a word. . . .*

> Yours truly,
> Tom Phipps
> *Urbana, Illinois*

---

down the tubes

Senator Henry Jackson is not a man given to vivid expression; of him, it was said that "if Scoop Jackson ever gave a fireside chat, the fire would go out." But this hard-line politician used a colorful bit of slang recently when he warned that unless the Soviets withdrew troops and planes from Cuba, the SALT treaty would go "down the tubes."

The phrase had been used in politics before. When Richard Nixon was asked in 1968 why he had campaigned for Barry Goldwater in 1964, he replied: "I did not just do it for Goldwater, but to try to save congressmen, senators and governors who were going down the tube with him."

Note the singular "tube"—that's the secret to the origin of the phrase. In surfing, "the tube" is a hollow tunnel which forms in the face of a long wave just before the wave breaks. "To shoot the tube" is to ride near the top of the wave under the curl, or through the hollow, or tubular, part of the curl, as it moves along the wave. (Is that clear? If not, pour a little suntan oil on the page.)

In time, surfers used the verb "to tube" to mean "to do poorly," since shooting the tube required an awkward-looking stance or an amateurish prone position. When surfers went to school and failed a test, instead of saying "I flunked it," they would say "I tubed it," or "I flushed it."

At this point—sometime in the 60's—plumbing metaphors merged with the surfing metaphor. "Down the drain" and the more recent "down the pipe" combined with the surfer slang to become "down the tube." Of late, the plumbing became more complex, and the phrase is "down the tubes," plural, distinguishing those tubes from the singular television, or boob, tube.

Were it not for lexicographers Peter Tamony and Sol Steinmetz, this phrase, as the surfers say, would have wiped me out.

Dear Safire:
"*. . . a hollow tunnel . . .*"? *Tsk, tsk, tsk.*

E. S.
(*Edward Salner*)
Baltimore, Maryland

---

due process, *see* stings and scams

---

eager, *see* anxious or eager?

---

eating your cake

Senate majority leader Robert Byrd, speaking two years ago in favor of tying a raise in Senate salaries to a cut in the amount that Senators could earn from outside sources, warned his confreres: "We have gotten our salary increase . . . but we cannot have our cake and eat it, too."

His figure of speech was inverted. "There is a popular proverbial expression which most people get wrong," writes George S. Hendry of Princeton, N.J. "They say: 'You can't have your cake and eat it.' You can—if you do the two things in that order; in fact, you must have your cake before you can eat it. The trick is to eat your cake and have it."

In the dark of one recent night, Senator Byrd reversed his position against the limitation of outside income and slipped a provision through the Senate that gives the Senators their salary increase and lets them keep their previous ceiling on outside income. That's eating your cake and having it, too.

---

effectificity

"One of these days," goes the caption on a famous cartoon of two guys with their feet on a desk, "we've got to get organized." Evidently that thought struck the White House recently, and a leading management consultant was hired as a deputy to the President's chief of staff.

Although he is widely known as "Ham Jordan's Haldeman," the real name of the man assigned the task of bringing crisp, businesslike efficiency to the center of power is Alonzo McDonald Jr. ("Alonzo" is a Spanish-Portuguese name, best known in the United States as a monicker for football coaches; combined with the Scottish "McDonald" it makes the roundest and most satisfying name to pronounce in Washington today.)

Alonzo McDonald speaks a special language. In a profile by Martin Schram of *The Washington Post,* his hard-driving patois was derided as "neo-Jeb Magruder" and—in an unkind cut—a sample of Alonzo's language was displayed:

"There's a hope that some of the cross-roughing will be done earlier . . . that decisions will be broadly based . . . that we can increase inputs.

"We need a process of involvement . . . a synthesization," the President's new organizer went on. "We've got to look at how problems interlink, the monitoring and the execution. . . . When there's an uncontrollable problem, that's the point in time when we must have analysis before we have ad hoc action."

I dialed Alonzo McDonald's number at the White House, spoke to one of his aides (called a "higby," after one of Haldeman's honchos), and explained I needed four and a half minutes for semantic instruction. There came a point in time when Alonzo returned the call.

Is he worried about being charged with speaking bureaucratese?

"It's not bureaucratese," he replied briskly but amiably. "It's a good solid business-operating vocabulary."

Cross-roughing?

"That's a term from bridge. It means taking an idea, rubbing it against different opposing ideas, so as to refine it. An idea that hasn't been cross-roughed has not been rubbed smooth by conflicting ideas." The word can be spelled two ways: "cross-rough," as in polishing a stone, or "cross-ruff," as in trumping a playing card ("ruff," the act of trumping in a game similar to whist, can be traced to 1598).

Interlink? Is that any different from the tired old word "connect"? Is it a combined form of "interface" and "linkage"?

"I use 'interlink' as it is used in electrical circuitry," said the highly charged executive. "It is not just connected—there's movement in there, current is passing through. It's important that we know how that current will flow, so that we don't hit a short. That way, we can improve our effectificity."

Effectificity? As a sucker for a neologism, I thought that one over carefully. When businessmen wanted to use the adjective "specific" as a noun, they rejected "specificness" and chose "specificity"; could it be that in turning the most important adjective in management consulting—"effective"— into a noun, they were setting aside "effectiveness" for the more electric-sounding "effectificity"?

"No," said Alonzo McDonald, less crisply. "Actually, I think I meant effectiveness."

My time was up and I thanked him.

"Any time," he said. "Effectiveness," he added, as if practicing the word, and hung up.

electronic journalism

"Eejay"—or "E.J."—stands for "electronic journalism," a phrase coined two decades ago by Eric Sevareid, and used today to denote a new, portable television camera that records on videotape and broadens the scope of television news coverage. By synecdoche the term describes the wide world of television journalism which is developing a lexicon of its own:

Voice Wrap: The use of a newscaster's voice to introduce and to close a piece of film or tape. Marine terminology is pressed into service for modifiers, as "fore" and "aft" sections of the voice wrap. Not to be confused with

Voice Over: Spoken commentary accompanying the film being shown.

Hot Switch: A change from one live event to another without a commentator's soothing transition, or a cut to tape. Not to be confused with a

Whiparound: A news-show technique in which an anchor man introduces the three successive reporters in one long breath, as the cameras cut from one to the other without new introductions.

Another Pretty Face: "A derogation of local anchor men, I like to think," says NBC's Tom Brokaw, who contributed "hot switch" to this glossary. A hatchet-faced or otherwise ugly newsman who finds himself replaced by a better-looking person scorns the replacement as "just another pretty face." However, a pretty face does not mean that you are "another pretty face": Neither Jessica Savitch nor Hilary Brown, for example, is "another pretty face," which is no derogation of their looks.

Piece of Manpower: A network term for "star." Roger Mudd is a piece of manpower. Not sexist: Barbara Walters is a piece of manpower. The phrase is usually spoken with awe.

Bite or Snatch: A short piece of film which comes inside the aforementioned "voice wrap," as: "Give us a bite of Carter."

Actualities: This is a reborn radio term for "what is actually happening," a snippet of on-the-scene reporting or a view of an event unfolding before the camera's eye, which the producer hopes will transcend verisimilitude and achieve verity.

Bird Feed: "Feed" is any transmission; the "bird" is a satellite, its name taken from the "Early Bird" designation of Telstar. A transmission via satellite is a bird feed.

Pubcaster: Not, as Daniel Schorr suggests, "someone who sounds off in a bar," but a news analyst on public radio or television, which Mr. Schorr now is.

It Looked Good Leaving Here (NBC version), or *It Left Here All Right* (ABC and CBS version): A sadly joking rejoinder to complaints of garbled reception. If you're broadcasting from Peking and a message from New

York says your transmission is a mess of squiggly lines, you are expected to utter the classic phrase. A recently ousted network president is thinking of making it the title of his memoirs.

Dear Mr. Safire:

Before your face gets eggier, let's go back to basics about the wonderful world of television:

No one I know of now working for the networks' evening news broadcasts ever calls what we do "eejay," "E.J." or even "electronic journalism." Eric Sevareid, I believe, tends to use his compound noun as a proper insult to those in radio and television news who have mastered the technology but lack traditional editorial skills.

Broadcasting's acronym for the last few years has been "ENG"—written without periods but pronounced "E," "N," "G." It (they?) means Electronic News Gathering (but don't ask me what happened to the hyphen, or why newsgathering isn't one word, because I don't know).

ENG seems to have been spread originally by equipment manufacturers, who needed a distinctive identifier during the three or four year transition from film to tape. (Advertisements in Broadcast Engineering *would talk about GETTING INTO ENG, and describe products as THE NEWEST IN ENG.) Network and station executives—who had to tell stockholders and accountants why they suddenly needed another $2 million—turned ENG into a coded signal for We're-Really-With-It!*

So everybody talked about "going ENG," and "getting new ENG equipment"—except inside 524 West 57th Street, where CBS News President Richard Salant decided that his organization definitely does not *gather news like leaves or lost marbles.*

CBS News, Salant felt, covers events, speeches and people, determining news-value not by indiscriminate harvest but through an editorial process involving correspondents, producers and (sometimes) executives. From that point on, your "E.J.," and others' "ENG," became "ECC" (pronounced "E," "C," "C.") at CBS News, for Electronic Camera Coverage.

Much of this alphabet-speaking is disappearing, since almost all broadcast news organizations have become—as they say—"all electronic." Today's verbal shorthand deals more with parts and products than the whole field.

Among workers and rivals, you hear about BVU-50's (Sony's new portable videotape recorder, half the weight of the widely used BVU-100's), HL-79's (Ikegami's latest, lightest camera, called "one-piece" because the battery for it is inside rather than having to be carried separately), 200-500 systems (a pair of Sony's large editing-units, connected and run through a button-studded control-panel), TBC's and Microtime 2020's (older and newer Time Base Correctors, essential for broadcast-quality playback of tape cassettes), Time Code Generators (add-on devices which record the time of day along with whatever else is being recorded on a cassette, to facilitate finding things during later

editing), Quads, Squeeze-Zooms, Soft-edge Wipes (all visual effects you'd recognize if you were to see them, but available only on the newest Control Room
Switchers costing a quarter-of-a-million dollars or so).

Your lexicon doesn't need those terms; they'll all be replaced eventually. But
you should be accurate in the terms you do use:

News—as generally understood to be an organized set of facts available at a
given time—is "broadcast," "reported" or "delivered" by "anchormen" ("anchorperson," if you insist), "correspondents" and "reporters." None of them is
a "commentator," and none of what they do is "commentary," a word the networks consistently have reserved for analysis. At CBS News, when conclusions
are offered from facts, it's called—without apology—"commentary." We even
"super" the word on the television-screen (as do the other networks).

It can get confusing: Marvin Kalb, for instance, is CBS News' Diplomatic
Correspondent. He does "reports," "spots" and "pieces" for CBS News, on
both radio and television. He's not, however, a "newscaster," since he doesn't
"anchor" a news broadcast. He does offer analysis of events on the CBS Radio
News broadcast First Line Report, but it's "billboarded" at beginning and end
as ". . . news and commentary . . ." Are you still with me?

Your use of "spoken commentary" in VOICE OVER is redundant and inaccurate; what you mean is "narration," which—these days—accompanies tape,
not film. VOICE OVER is an interesting form: one can "do a voice over," "do

it (a spot) voice over" (no preceding article), or be "all voice over" (not seen on camera anywhere in the piece).

A special kind of VOICE OVER— which is never called that—occurs when an anchorperson in a studio begins reading a story on camera, then, five or 10 seconds later, is "covered" (replaced on the screen) with pictures of what's being talked about, say, a fire, while the anchorperson continues reading. That's called a "telop," and network television uses a lot of them. The word originally described the optical projection of a still picture—using a special slide-projector—"full-screen," as opposed to being behind a correspondent's shoulder. Full-screen moving pictures, with an anchorperson's narration, became "living telops," abbreviated on "lineups" or "rundowns" as "LTP."

I'm not familiar with using FORE and AFT for anything in television news. We sometimes talk about WRAPAROUNDS, or "wrapping around" a sound-cut, but, usually, we discuss pieces by type, or by parts.

The simplest spot is a "straight standup," in which a correspondent delivers a report directly into the camera. The White House and the State Department yield more of these than other beats, because so few pictures of what's being reported exist at either place. Sometimes, part or all of a standup can be "covered," after being recorded, by editing-over "stock footage" of the subject of the piece. Some kinds of "stock footage" are so easily available—Pentagon handouts, for example—that the "cover picture" is referred to, casually, as "wallpaper." ("Stock footage," by the way, is a film term—film being counted in feet. Videotape is counted in minutes-and-seconds, but no word has come along yet to replace "footage.")

When figures or quotes are thought helpful to understanding a spot, they're "fonted" over the cover picture. The letters and numbers are called "font" because (1) they come in different styles, like type, and (2) they're generated electronically by a "vidifont machine," operated from a typewriter keyboard.

The second common network news piece has no name at all; it's the one which involves those WRAPAROUNDS. These pieces typically begin "voice over" (a hearing, a news conference, scenes of a flood, etc.), which continues to "the set-up" (specifically showing the person who's about to be heard from), which is followed by a "sound-bite" or "sound-cut," and a close.

Once a producer and a correspondent (and, very often, the editor who's going to cut the spot) work out the mechanics, a script is written. Either the producer tells the correspondent how long to write each segment, or the correspondent writes the script and presents it to the producer for approval.

> PRODUCER (WHO LIKES FIRST METHOD): *"I'll give ya 10-to-15 seconds voice over at the top, then a five second set-up shot; 20 seconds at the outside."*
>
> CORRESPONDENT (WHO LIKES SECOND METHOD): *"Nah; I've already written 25 seconds for the top. Lemme lay down that track (record it) so I can write the rest of this."*

All of the preceding concerns "spot news," which is most of what appears on the evening news broadcasts. But there are a couple of other kinds of stories worth mentioning: "takeouts" and "end-pieces" (or "kickers").

A "takeout" is longer than a regular news report, and the term implies that considerable time and effort have gone into the piece, usually over a number of days (or, rarely, weeks). A "takeout" is a serious look at a serious subject, and when a peg pops up earlier than expected, or news events dictate instant, complex sidebars (e.g., Three Mile Island's near-melt meant a detailed look immediately at nuclear power nationwide), a "takeout" will be done "quick and dirty." That doesn't mean it won't be almost as good as one that takes days to finish; it does assure that everybody will have their tongues hanging out before it "makes air."

Light, feature-y, funny or bizarre subjects may lend themselves to becoming "end-pieces" (or "kickers"). As in print, stories of this kind sometimes are very, very hard to pull off successfully.

BIRD FEEDS? Well, yes, but everybody has dropped one of the two words. What you hear is, "What time's the bird today?" or, "Ya got somebody back there (in videotape) taking in this London feed?" Satellite transmission doesn't cause the flurry it once did, especially now that domestic stories from Los Angeles, Chicago and Dallas can "get on the bird" to New York—and do, daily. (One New York producer calls what comes in by satellite "bird droppings," but the terminology's never caught on.)

PIECE OF MANPOWER is new to me. I most often hear "on air talent" graded on what you might call the "gorilla scale," which hardly is unique to broadcasting. There are "800-pound gorillas"—sometimes known, when out of ear-shot, as "The Gorilla," or "The 800-pounder." Lesser but important correspondents occasionally are called "400-pounders." We also use some odd noun-forms: "Who's the voice on this piece?" Or, "See if the talent is back from lunch yet." Or, "Look out, the star's not in a very good mood today."

There are some words that everyone uses seriously and sparingly, since they convey a message of doom. "To crash," in all its forms, describes harried work against a deadline. When someone announces that "we may crash with the lead piece," or "Chicago's crashing on both pieces tonight," they're telling the producers putting the broadcast together in New York to start thinking of other options. "Going down in flames" is another no-kidding warning that a piece may not be finished in time to make the broadcast. Everybody trying to help "throw it together" is said to be "doing a crazy dance."

Pieces that don't make a broadcast—although they were finished and ready—have been "dumped," "pushed out," or, simply, "passed." When a late feed has not come in and the start of the broadcast rapidly is approaching, a New York producer may order that a completed piece not in the lineup be ready to go:

PRODUCER: "Y'know that Memphis piece we dumped? Well, Cleveland isn't in yet, so ya better get it up somewhere (have it cued on a videotape machine)."

"Takeouts" that are "passed" for a particular broadcast—"pushed out" for other news, usually—are "put on the shelf," or "kept in the bank." Sometimes, a "takeout" will sit on the shelf so long that it's judged to have "grown a beard," and dies—never to be seen, unless another broadcast will take it.

Otherwise, words are less colorful. Good producers and correspondents and "can-do." Good pieces are "winners." Bad people and bad pieces are "losers." A terrible piece is "the pits." A broadcast that "blows up" on air—technical breakdowns, pieces out of sequence—is (or was) "a disaster." Profanity is common: we "kick the shit out of the competition," although sometimes they "kick the shit out of us." A truly dreadful spot is—what else—"a piece of shit."

I'm sorry to have run on like this; I started out to write you a short letter about your column, which I enjoy very much.

If I don't stop here, we'll soon be into "long throws," "quick outs," "loops," "jump-cuts," "editek pairs," "drops" and "cold opens." I don't know if either of us could stand it.

Sincerely,
John A. Armstrong

P.S. C'mon with PUBCASTER; Dan, I'm sure, made that up.

---

epitaph

Two giants in the world of words died recently: Eric Partridge, the lexicographer of slang and hunter of clichés, and Theodore Bernstein, *The New York Times* authority on usage who exorcised "Miss Thistlebottom's Hobgoblins."

Both were generous with their time and would unfailingly respond to the queries of budding word-watchers. An epitaph for both can be found in some lines from a poem W. H. Auden wrote on the death of Yeats:

> *Time that is intolerant*
> *Of the brave and innocent,*
> *And indifferent in a week*
> *To a beautiful physique,*
> *Worships language and forgives*
> *Everyone by whom it lives.**

erosion, *see* slippage

ethnic and other slurs

When Iran threatened to withdraw its money from United States banks, and the United States countered with a freeze on Iranian assets, a London foreign-exchange dealer who was buffeted by the action and reaction was reported to have exclaimed "It's bananaville down here."

He was in error. "Banana," singular, is used to derogate Latin American nations, as in "banana republic"; "bananas," plural, is used to mean "crazy," or—in the sense intended by the London trader—"crazily frenetic."

Bananaville, then, would be a disparagement of a lazy tropical town, a world apart from Bananasville, that frantic city across the river from Shrinksville. Let's try to keep the singular and plural meanings separate.

On the subject of national or regional derogation, one reader—who signs herself "Rachel Slurz," but that cannot be her real name—asks: "What is the origin of the phrase 'Mexican standoff'?"

Long before Polish jokes, American English incorporated ethnic putdowns in various phrases. Just as the English knocked the Dutch ("Dutch treat" for no treat at all, and "Dutch courage" for drunken ferocity), Americans knocked the Mexicans: In Texas, a "Mexican breakfast" is a cigarette and a glass of water, offering no nourishment, and the phrase "Mexican standoff" came to mean one of those impasses from which no good would come.

In recent years, with the assertion of ethnic pride, the language has tended to purge itself of stereotyped national characteristics (although kids still call other kids who take back presents "Indian givers"). In one usage about Mexicans, the change has been extreme, from slur to neutral description and finally to euphemism: "Wetbacks" (from having entered the United States by swimming the Rio Grande) became "illegal aliens"; as that category came to include millions of people, it was changed to "undocumented workers." The objection to the use of this bureaucratic euphemism has led nowhere, or to what can best be called an American standoff.

Dear Mr. Safire,
*   . . . As to "Mexican standoff," I believe it originated as a derisive description of a battle in which opposing forces would do a lot of posturing and fire a lot of*

shots, and would then mutually withdraw without settling the issue. Thus, it
would be more accurately described as "one of those impasses from which no
decision *would come."* ...

Sincerely,
Harley E. Barnhart
Sarasota, Florida

---

euphemism

The art of euphemism—refusing to use painful words like "dying"—has not
passed away.

At Harvard's Graduate School of Business Administration, Professor
Howard Raiffa teaches a course in Competitive Decision Making that realis-
tically faces up to a negotiator's need to lie: Students must realize, instructs
Professor Raiffa, that occasions will arise when they will be particularly
vulnerable if they honestly reveal information that could be exploited by
less scrupulous adversaries. The name he has adopted for one option to be
considered when bluffing, or misleading, seems called for is "strategic misrepresentation," which the earliest residents of this continent called "speaking with forked tongue" and which we honestly call "lying."

To some degree, euphemism is strategic misrepresentation. A few years
ago, I wrote a column which contained what a State Department spokesman
denounced as a "contemptuous lie." (He meant "contemptible," and, when
corrected, growled, "That, too.") Henry Kissinger, who was Secretary of
State at that time, was more restrained in his public reaction; he called it "a
canard." As one who smacks his lips over *canard rôti à l'orange,* I wondered
why the French word for duck—*canard*—means lie or great hoax. A nervous
man at State's French desk, who kept saying he did not want to get involved,
explained that the original expression was *vendre un canard à moitié,* "to
half-sell a duck"—that is, to pretend to sell it with intent to cheat. In English, though, "canard" has come to mean "lie"; it carries an overtone of tall
story that euphemistically takes much of the sting out of such an accusation.

A Park Ranger in the Grand Canyon has an assignment to kill the wild
burros who eat the scrub and cause erosion. Just as C.I.A. operatives used
"termination with extreme prejudice" to describe liquidation, itself a euphemism for "assassination," the Park Service calls its necessary interces-
sion with natural ecology "direct reduction." "Are you going to kill the
burros?" asked a CBS reporter. "Well, sir, we call it 'direct reduction.' "

Calling this to my attention, newsman Michael Winship wonders: "What do you suppose *indirect* reduction of burros constitutes? Birth-control lectures?" (Birth control, by the way, is not a euphemism; it is a more understandable term for contraception.) Another reader, David Silberstein of Connecticut, suggests that the next euphemism for "birth control" will be "evading the issue."

The best new advertising sweetener was sent in by editorial writer Harold Lavine of *The Arizona Republic:* "There is a used-car dealer on Camelback Road in Phoenix who sells 'pre-owned Cadillacs.'" This usage, which eschews "used," can also be heard hawking a previously owned Mercedes in Maryland. Cheap cars become used; expensive cars become previously owned. (Would you buy a previously owned car from this candidate?)

"Sweeten," ironically, is a word advertisers are shying away from in these drying times. An apple-juice manufacturer who adds a sweetener to his product has rejected "sweetened" in favor of a new participle: "sophisticated." Apple juice is less tart when it has been sophisticated by a ton of sugar.

The most significant euphemism of the year was introduced into the field that understands opinion-molding best: public relations. That phrase was coined by Ivy Lee, who burnished John D. Rockefeller's image; it was shaped into "public relations counsel" by Edward L. Bernays, who detested "press agent," and was replaced in the military by "public information," which seemed less manipulative; it has been further euphemized into "public affairs" and "corporate communications."

Comes now the Environmental Protection Agency (populated by what used to be called "conservationists") to comb its flacks in a new and far more other-directed way: the Office of Public Awareness. "There's been a tendency to P.R. the public," explained Joan Nicholson, director and namer of the office, who uses the initials of "public relations" as a pejorative verb, "about how groovy the agency is. I wanted to somehow signal the public that we were wanting to hear from them. . . ." Evidently public awareness is an offshoot of what used to be called "outreach" until it was hooted out of existence, and will one day be followed by an Office of Public Sympathy, headed by a chaplain handing out punchable cards.

Miss Nicholson ought to be made publicly aware that few people use "groovy" anymore. Also, please be aware that calling a flack an awarenik denigrates the pervasive function of public relations, sophisticating a previously owned expression to the point of strategic misrepresentation.

Dear Mr. Safire:

In reading your article on euphemisms, I was reminded of a small subset of expressions in illness-related matters.

Consumption led to the use of the more scientific tuberculosis; this, in turn, gave rise to the substitute initials TB. There is a similar development in the changes that led from tumors to cancer to CA. Gall-bladder disease now masquerades as GB.

The use of initials reminds me here of another construction. The impolite expression (from the German) given in Yiddish as putz, to mean a person with faulty thought processes and other aberrant behavior, shifted from not being spoken but to be spelled out. This then transforms to pay, tzadik. In the mouths of American "Yeshiva boys" the expression in Williamsburgh, Brooklyn and other communities came out as "stop being a big pay tzadik." This exhortation was intended to redirect someone who was behaving foolishly and to get him to change his behavior at the moment. A further transformation has taken place and now we can hear someone hollering out "stop being an 80-90." In Hebrew the letters of the alphabet have numeric values and the most polite and benign way of calling someone a putz is to call him an "80-90."

Sincerely,
Donald Meyers
Flushing, New York

Dear Mr. Safire:

When you write about doctors, do you use the term "quack"? And when referring to attorneys, do you call them "shysters"? Then why, when writing about public relations people, as you did in your column on euphemisms, do you call them "flacks"?

"Flack" is a pejorative, not a euphemism. Is there some reason you want to disparage a useful (if not noble) profession that gave you your start?

Sincerely yours,
Bernard E. Ury
Chicago, Illinois

Dear Mr. Safire:

I enjoyed your comments on euphemisms, particularly the emphasis placed on Harvard's Graduate School of Business Administration on the phrase, "strategic misrepresentation." Note well that the Reverend Moon in contemporary pop-faith uses and indoctrinates his followers in the phrase "heavenly deception." A lie by any other name. . . .

Euphemisms can be delicate exercises in gentleness. The Talmud refers to a blind person as one possessed with "extra light." This may be due to the fact that a blind person is endowed with sensory perception not given the rest of us.

Sincerely,
Rabbi Israel C. Stein
Bridgeport, Connecticut

Dear Mr. Saphire:

That apple juice man who sells "sophisticated" instead of "sweetened" juice has the language on his side, and probably figures, correctly, that most people are somewhat in awe of the word and those people and things alleged to have that attribute (speaking euphemistically). My dictionaries define "sophisticated" as "mixed with some foreign substance; adulterated . . ."

I still recall, as a schoolboy, running across the picture of an English pub, probably in a National Geographic Magazine, with a sign advertising "Unsophisticated Ales & Beers." This provided great amusement to those of us who imagined ourselves "sophisticated" until we looked the word up.

Sincerely,
Clifford H. Ramsdell
South Orange, New Jersey

Dear Mr. Safire:

Your article on euphemisms gives credit for "pre-owned" to sources in Arizona and Maryland. Actually, for many years the firm of Becker and Becker in Philadelphia, Pa., has been advertising "pre-owned minks" on television. If you can find out whether the Beckers themselves or their advertising agency coined the phrase, you will have the rightful inventor of this charming word.

Also, you have not mentioned the most ingenious euphemism—(I use it every semester to illustrate the meaning of "euphemism" to my communications seniors) and that, I think, is "life" insurance. If you can trace the man who came up with that one, you may be able to give the P.R. profession what Freud is to psychology and Einstein to science.

Sincerely yours,
Eva B. Neisser
Vineland, New Jersey

---

euphemisms, *see* banana

Experience counts

The business world is doing to "experience" what the academic world is doing to "arts."

We all know how status-conscious school administrators have changed the name of English courses to "The Language Arts"; this will one day produce legions of language artists, much as the teaching of "the confidence arts" produces con artists. Other courses have been named "communications arts" but the message about what is taught cannot get through the underbrush of the overview.

Other academics have used the word "experience" to enliven the names of courses with a trendy sense of totality: Thus, "American Literature" becomes "The Reading Experience," which presumably includes Music-Appreciation While Reading, Reading on the Grass While Relating to Friends, Looking at the Written Word and Scratching Yourself, etc.

Businessmen have been drawn to this cathedral of archness. Advertising for Miami Beach, Fla., promises "a whole new experience." At the spruced-up Fontainebleau Hilton, the indoor pool is being replaced by a running track, roller-skating rink, and weight-lifting center called "an athletic experience"; the old stores are being replaced by chic boutiques to offer "a shopping experience"; the restaurants that used to offer a nibble here and a nosh there are being coordinated and "themed" into "an eating experience."

I don't mind the merchandisers doing their thing; I do mind the academics doing the merchandiser's thing. In business, "experience" counts, but in school, "arts" is crafty.

---

eyeball to eyeball, *see* meta-fore!

Fair's not fair

In a recent Associated Press/NBC News poll, only 19 percent of those polled gave President Carter a "good" or "excellent" rating. Forty-nine percent rated Mr. Carter's work as "only fair," and 30 percent called it "poor," with 2 percent "not sure."

Meeting with non-Washington reporters, the President dealt with this poll—which would distress most politicians—in an upbeat way. He suggested that the word "fair" reflected positive feelings: "Where I come from, which is southwest Georgia . . . if somebody says, 'I think he's doing a fair job,' that is high approbation."

What does "fair" mean? Perhaps, as the President suggests, there is a regional difference in meaning, with Southerners taking "fair" to mean "doing fairly well." Not all Southerners agree: "I wish that I were back in grade school," writes Denton Hall of Delray Beach, Fla., "so that I could explain to my parents that my marks of 'Fair' were really 'high approbation.' " (The President probably meant "approval"; "approbation" means "official approval.")

In most of the country, "fair" is a word that has been taking a beating. In its sense of "just," the meaning is stable: When Mr. Carter said two years ago, "There are many things in life that are not fair," he used the word in the same sense and value as did John Kennedy with "Life is unfair." But in the sense of "average"—as in "I'm feeling fair"—the meaning is slipping to "below average." When a scale runs from "excellent" to "good" to "fair" to "poor," the dividing line seems to be above "fair," especially when the adverb "only" is added—"only fair" is synonymous with "not so hot."

To the grimly optimistic, however, the word retains its clear-sky connotation: In Mr. Carter's estimation, only the brave deserve a "fair."

Dear Mr. Saffire,

I think you made a mistake in your column On Language. *You ended with the expression: 'only the brave deserve a "fair." ' In my opinion you should have written 'none but the brave deserves "a fair." ' The quotation is from* Alexander's Feast *by Dryden.*

> Yours truly,
> Harriet Epstein
> New York, New York

fashionese

The F.B.I.'s list of "Ten Most Wanted Criminals"—mug shots on display at your local post office—owes its origin to the fashion industry in New York. In 1940, fashion publicist Eleanor Lambert turned a French promotion into an international survey: "The Ten Best Dressed Women." In 1950, Miss Lambert's husband, the late Seymour Berkson, then head of the International News Service, sent I.N.S. rewrite man James Lee to the F.B.I. with the catchy "Ten Most Wanted Criminals" idea; three decades later, both lists are going strong.

It was natural, then, for a word-watcher to turn to Miss Lambert for her list of the ten words women need to know to be well-dressed this season. Here is her response:

- Bias
- Body suit
- Retro
- Bustier
- Tailleur

- Blazer
- Pillbox
- Jacquard
- Cinched
- Maillot

With the help of a 1939 fashion dictionary by Mary Brooks Picken, and some calls to French-speaking seamstresses, here are the meanings of this year's ten most-wanted fashion words:

Bias: In cutting material, a line taken diagonally across the warp and woof threads. Clothes cut on the bias hug the figure closely.

Body Suit: A one-piece undergarment of some elastic material used to gently shape or firm the body, or to give an illusion of nudity. ("Pantyhose that go clear up to the neck" is not a suitable definition.)

Retro: Fashion slang for "retrogressive," the opposite of futuristic. Describes a harkening back to a distinctive look of another era, now applied mostly to the 40's and 50's.

Bustier: A strapless top or dress held in place by its clingy knit or elasticized fabric.

Tailleur: A tailored suit with crisply finished edges, often mannish in feeling, as opposed to softly draped or flowing styles.

Blazer: A lightweight sports jacket, now usually a solid color, originally so-called because it was made in brilliant vertical stripes, blazing away along with the "school tie."

Pillbox: Not, as commonly thought, "a low, concrete emplacement for antitank weapons," but a small round hat with flat top and straight sides, such as once worn by a short bellman calling for a cigarette manufacturer.

Jacquard: A fabric with a figured weave made on a Jacquard loom.

Cinched: Tightly girded, as a waist made to seem smaller by the sucking-in of guts before fastening. From the Latin for "to gird," used in Spanish to apply to horses' saddles. Since the meaning is "to get a tight grip on," this led to "easy to handle," and thus to the American slang noun for a simple matter, a "cinch."

Maillot: A one-piece swimsuit (formerly called a bathing suit), cinched all over; also any form-fitting garment. From the French word for tights.

Now you are armed with the necessary lingo for a sybaritic stroll with a *soignée* swinger. If these words soon lose their vogue, Miss Lambert has a second list of ten (much as the F.B.I. has a fresh group of suspects and escapees to replace their top ten when caught). You'll have to work these out for yourself:

- Tank
- Bermudas
- Bandeau
- Canotier
- Deco

- Sarong
- Fagoting
- Tussah
- Iridescent
- Feathered

To hold down the volume of mail, I'd better define "fagoting": It is the thread, yarn, or braid used straight or crisscrossed in the open seam to form openwork trimming. The technique of fagoting, or enlarged hemstitching, joins two pieces of cloth so as to give a lacy effect. One "g," one "t."

Follow-up to "fashionese"

An item cluttering up the shame-on-you file is my misuse a few weeks back of "hearken," as "hearkening back." Ain't no such thing. "To hearken" means "to pay heed, to listen closely"; but "to hark back" means "to revert." I meant to say that "retro" fashions were a harkening-back to a previous day.

The important thing, in writing a column on language, is not to let mistakes make you self-conscious—otherwise, you can never finish a sentence. So I'll just plow ahead (plough?), and if I make mistake, the hell with it (*to hell with it?*).

Dear Mr. Safire:
    Shame for not knowing that the American farmer turned the prairie sod with a "plow." (Perhaps he uses a computer now.) The English farmer tills his soil with a "plough."
    The difference in the spelling of this implement was one of the few significant clues that Dr. Watson spotted in The Adventure of the Three Garridebs. *Sherlock commended him with "you improve all the time."*
    That "clew" helped Sherlock Holmes identify the benefactor/murderer, who was, of course, the notorious American Killer Evans, a.k.a John Garrideb, a.k.a James Winter, a.k.a Morecroft.
    You should have known.

        many thanks
        Arthur Hopkins Hudson
        Fairhope, Alabama

feisty

"Feisty" is one of the hottest new words around. Newsmagazine profilists find it impossible to describe China's Deng Xiaoping without hailing his feistiness; television commentators cannot refer to Israel's Menachem Begin without wondering why he is so feisty. "Feisty" is to with-it wordsmiths as "perceived" is to academics, "luminous" is to theater reviewers, "asymmetric" is to SALT sellers, "trenchant" is to book blurbers, and "abrasive" used to be to political writers before Bella Abzug left the scene.

The word is in the American Heritage Dictionary with its two different meanings: (1) "touchy, excitable, quarrelsome" and (2) "spirited, frisky."

Which meaning is taking over? Is Deng a sassy troublemaker, or an ebullient free spirit? Is Begin an irascible curmudgeon, or a lively effervescent? (And why can't I use "effervescent" as a noun?)

A clue can be found in the word's root: A "feist" is a small dog of mixed ancestry, a flatulent mongrel. Since a mutt has a reputation for friskiness and self-reliance, the Southern regionalism seems to picture frisky tail wagging rather than snarling hackle raising.

I think the word is being used mostly in grudging admiration; to be "feisty," in the positive sense, is to be self-assured to the point of cockiness, willing to take issue and provoke discussion.

But the negative sense is there, too—"belligerent," "arrogant"—which makes "feisty" confusing. The hottest word around turns out to be a Humpty-Dumpty word, a voguish befuddler, meaning what the speaker chooses it to mean.

Mr. Safire—

The word "feisty" has but one meaning—"short." Never has the word been used to describe a person over 5'10", except in the NBA.

John Skinner
South Euclid, Ohio

---

flakes and kooks

The Kook is dead; long live the Flake.

The vocabulary of eccentricity is one of the richest veins of slang; only copulation and drunkenness offer a greater variety of colorful descriptions. The idea of *coming apart* is central: On the notion that one is held together by nuts and screws, we have "nutty" (which leads to another kind of nut, as "nutty as a fruitcake") and "screwy," or "screw-loose." Another metaphor is *emptiness:* Some minds are so empty there can be "bats in the belfry" (followed by "batty"), or "nobody home," "out to lunch," "not all there." The idea of *damage* is also prevalent: "cracked," "lamebrain," "blown his stack," "off his hinges," "a leak in the think tank."

In the late 1950's, a term came sweeping in from the West that engulfed all these expressions: "Kook"—probably derived from "cuckoo" and popularized by California surfers who used it to deride those who could not ride in The Big One—became the central term to describe someone who was

"slightly crazy." Politics snapped it up: In 1964, some followers of Senator Goldwater were derogated as "nuts and kooks."

"Kooky," after two decades, has begun to fade. In the early 70's, the terms for eccentricity came from the drug culture. In the Southwest, "He's got snakes in his head" was derived from the use of peyote; the hallucinations of those who ingested the substance were said to feature snakes. In urban areas, "spaced-out" was a favorite, with the derivatives "spacey" and "space cadet," perhaps rooted in the interest in the space age, but surely influenced by removal from reality, as drug users sought to be "out of touch."

In recent years, the name for nutliners has become "aired out," or "not wrapped real tight," as if the admired "hanging loose" had gotten out of hand. Teen-agers today prefer "jelled"—as in "he's jelled," "he's a jell-brain"—or the derivate "shaky."

The more significant term, however—which may show the generation-spanning shelf life of the now-archaic "kook" (I have to do a piece on hyphens soon)—is "flake," with its offshoots "flaky" and "flaked-out."

Shakespeare used the word in *Richard III*—"and flaky darkness breaks within the east"—as an adjective to picture the mottled dawn sky, as if white snowflakes were breaking up the gloom of night. Later, as a verb, "to flake" meant to peel off, as decaying enamel came away from wood in little strips.

Baseball gave the word its current meaning. In the early 60's, the noun "flake" was used to denote a colorful or eccentric player. Leonard Koppett, *New York Times* sportswriter, reported in 1964 that the Yankees had accumulated an "amount of 'flake' in such young players as Joe Pepitone, Jim Bouton, Phil Linz...." Mr. Koppett recalls that, at first, the meaning was "off-beat, original, far-out"; later, it became "slightly crazy, eccentric, wild." "Flaky," which began as an adjective in the late 50's, was turned into the noun "flake" in the 60's, and is now back to its original, far-out, adjectival form.

As such, the word is a label that Carter White House staffers have been trying to pin on Governor Jerry Brown of California, and the accusation of "flakiness" may be as important politically as the charges of "kookiness" and "trigger-happiness" were in 1964. Sensing the danger, Governor Brown promptly counterattacked: "I think those dinosaurs of the Democratic Party who believe it is 'flaky' to balance the budget and fight inflation in a serious way or try to slow down the addition to nuclear power are going to find out they are the flakes."

That statement lacks brevity and punch. Somewhere along the trail, we may hear a candidate lay it on the line: "I am not a flake."

---

flat

We cannot watch the forthcoming Super Bowl without an understanding of the hottest cliché in the hotbed of stereotypes that is professional football: "flat."

When a team is not playing as well as it should; when that spark, that esprit, that motivational *je ne sais quoi* that leads to the nirvanalike "momentum" is missing, a team is said to be "flat." "The Steelers weren't as crisp as usual," said Oiler linebacker Art Stringer. "I don't know if they got flat sitting around the hotel room . . . or what."

Origin? "Oh, how stale, weary, flat and unprofitable seem to me all the uses of this world," said Hamlet in soliloquy. (In pre-Copernican times, astronomers were also quoted as observing, "The world seems flat," but that was in a different sense.)

Wine that lost its sparkle and zest was described as flat three centuries ago; today, the meaning is the opposite of "effervescent," as when the top is left off a bottle of soda pop and the fizz disappears.

From that, one might expect the opposite of "flat" to be "bubbly" or "fizzy," but it is not: The opposite of "flat" is sometimes "crisp" but more frequently "up." A sportscaster, viewing a nonflat aggregation of players, will first say, ritually, "They came to play," and add, "The team is really 'up' for today's game." (I can imagine the astronomer-geographer Copernicus insisting to doubters: "No, the world is 'up.' ")

Football metaphors are often adopted into general speech. For example, "opportunistic" used to be a derogation of politicians but it is praise for a football team, and the word will soon take the favorable connotation even as applied to fast-compromising pols. In the same way, we can expect flatness to be used in descriptions of all lifeless performances. Ultimately, the reaction of a crowd that refuses to roar on cue will be described as "flat," as the people in the stands watch their hopes fizzle.

"Quois"?
Who added the "s"? Pas moi!
Was the printer an Iroquois,
Who shrugged and asked,
"Pourquoi pas?"
Or did the "s" by some mistake
Make a hissing escape
From a football getting "flat"
In a later paragraph?
Ma foi!

> Yours very truly,
> Helen Geberer
> Bronx, New York

Dear Mr. Safire:

Vis-à-vis the final paragraph:

"Opportunistic" has recently acquired yet another connotation (if not definition) courtesy of the New England Journal of Medicine. *Two separate articles in a recent issue (Volume 301, Number 18—1 November 1979), by researchers in Pittsburgh and Charlottesville, Virginia, are respectively titled "Opportunistic Lung Infection" and "Opportunistic Pneumonia." Both are reports on cases of pneumonia caused by what seems to be a newly identified bacterium (or perhaps two different bacteria) distinct from the agent of Legionnaire's Disease.*

I'm sure you're familiar with the American Heritage definition of the word, which suggests it can be used solely to describe human beings. Well, anthropomorphically, I guess it might be applied to bacteria as well. But an infection—a condition, as opposed to the causative agent(s) thereof? Neither article, nor an editorial in the issue commenting on them, offers a clue to that twist. But the editorial comments that of the 13 patients described in the pieces (eight in the Pittsburgh report, five in the other), all had been receiving immunosuppressive therapy (ten were recipients of kidney transplants). That suggests—my guess— that the editors intended "opportunistic" to mean "an uncommon opportunity for bacterial invasion was offered (to the bacteria)."

C'est la langue.

> Dodi Schultz
> New York, New York

Dear Mr. Safire:

One line of metaphor that you might wish to explore before the Super Bowl: A team that is the opposite of flat is not only described by sportscasters as up. *It is also called just what one might expect, antonymically speaking:* sharp.

The musical metaphor makes perfect sense, since in musical notation "flat" denotes one notch down from the natural (sorry, redundancy: flat denotes) and "sharp" one notch up.

Whether notes were flat before wine I would not presume to say. The metaphor, furthermore, may be shared by food and music on the upper side of the scale as well. A sharp cheese is one that is piquant. The usage possibly arises from the cutting sense of the word. But a sharp cheese is also one affording us a physical (not mental) sensation that is stronger, more intense, and on a higher plane—which is just what a sharp team is.

The question of whether gustatory metaphor shaped the language of music, or the other way around, or whether both arose simultaneously from the use of the common meanings of the day could be interesting homework for another sharp cookie.

Yours sincerely,
Andrew Kupfer
New York, New York

O Solecism Mio

Shakespeare's Hamlet was misquoted in this space as having said "How stale, weary, flat and unprofitable seem to me all the uses of this world!" 'Twas an unweeded garden, switching "stale" and "weary." Lyris Hyatt of Bryn Athyn, Pa.—no Y's guy, she—explains that "part of the charm of Shakespeare's line is its neat phonetic pattern: the front *ee* in *weary,* through the vowels in *stale* and *flat,* to the open *ah* in *unprofitable.*"

And then I wrote that astronomers in "pre-Copernican times" thought the earth was flat. (Earth is lowercased, along with sun and moon, unless used in a sentence with other planets, in which case all are uppercased.) Gordon K. Lister of New York writes that I have confused "the sphericity of the earth and the heliocentricity of the solar system." That is confusion on a cosmic scale. It seems that many educated people since Aristotle have believed that the earth was round, and if Copernicus is to be used in an example of revolutionary thinking, it should be because he challenged the common belief that the sun revolved around the earth. Sorry, Nick.

Don't you enjoy watching pretentious writers sprinkle their language with foreign words and phrases and spell them wrong? *Je ne sais quois* should have been *Je ne sais quoi* and ridiculing a goof like that is part of the *raison d'être* of this column.

Dear Mr. Safire:
... Would not "capitalized" serve you better than "uppercased"? The latter strikes me as printer's jargon brought into more general use. The former is the more widely used word, I suspect, as a result of its place in schoolwork. (At

*least no teacher of mine ever told me to be certain to uppercase the first words
of my sentences.) In addition, the word "capitalize" has a secondary meaning
that "uppercase" appears not to possess; namely, the printing in uppercase type
of the initial letter of the word. I think that the distinction is worth preserving,
for it is in fact the very one you want here. You do not mean to print the whole
of the word "Earth" in uppercase letters, only its initial letter. The word "capitalize" seems to carry that sense. To me, at least, "uppercase" (which suffers
the additional problem of inelegance) does not. . . .*

*Roger F. Stacey
Department of English
The Taft School
Watertown, Connecticut*

flew out/flied out

"Last time up at bat," said the NBC baseball sportscaster, "he flew out."

This egregious abuse of sports grammar was brought to my attention by
James Reston of Fiery Run, Va., a former traveling secretary of the Cincin-
nati Reds.

"He flew out" is an example of incorrect correction, as in the way "spit 'n'
image" is miscorrected to "spitting image" by misguided zealots of confor-
mity.

When a batter has hit a fly ball which is then caught, the past tense of his
action is "flied out." The only time "flew out" would be correct is if the batter dropped his bat, flapped his arms, and soared out of the stadium, thereby
earning himself the frothiest head in the *Guinness Book of World Records*.

floutsmanship

"The Government of Iran must realize," read *The New York Times* transcript of President Carter's request to the United Nations for sanctions,
"that it cannot flaunt, with impugnity, the expressed will and law of the
world community."

When a President makes a blatant error in English in a formal address,
that's linguistic news—and needs prompt correction, lest the force of the
usage by the Highest Authority legitimate the error.

"Flaunt" means "to display ostentatiously"; its early uses had to do with coquettish strutting about, showing off gaudy silks, and the word still means "to parade one's possessions in a way to invite envy."

President Carter meant "flout," which means "to show contempt for." That quite different verb is akin to the noun "flute," and is rooted in whistling noises made in derision, as if by a flute. You can flout convention and you can flout authority, but you cannot use "flaunt" for "flout" when you are talking about expressing contempt.* The confusion between the two similar verbs is common, but Presidential writers are expected to avoid making common mistakes in seeking to gain the common touch.

"Impugnity" is not a word. This was not Mr. Carter's fault; he said "impunity," which sounds the same, and the sound was mistranscribed. The "pun," pronounced "pyoon," is allied to "punishment"; the word "impunity" means "without punishment." The other spelling, based on the verb "to impugn"—"He's impugning my integrity"—is allied to "fight," as in "pugnacious" or "pugilist." Forget "impugnity," a nonexistent fighting word.

Another catchy usage in the same sentence is "world community," which has been bruited about lately as a substitute for the apparently sexist "mankind," with the special meaning of "the nations of the world gathered together." In 1888, the Earl of Carnarvon first spoke of "the community of Europe," and, in the early 1940's, Walter Lippmann popularized "the Atlantic community." Since "community" had a warmer connotation than "establishment," generals and spooks have been moving to "the defense community" and "the intelligence community." Mr. Carter's global village greening has enshrined "the world community," and we can leave it to NASA to replace the solar system with "the planetary community."

Lots of nourishment in that single sentence. As for the subject of the President's request, the word "sanction" is one of those rare terms (like "sanguine") that mean the opposite of themselves.

"Sanction" means "official approval," from the same root as "sanctify" and "saint"; as a verb, it means "to give permission." At the same time, "sanctions" have come to mean those actions, usually economic, used to punish a nation. In one sense, the word means "permission," to be coveted, and in the other sense, the word means "penalty," to be abhorred.

Strangely, nobody seems confused by this contradiction. Here's why (the most useful contribution advertising copywriters have made to the language is "here's why"): *The plural turns the meaning around.* When a sanction becomes "sanctions," its meaning switches from approval to restriction. This is not always the case—if you start to examine each of the sanctions, the individual sanction takes the negative meaning of the group—but, as pundits say, it is a useful rule of thumbsucking.

Got it? If you've got it, flaunt it.

* *J. D. Shulman of Silver Spring, Md., pointed out that my condemnation would have been improved by changing the last "can" to "may."—W.S.*

Dear Mr. Safire,

I cannot resist flaunting my new found ability to spot sneer words. Hence, I point out to you your use of "apparently" in the phrase 'apparently sexist "mankind." '

"You can flout convention and you can flout authority," but you may not flout with impunity, the women's movement's plea for equality in language and terminology.

I have no wish to impugn your integrity but blow your flute elsewhere.

> *Yours truly,*
> *Melanie Belman Gross*
> *Orange, Connecticut*

P.S. The pugnacious spirit of this letter is entirely unintentional.

To the Editor:

William Safire took President Carter to task for using the word "flaunt" instead of "flout." ... Checking the point in the Third Merriam-Webster Unabridged Dictionary I found, quite to the contrary, that the second definition of "flaunt" was given as: "to treat contemptuously: [to] flout." Similarly in the Unabridged Random House Dictionary the usage of "flout" is listed under the definitions given for "flaunt."

Blatant error indeed! The President was following accepted American usage. I can only conclude that Safire had let political partisanship color his amateur linguistics.

> *Lytt I. Gardner, M.D.*
> *Syracuse, New York*

---

football metaphors, *see* flat

---

fortunate/fortuitous

A curious sentence, or an odd collection of words preceding a period, recently appeared in *The New York Times:* "The least fortuitous time to go abroad probably is with your children, or when you are a child." We can assume that the writer meant "The worst time to travel abroad is when you are a child, traveling with your parents."

Venal syntax aside, consider the misuse of "fortuitous." "Fortunate" means "lucky"; "fortuitous" means "by chance," "accidental."

Both "fortunate" and "fortuitous" come from the same Latin roots as "fortune," which means "chance"; but the different endings are designed to separate the elements of chance. "Fortuitous" denotes the workings of chance, while "fortunate" describes the happy results of those workings of happenstance.

The only reason for the existence of the word "fortuitous" is to separate those meanings. If it is used as a pompous synonym for "fortunate," the word loses its purpose.

Unfortunately, both Merriam-Webster's Eighth Collegiate and Webster's New World Dictionaries admit, as a second definition, the "fortunate" meaning of "fortuitous." That's too complaisant: An error should be described as such. Properly, the American Heritage Dictionary writes "fortuitous is often confused with fortunate," and condemns it as "loose usage."

When in doubt, remember the immortal words of General Sherman at the Battle of Allatoona: "Hold the fortuitous!"

frontrunning

Even before his victory over Ronald Reagan in the Iowa caucuses, candidate George Bush was described by columnist Mary McGrory as being in "the front-runner's position for second place" in the long race for the Republican Presidential nomination.

Political savant Richard Moore considers that to be an authentic political oxymoron, like "loyal opposition" and "unthinkable thoughts." When Bush "broke out of the pack"—the ringing cliché, after Iowa—his position became, at the least, the chief challenger to President Carter's chief challenger.

A neologism is needed—just a temporary language fix, really—to describe the scramble for second place that precedes the scramble for first place. A suggestion: "front runner-up."

fumblerules of grammar

Not long ago, I advertised for perverse rules of grammar, along the lines of "Remember to never split an infinitive" and "The passive voice should never be used." The notion of making a mistake while laying down rules ("Thimk," "We Never Make Misteaks") is highly unoriginal, and it turns out that English teachers have been circulating lists of fumblerules for years.

As owner of the world's largest collection, and with thanks to scores of readers, let me pass along a bunch of these never-say-neverisms:

- Avoid run-on sentences they are hard to read.
- Don't use no double negatives.
- Use the semicolon properly, always use it where it is appropriate; and never where it isn't.
- Reserve the apostrophe for it's proper use and omit it when its not needed.
- Do not put statements in the negative form.
- Verbs has to agree with their subjects.
- No sentence fragments.
- Proofread carefully to see if you any words out.
- If any word is improper at the end of a sentence, a linking verb is.
- Steer clear of incorrect forms of verbs that have snuck in the language.
- Take the bull by the hand and avoid mixed metaphors.
- Avoid trendy locutions that sound flaky.
- Never, ever use repetitive redundancies.
- Everyone should be careful to use a singular pronoun with singular nouns in their writing.
- If I've told you once, I've told you a thousand times, resist hyperbole.
- Also, avoid awkward or affected alliteration.
- Don't string too many prepositional phrases together unless you are walking through the valley of the shadow of death.
- Always pick on the correct idiom.
- "Avoid overuse of 'quotation "marks."' "
- The adverb always follows the verb.
- Avoid commas, that are not necessary.
- If you reread your work, you will find on rereading that a great deal of repetition can be avoided by rereading and editing.
- A writer must not shift your point of view.
- Eschew dialect, irregardless.
- And don't start a sentence with a conjunction.
- Don't overuse exclamation marks!!!
- Place pronouns as close as possible, especially in long sentences, as of ten or more words, to their antecedents.
- Hyphenate between syllables and avoid un-necessary hyphens.
- Write all adverbial forms correct.
- Don't use contractions in formal writing.
- Writing carefully, dangling participles must be avoided.
- It is incumbent on us to avoid archaisms.
- Last but not least, avoid clichés like the plague; seek viable alternatives. .

Fumblerule Follow-Up

Late entries in the Fumblerule Derby:

- Never use a long word when a diminutive one will do.
- If a dependent clause precedes an independent clause put a comma after the dependent clause.
- One will not have needed the future perfect in one's entire life.
- Unqualified superlatives are the worst of all.
- If this were subjunctive, I'm in the wrong mood.
- Surly grammarians insist that all words ending in "ly" are adverbs.
- De-accession euphemisms.
- In statements involving two word phrases, make an all out effort to use hyphens.
- It is not resultful to transform one part of speech into another by prefixing, suffixing, or other alterings.
- Avoid colloquial stuff.

Dear Mr. Safire:

A question about a passage in today's "The Fumblerules of Grammar." You wrote:

> *"As owner of the world's largest collection, and with thanks to scores of readers, let me pass along a bunch of these never-say-neverisms:"*

It seems to me this might be clearer in one of three different ways to avoid that initial dangling element.

1. *As owner of the . . . scores of readers, I'd like to pass along . . .*
2. *Let me, as owner of the world's . . . readers, pass along . . .*
3. *As readers of my column, let me pass along . . .*

Doesn't your sentence give the impression your readers own the largest collection? You appear to be the understood subject of let.

Your hair-splitting disciple & admirer,
Dawes Potter
White Plains, New York

fungible

"The rationale," writes economics columnist Hobart Rowen, "is that oil is 'fungible'—that is, if Iran sells more oil to, say, Japan and West Germany, other oil will be available for sale here."

"Fungible" is the vogue word to know if you intend to impress anybody with your grasp of the tricks of international trade. It has nothing to do with good times (no place is called "Fungible City"), and the word does not denote a special susceptibility to athlete's foot (although the Latin "fungus," meaning "mushroom," has a plural of "fungi," that unexpected growth has nothing to do with the mushrooming use of "fungibility.")

Fungible, soft "g," is a term in contract law for "capable of mutual substitution." It comes from the Latin *fungi vice,* "to fulfill the office of," or "take the place of."

When Libya wanted to steer some money into the hands of Idaho farmers—thereby to lean on Senate Foreign Relations Committee chairman Frank Church of Idaho—that nation bought grain from the boys in Boise; however, since the Libyan consumer prefers a different kind of grain, delivery was made in the type of grain grown far from Idaho. That substitution could be accomplished because grain is fungible.

Similarly, when the United States stopped buying oil from Iran, we expected Iranian oil to be bought by other nations, which were then expected to buy less from Saudi Arabia, as we switched our Iran purchasing to the Saudis. That's because oil—like grain and like money—is fungible.

The hot new word (traceable to 1765) has also gained a metaphoric use in Washington: "The new-boy network is fungible," a National Security Council staffer told me. He meant that members of a clique of foreign- and defense-policy planners, who have the same ideological bent and mental set, can be slipped in and out of government without upsetting policy. Fortunately, there are two different new-boy networks—accommodationist and hard-line—which limits fungibility within each mind-set.

Fungible is interchangeable with "interchangeable," but that outmoded word is too widely understood for insiders, who find fungible more fun.

Dear Mr. Saffire:

My understanding of fungibility (as of interchangeability or mutual substitutibility—all three are fungible) is that all units of a commodity with such property are either indistinguishable from each other or meet the specifications contained in a contract (written or verbal, explicit or implied) calling for delivery of one or more units of that commodity. Those specifications can, of course, range from very general to very specific.

Grain may or may not be fungible. The Idaho grain is precisely an example of a commodity that is not fungible because the Lybians wanted another type of grain. Presumably, the Idaho farmers had to acquire the specified type of grain at market price before being able to arrange for delivery. (It isn't really clear to me what the Idaho farmers got out of this transaction, except perhaps for a commission.)

Money may or may not be fungible. If I have specified payment in U.S. dollars, I do not have to accept the equivalent in French francs. If I have specified payment with a certified check, I do not have to accept payment with an uncertified check, a credit card or even cash. When it comes to vending machines, pennies and dimes are not fungible.

Your understanding of fungibility as it comes across in your column actually corresponds with "marketability": the quality of being readily saleable at near market price, which is the characteristic all commodities have in common.

> *Sincerely yours,*
> *Ottho G. Heldring*
> *New York, New York*

Dear Mr. Safire:

... Your friend Dick Nathan (who, as you may know, is now at the Woodrow Wilson School, at Princeton, and for whom I worked at Brookings) talked about "fungibility" to describe the difficulty of tracing general revenue sharing funds once they had been absorbed into the general fund of a recipient government.

In testimony in front of the Senate Subcommittee on Intergovernmental Relations on June 5, 1974, he said:

> *"The essential problem in this area is 'fungibility,' referring to the extent to which state and local officials can use financial resources interchangeably. All money is green." ...*

> *Yours sincerely,*
> *André Juneau*
> *Federal-Provincial Relations Division*
> *Department of Finance*
> *Ottawa, Ontario*

---

further/farther

The last time I was wrong, as the saying goes, was when I thought I made a mistake.

"Thems as dishes it out ought to be able to take it," I wrote gallantly if colloquially not long ago, putting forward a reader's correction of my use of "a step further." With an excess of obsequiousness, I accepted the correction of "a step further" as differentiated from "a degree further."

Comes now the rex of lex, Webster's New World Dictionary editor David Guralnik, to say I was wrong, because I was right: " 'Step' in your context does not refer literally to distance, but is used in its extended sense of 'degree.' " So "a step further" not only is correct, but (in my view) is better usage than "a step farther," which is too narrow a construction.

Furthermore, I intend to stop bothering my head about the metaphoric difference between "farther" and "further." Rule: Use "farther" only when you're talking distance, otherwise use "further" allatime.

Further protest will be unavailing. As Guralnik says, "Them that dishes it out need not fall over every time someone blows hard."

Dear Mr. Safire:

Re "farther-further" and the "eagle-eyed" gentleman from Bronxville. You should not have accepted his distinction between the two words.

In the first place, your phrase, "taking it a step further," used "step" metaphorically, not as a measure of literal distance. Even those who insist on the distinction reserve "farther" for literal distance.

Second, according to Fowler and the Oxford English Dictionary, etymologically "farther" is merely a spelling variant of "further," which began life as the comparative of "fore" and later "far."

Fowler, Copperud, Bernstein and others are perfectly willing to let "farther" die and "further" take over completely. Only the American Heritage usage panel and like-minded traditionalists would maintain the distinction for literal distance.

You have been foiled by School Marm, who is the older sister of Wise Guy and Nice Nellie, all three of them being members of the grubby Wisenheimer family of Wiseacre Estates. Foreclosure is too good for them!

> *Sincerely,*
> *Mark Isaacs*
> *Maggie Isaacs*
> *Perkasie, Pennsylvania*

---

fuzzwords

"Be advised," as the bureaucrats say (a written form of "Now hear this!" on a Navy squawk box), that we are losing some and winning some on the fuzzword front.

The verb "to check"—which originated in the checkmark made after determining whether a written datum or statement was correct—after losing ground to "cross-check," has now been overwhelmed by "cross-validate." (As the fellows who hand out fliers for massage parlors in Times Square will soon say, "Cross-validate it out." The same massaged metaphor can be found in another bureaucratic favorite—"hands-on experience"—which means knowledge gained in life rather than gleaned from textbooks.)

The word "traveling" is also moving on. No longer does the compleat bureaucrat say "I will be traveling next week." Instead, the freshly minted pomposity is "I will be *in travel status.*"

However, that sinking feeling stops when it comes to the bureaucratese for "life preserver." Commander Neal Mahan, executive director of the National Boating Safety Advisory Council, a civilian front group of the Coast Guard, has announced his group has just tossed in the sponge on "Personal Flotation Device," or P.F.D. That leaden coinage was "frequently misunderstood by the average boater," says the commander, his voice like thin ice breaking. Someday, when the antibureaucratic word gets through to the airlines, the little signs that say "Your seat cushion may be used as a personal flotation device" may be conformed to ordinary English usage, as "Use your seat cushion as a life preserver." More likely: "Be advised: your seat floats."

---

gatesmanship

The "Dome" of "Teapot Dome" was never used as a suffix to denote financial chicanery in subsequent scandals, but the "gate" of "Watergate" is becoming the standard label for any new political shenanigans.

Some uses of "gate" are apt: When Bordeaux wine shippers in France were caught with their large toes on the scales, "Winegate" was appropriate because of the relationship of water to wine.

Some other cases were borderline: As a popularizer of "Koreagate" and as perpetrator of "Lancegate," I am ambivalent (a word I am of two minds about) about those two, but it seems stretching it to call the investigation into South Africa's former Information Minister, Cornelius Mulder, "Muldergate." Also, calling the probe of the Carter warehouses "Peanutgate" seems both to condemn and minimize.

The excessive use of this suffix is becoming a linguistic gategate. The only excuse for its perpetuation is in those instances where rhyme or punning gives special dispensation, as when the furor over New York City's Comptroller Harrison Goldin's dealings were dubbed "Goldingate." That bridged the gap for gateniks.

Generic: What's in a name?

Five years ago, I described a possible shift of Administration officers as "Cabinet scrabble." Promptly, the Selchow & Righter Company complained of my "improper" use of its trademark: "There are as many crossword games being sold as there are cola drinks and cameras," wrote the advertising manager, "but there is only one Scrabble brand, one Coca-Cola brand, and one Kodak brand. The descriptive name of our product is crossword game. The trademark is Scrabble." Testily, I replied I would not soon again plug its headbreaking entertainment; besides, I can never get the "J" on a triple-scoring square.

Of late, we have all been watching a television commercial starring Robert Young—a doctor who plays an actor, or vice versa—who was using a locution no human being in a normal situation would ever use: "Try Sanka brand decaffeinated coffee." Why the strange turn of phrase—why not just the conversational "Try Sanka"? The viewer could almost hear the ad manager in the background, afflicted with coffee nerves and surrounded by lawyers, whispering: "The descriptive name of our product is decaffeinated coffee. The trademark is Sanka."

The Scrabble and Sanka lawyers are absolutely right to worry about familiarity breeding contempt: If a trademark becomes generic—applicable to a genus, kind, or group—anybody can use it.

Recently, the Federal Trade Commission struck terror among the companies with trade names by moving against Formica, a corporation that makes plastic laminated counter tops. In the past, trademarks were lost because they fell into disuse, but now—for the first time—the Government is seeking to remove the trademark for a linguistic reason: that the word has become generic.

This is not merely a case of companies fighting over trademarks, as when United Drug wrested the exclusive use of *aspirin* from Bayer, or when Du Pont unsuccessfully sued Waxed Products for infringement of *cellophane,* or when Otis lost *escalator* to another elevator company and later to critics of the Vietnam War. This was Uncle Sam acting as Uncle Same, and shudders went through all the household words: "Don't put the *jello* in the *plexiglas* dish in the *deep-freeze,* Dr. Welby—put it in the *frigidaire*—while I change into my *levi's* to throw a *frisbee* around."

When a trademark gets into the dictionaries, it may be in trouble. When Merriam-Webster's Third Unabridged came out in 1961, the brand-name crowd was dismayed: "The only word capitalized was 'God,'" moans Dorothy Fey, executive director of the U.S. Trademark Association. Since that time, most dictionaries—including Merriam-Webster—capitalize such

household-word trademarks as "Deep-freeze," and identify them as trademarks. (Anybody can call a dictionary "Webster's.")

Now the battle is joined. The F.T.C. says the householding of Formica would save the consumer money; industry replies that the trademark assures the consumer of known quality, and businessmen are urging Congress to induce the F.T.C. to back off. Meanwhile, F.T.C. official Alfred F. Dougherty Jr. has said that manufacturers would be better advised to avoid saying "Buy Dougherty's" and instead to specify "Buy Dougherty brand widgets." Admen everywhere are *xeroxing* that and *scotch taping* it to the wall; that's why Robert Young cannot say "Try Sanka."

I think the Government attack on names is an egregious example of overregulation. To put the shoe on the other foot: The Feds would hold it illegal for your local Lethargic Messengers to call themselves the U.S. Postal Service. A counterattack is called for: If my name were Fred T. Cookie, I would start issuing "The F.T.C. Report." (That's not so outlandish: When a bluejeans manufacturer named a line "F.B.I. Blue Jeans," the Government sued and lost—the judge ruled that nobody would think the F.B.I. had gone into that business. No ruling yet on black bags.)

If some enterprising manufacturer now goes out and registers the name "Generic Drug Company," you will soon read about it in *The New York Times* brand Sunday-issued *Magazine*.

Dear Safire,

. . . Scrabble, unlike formica, aspirin, sanka or even deepfreeze, is an English word which antedates the crossword game.

"And he changed his behavior before them, and feigned himself mad in their hands, and scrabbled on the doors of the gate, and let his spittle fall down upon his beard."

"He" was David, and the quotation is from 1 Samuel XXI 13.

"Scrabble" here means to claw or scratch. It can also mean to scribble. The trademark refers to a game, which is a new and (probably) protectable use. But I'd spit in their eye if they tried to stop me from using the word in its pristine senses.

> *Cordially yours,*
> *Arthur J. Morgan*
> *New York, New York*

God damn

The story on the United Press International wire had what wire-service editors call an "attentioner" on the top, calling attention to the use of a profane word in the copy that followed, in case the receiving editors wanted to blank it out.

That drew my eye down to the dangerous paragraph, which began " 'William Safire is a goddamn liar,' Mr. Sinatra added."

I was, needless to say, shocked. "Goddamn" as one word with an "n"? I called U.P.I. in New York and was told that U.P.I. style calls for one word, a lowercase "g" and the "n" at the end of "damn." The man at the desk added that the crooner's remonstrance had come to U.P.I. on a telex spelled "g—d damn," two words, which the wire service fixed to conform to its style. (Some writers spell "God" "G—d" because they believe the name of God should not be written, but that should not apply to a small-g god.)

I had always thought that "goddam"—written as one word, with a lowercase "g"—carried no final "n." However, diligent research shows that *The New York Times Manual of Style and Usage* agrees with U.P.I. in using an "n" in writing "goddamn" (and adds a warning that it "should not be used at all unless there is a compelling reason"). So does Merriam-Webster's Eighth Collegiate, although that dictionary gives "goddam" as an alternate in its noun form ("I don't give a good goddamn/goddam"); in its verb form ("I'll be goddamned/goddammed"), and in its adjective form ("goddamned/goddamn/goddam liar"), as in the U.P.I. version of Mr. Sinatra's usage.

I think the style books and the dictionaries are wrong to prescribe or prefer the use of "n." Here's why: Everyone agrees on the noncapitalization of "g"—in this case, god is not the Supreme Being, but a smaller god, as in "godfather" or "godforsaken."

I'd take that nondiety* notion a step further: The last half of "goddamned" doesn't mean "damned" in the sense of "accursed" either. Most dictionaries have that wrong. A "goddamn liar," to use U.P.I. style, is not a liar divinely accursed but is simply *very much* a liar. Since the damnation has been removed from "damned," ought not the "n" be removed as well—to signify the change from curse to general emphasizer?

I think the "n" should go—it's not pronounced, anyway. In the same way, the phrase as used as an expletive—"Goddamn! There goes another nuclear plant"—calls up no meaning of a stern diety*; rather it is a whoop of admiration or exasperation, like "gosh darn" or the western-movie "goldang." The "n" preserves a previous, and now erroneous, meaning, and should be dispensed with.

Thus—"Goddam! That Sinatra is one goddam good singer." (I left out another use of the phrase, in its mock-cursing sense, but it's too late now, goddammit.)

Dear Sir:

Twenty years ago, or so, I roomed in the house of a Lithuanian refugee, in Valparaiso, Indiana, and our conversation was a mishmash of English, German, and Russian, which we both knew to varying degrees.

There were lots of bull sessions, about a wide range of subjects, and there was a definite difference in tone between discussions sacred (the family he had to leave in Lithuania, opportunities in America, etc.) and discussions profane (mostly international jokes and put-downs). At one point, he was sad to report that his daughter had been admitted to the university: he knew that one of the prerequisites, in the Soviet scheme of things, was political reliability. As he amplified on this, he said, "I think she doesn't believe in Gosh anymore."

Sincerely yours,
W. W. Keen James
New Hope, Pennsylvania

* *Deity, several spelling-bee winners pointed out.—W.S.*

goodbye girl

Appearing on a Houston television show, and fulminating about Leon Jaworski's cover-up of Koreagate, I noticed a good-looking blonde taking still photographs on the set.

In the course of plugging a novel, I mentioned that the heroine was also a girl photographer—"like the one you have right here."

After the show, an icily formal person with cameras around her neck asked: "If I were a man, would you call me a 'boy photographer'?"

Chagrined, but bearing it, I apologized. Although "girl" is not as pejorative as "boy" (the racist put-down of a black of any age), the word—once the embodiment of carefree femininity—has fallen on hard times. Young women sensitive to slights take "girl" as a slight, just as they do "blonde," an adjective turned by sexists into a noun, meaning a woman with hair of that color but also connoting allure or blowziness.

Although alerted to this sensitivity by the woman photographer—rather, the photographer who was a woman—I fell into sexist ways again in a column about the Chappaquiddick incident, referring to "the 'boiler-room girls' at the party."

A woman's voice came on the telephone the day the column appeared to say: "I am outraged." Asked to be more specific, she identified herself as one of the six young women at the party on what is often called "that fateful night," and she resented—as a sexist slur—being referred to as a "girl." As she put it, using the same example I had heard on the TV set: "You don't talk about the men at that party as 'boys.' "

Forgetting for a moment my primary role as a student of language, I invited her to recount the full story of what happened that fateful night. She declined—as she has these ten long years—and pressed her feminist cause. I objected: Didn't everybody say "boiler-room girls" in 1969, referring to the persons who man the telephones in a political campaign? "You could say 'girls' in 1969," she responded, "but not in 1979."

She has a point, to a point; women who are secretaries resent their bosses' saying "Talk to my girl about that," especially when girlhood is long gone, and the self-description of a group of women as "the girls" seems to be on the wane.

Girls are getting younger. That is, the word is being used now to denote females of a lower age. "Young woman," which often used to be sternly admonitory—"Young woman, that's my hat you're sitting on"—is now the desired form of address to a maturing ex-girl whose address you'd like to have. "Don't refer to *the fair sex* or *the weaker sex*," writes resultful David

Ewing in *Writing for Results.* "Say *women.* Diminutive forms such as *usherette* are being ushered out in favor of just *usher.* And, of course, *girls* instead of *women* is a solid no-no."

The only place "girl" seems to be welcomed these days is in rock music, which refers to all women of all ages as either "milady" or "gurl." Rodgers and Hammerstein lyrics are passé: We will soon hear a lusty chorus roar "There Is Nothing Like a Young Woman" ("dame," like "broad," "chick," or "skirt" or "bird," is even further beyond the pale). A piquant Oriental singer will soon belt out "I Enjoy Being a Young Woman."

Use the word "girl" at your peril. The Working Girl, long harassed and patronized, has earned her way to linguistic equality; a sign of the changing times is that it is not possible to say that Heaven protects the Career Woman.

Dear Mr. Safire,

It is because I get such pleasure from reading your column about our language that I take this time to write you about your lack of understanding of the implications inherent in the word "girl."

You wrote, "although 'girl' is not as perjorative as 'boy' (the racist put-down of a black of any age)." But you were wrong. "Girl" is just as insulting to a woman as "boy" is to a black man, (you left out the "man") for the same reasons. They both imply in the person so described an inability to grow up and assume the responsibilities of the adult segment of our society. They both, therefore, by definition, deny to that person the rights and privileges of adult status.

It was due to the thought process that was manifested in the use of the word "boy" that whites could, in good conscience, subject blacks to a "protected" position in our society, one lacking in all the respect and honor we confer on our adult members.

Women, too, have been subjected to this patronizing oppression and were taught to think, as they shuffled from kitchen to party to bed, that they were lucky to be so treated and to fear their emancipation. Many still do. I still do. But I'll fight myself and "enlightened" men like you all the way to freedom.

Sincerely,
Joyce Stillman-Myers
Northport, New York

Writing that something is "a no-no" is using an impermissible cuteism, no?
William Cole
New York, New York

Dear Safire:

Some half a dozen years ago one of the Negro (Black) civil rights periodicals ran a cartoon that depicted a nine-year-old male at a coin phone, standing on a chair; the setting made it clear that this was a maternity hospital waiting room. The young person was crying exultantly into the phone:

"It's a woman! An infant woman!"

Yours etc.,
Howard N. Meyer
Rockville Centre, New York

Dear Mr. Safire,

I have just been enjoying your piece on the use of the word "girl." On this subject may I point out that recently a woman of a certain age said to me, "We girls meet for bridge on Tuesdays."

My reason for writing, however, is to request—implore—that you comment on the use of the word "lady" when "woman" is more appropriate. In this age when wounded egos are to be avoided at all cost, this appears to be a popular euphemism. I can only repeat the old story of the person seeking employment who inquired, "Are you the woman who advertised for a washlady?"

Sincerely,
Sidney V. Chrysler
Chaplin, Connecticut

Dear Mr. Safire:

I enjoy "On Language" very much, and your column has inspired me to write, not to wag a finger at your trading-stamp spelling of "possibly" but to comment on your conversation with the camerawoman.

Apparently she clarified for you the implications of the word "girl" in 1979, but her anger at your calling her a "girl photographer" may have been misplaced. After all, calling someone a "girl photographer" indicates nothing about the photographer's age or gender; rather it describes the age and gender of the photographer's subject. A "girl photographer" is, quite simply, one who photographs girls.

As more and more women have stormed into the professional world, phrases like "woman doctor," "woman writer," and "woman lawyer" have appeared with increasing frequency, and such misuse sets this feminist's teeth on edge. A "woman doctor" is a gynecologist, a doctor specializing in the treatment of women. A "woman writer" is one who writes women—either writes them letters or writes the word "woman." I'm not quite sure what a "woman lawyer" is, but I suspect Marvin Mitchellson is one.

"Woman" is a noun, not an adjective. A female writer, I count among my closest friends a female doctor and a female lawyer, and I once made an appointment with a female doctor who also happened to be a woman doctor. I can't help but wonder why men who have entered traditionally female fields are correctly labeled "male nurses," "male secretaries," and so on, while professional women are constantly called "women professionals," as if being a woman were part of the job. If you could do anything to erase such subtly offensive usage, you'd be doing us all a big favor.

> Sincerely,
> Barbara J. Keiler
> Albany, New York

Dear Mr. Safire,

Enuff is enuff.

If, in fact, spoken language is for communication I wonder how any of us will ever communicate if every word is going to be taken in some kind of a personal manner. If I must concern myself about the possible connotation of "boy" or "girl" I really don't know how I am going to get a sentence in order. I suggest that if anybody has a "hang up" on any particular word that they verbalize that hang up to the communicator. Then, if the talkor so desires he can change the word to the talkee's satisfaction. Or the talkor could turn around and walk away. The latter course would be my gut reaction. If I have to watch every word I say I really would rather not have the conversation.

To wit; man kind, manual labor, mendacious. How about hurricane? I feel that is discrimination. I would like to see the word himacane. I resent the term manhole—I don't believe a manhole is a very elegant thing and do not wish to *be associated with it. Remember the man eating tigers? I resent that too, why don't they ever eat woman. Also, William Shakespeare has some nerve. I suggest we change the title of his play to* Two Gentle Persons from Verona.

I do believe, Mr. Safire, that my point is made. If, in-fact, language is for communication, then some of our hangups will have to go down the drain.

Thank you,
Cordially,
Arthur L. Finn
Los Angeles, California

Dear Mr. Safire:
You are incorrigible. Boiler-room girls do not "man" telephones. See Webster's New International Dictionary, Second Edition: "Man" = "to supply with men; to furnish with a sufficient force or complement of men." Here your toes as a boiler-room girl operated switchboard, blinked again in the usual sexist manner.

Sincerely,
David Toren
New York, New York

---

gorilla

"Gentlemen," beams the chief executive, "I am pleased to announce that we have a gorilla."

The speaker is not a zoo keeper; nor is he the head of an underworld organization, using "gorilla" to mean "strong-arm man," or hoodlum imported for intimidation. The speaker is the boss of a music-publishing business, using the newest noun that denotes "smash hit" throughout an industry that is neologistically fecund to none.

Why "gorilla" to describe great success? Edward M. Cramer, president of Broadcast Music Inc., surveyed his branch offices on my behalf. He and his associates think the word is derived from the previous word for huge success, "monsters": It is but a short leap from "monster" to "gorilla."

Other terms tootling through the music field at present are "sweeten" (adding instrumentation, usually strings, to build up a record's sound), "pass" (a euphemism for "turn down"), "blows me away" (replacing the archaic "knocks me out"), "matted down" (for "perfected," or "made first-rate"), "chump change" (a small amount of money paid a poor artist to aid

his survival), and "plug in the door" or "close" (the up-against-it condition of the artist who gets "chump change").

In addition, to "get down" is to lose one's inhibitions, and to be "wrapped tight" is to be in good shape, replacing "uptight," the meaning of which has changed to "tense." "Boss" and "tough" are adjectives used to replace "far out," or "wonderful" ("That's tough" no longer offers sympathy, but high praise). An individual in any sort of difficulty is "losing the ball" or "coming undone" and will soon find himself "alley-whipped," or unpaid.

Thus, an alley-whipped, plug-in-the-door kid on chump change can—if he will only get wrapped tight and his work matted down—be able to produce boss music, blowing them all away with a gorilla.

Curiously, a parallel use of "gorilla" (a Greek word for a race of hairy women, later used for an animal species) can be found in television news lingo, the patois of a related form of show business. Commentating on a piece here a few weeks ago about "the word from eejay," or electronic journalism, a network producer who insisted on namelessness writes: "I most often hear 'on-air talent' graded on what you might call 'the gorilla scale,' which hardly is unique to broadcasting.

"There are '800-pound gorillas,' or top stars, sometimes known, when out of earshot, as 'The Gorilla,' or 'The 800-Pounder.' Lesser but important correspondents occasionally are called '400-pounders.'"

The nameless networker went on to commentate about a word I have been tracking remorselessly: the verb "to crash." Originally, the word—a variant of "cracken"—meant "to collide noisily." In 60's slang, "crash" came to mean "to arrive uninvited and plunge deeply into sleep," as in a "crash pad." Recently, it picked up the hurried connotation of "crash program" and today means "to race against time."

" 'To crash' describes harried work against a deadline," writes the keeper of the 800-pounders. "When someone announces, 'We may crash with the lead piece,' or 'Chicago's crashing on both pieces tonight,' they're telling the producers putting the broadcast together in New York to start thinking of other options." (In this new meaning, a "crashing bore" is one who hastens to be tiresome.) A related terminological development in the minor-disaster area: " 'Going down in flames' is another no-kidding warning that a piece may not be finished in time to make the broadcast. Everybody trying to help 'throw it together' is said to be 'doing a crazy dance.' "

The gorilla and crashing metaphors mix well. Whether in the forest primeval, or in the jungles of the music or television business, when an 800-pounder starts to crash—better let him crash.

Dear Mr. Safire:

... On the subject of unsavory origins for popular expressions, today's column discussed the use of the term "crash" in 60's slang to mean "to arrive uninvited and plunge deeply into sleep," as in a "crash pad." Actually, the word "uninvited" could be deleted from the definition. Arriving anywhere uninvited (particularly a party) was called "crashing" long before the 60's use of the term, presumably because you had to crash through doors or bouncers to gain entrance. The use of "crashing" and "crash pad" in the 60's was, like so many of the more obnoxious usages to come out of that era, a direct reference to a particular drug experience. Coming out of an hallucinogenic "high," whatever the chemical source, was generally referred to as "crashing" because coming back "down" to reality from the artificially-induced "high" was the equivalent of a plane making a crash landing. And the experience generally left the victim drained and in need of deep sleep. (I'm not sure about this, but the "pad" part of "crash pad" could be related to the space-center term "launching pad" as its exact opposite, the place where you come back down.)

If you're at all interested in tracing some of the ways in which drugs continue to influence popular language expressions even when the speaker or writer is unaware of the source, note the sudden popularity of the word "munch" and its variations "munching out" and "the munchies." The term has been innocently (or perhaps not so innocently) utilized by advertisers of potato chips and other noshables who wish to sound modern. Any high school student can tell you that the term refers to the craving for junk food that usually accompanies or follows being stoned on pot. ...

Sincerely,
Michael K. Brush
Yaphank, New York

Dear Mr. Safire:

All of your comments about "up tight" have neglected the initial sexual connotation of that phrase: In black slang, a man was said to be "up tight" with a woman—for reasons that should be anatomically obvious—when she was his regular lover; and vestiges of that usage still persist when a person describes his close (but not necessarily sexual) relationship with another person as "tight" (e.g., "He and I are tight").

I think you are similarly off the mark with respect to "boss" and "tough," neither of which is particularly new in youth and music circles. As an undergraduate at the California Institute of Technology late in the 1950s, for example, my good friend and journalistic associate Tom Dodge always described one of the departmental secretaries as a "tough dolly," indicating her abundant physical attractions. Likewise for the antiquity of "boss" as an adjective. Jerry Garcia, lead guitarist of the Grateful Dead for around fifteen years, constantly sprinkles his discourse with "boss" as a term of highest praise; and toward the close of the 1960's, several record companies tried to hype some rock groups from Boston by references to the allegedly new "Boss-town Sound." Both of these illustrations indicate that use of "boss" in the sense of "top-flight" or "first-rate" is anything but new. . . .

Sincerely,
Frank Kofsky
Professor of History
California State University
Sacramento, California

Dear William Safire,

From the old joke bag:

Room Clerk: I guess the most unusual guest was the 800-pound gorilla.
Interviewer: Gosh, where does an 800-pound gorilla sleep?
Room Clerk: Anywhere he wants!

Sincerely,
Sondra Gordon Langford
Chatham, New Jersey

Dear Mr. Safire:

"In 60's slang 'crash' came to mean to arrive uninvited. . . ."

I do not know when "crash" came to mean "to arrive uninvited," I do know that in the distant past when I was a College freshman in 1912 it had that meaning. The great excitement in those days at that College was the rivalry between the "Evens" and the "Odds." The Odd Sophomores planned a party for the Odd Seniors, a regularly scheduled event. Scouts informed alert Freshmen that refreshments for the party were to be unusually varied and abundant, so four or five of the more daring studied the layout and found a rarely used entrance to the scene of the party. Thinking Sophomores would not recognize or even be able to see a mere Freshman, they crashed the party and were revelling in the goodies when they were discovered and forcibly ejected. It was always a good story to tell.

Random House Dictionary, Unabridged, 1966, gives one of the definitions of "crash" as "to go uninvited to a party." It gives no date for the commencement of this use of the word.

The Oxford Dictionary, 3rd Edition, Abridged, 1955, does not give this definition of "crash." Surely the British have indulged this sport.

> *Very truly yours,*
> *Lucy Somerville Howorth*
> *Cleveland, Mississippi*

Dear Bill,

The computer business is one of the great sources of new jargon. "Crash" in computerese first was a "head crash," as applied to the read/write head of a disc storage unit. The clearance between the rapidly spinning disc and the head that reads the magnetic information was very, very small. Dust of a diameter of a few microns would cause great problems if it got in that space, thus super-clean and air-conditioned computer rooms. A really bad incident of dust or misalignment of the head would wipe out the data, the disc, or even the entire machine, thus a "head crash." Next, any more or less major failure of the entire system became a "crash," i.e. the computer was "down," and everyone who was using it was grounded until the computer room found the failure, powered the thing back up, and got it running again.

> *Gordon Eliot White*
> *Washington Correspondent*
> Deseret News
> *Alexandria, Virginia*

---

graduated from

I was never graduated from college; dropped out of Syracuse University in my sophomore year. This is said wistfully, not because of any regret at not having been graduated from a university, but to recall a useful usage of yesteryear: "to be graduated," which has been replaced by the simple "graduated."

The former distinction had a function: Graduation (from the Latin *gradus,* "grade," or "step") meant a "a step up," and that step was conferred by an institution of learning, not snatched by the student. Syracuse graduated the student; the student did not graduate the university.

Okay; the old "to be graduated," with its nice nod of respect to ivied halls, is now taken to be pedantic; "to graduate" is now activist. You go to college, your parents pay a whopping tuition, you graduate.

But—to be both accurate and correct—you do not merely graduate; you graduate *from* a school. Without the "from," the verb "to graduate" means to make little marks on a test tube, to calibrate, to move someone to the next gradation or step. To say "I graduated" rather than "I was graduated" may now be acceptable, quite correct, even modish—but to say "I graduated college" rather than "I graduated from college" is to be a language slob and a discredit to whatever learning factory mailed you a diploma.

With that "from" as the mark of an educated person, consider this recent display advertisement conceived by a presumably college-educated copywriter, and approved by some former Big Man on Campus at NBC's local television station in New York:

> "WARNING: YOUR CHILD WON'T GRADUATE HIGH SCHOOL IN NEW YORK IF HE FLUNKS THIS THURSDAY'S TEST! Find out why, tonight at 8 o'clock, on 'Education: At Whose Cost?' "

At all our costs. I have no quarrel with a copywriter's using a gum-chewing vernacular ("like a cigarette should") in advertising chewing gum, but educating people about education calls for the use of educated English.

Bravo, Mr. Saffire!
. . . Why is it that the writers best known for their nice language are usually slightly to the right of Attilla in their political positions?

Very truly yours,
Bill Schnirring
New York, New York

Dear Sir:
I very much enjoy your columns on language and was particularly interested in the one dealing with "graduating college." I wondered if you had shared my pain at a recent nationally televised commercial which began "I teach college . . ." thus instantly losing any credibility it might have had, as obviously no college professor would ever have said such a thing! I had thought no one but me cared!

With best wishes,
Marjorie Veronneau
Cheshire, Connecticut

Have a nice day

"Goodbye" sounds too final. "So long" is too casual. "Take care" and "take it easy" are passé; "keep the faith" and "peace" are not sufficiently irreverent; "be well," "be good," and "God bless" never made it to a wide circle. Perhaps because of a recent aversion to welfare, "farewell"—the most poetic of remarks at parting—seems overblown.

What, then, do we say to somebody as we take our leave? Universal answer: "Have a nice day."

The expression has taken the nation by its throat. A cartoon shows a minister pronouncing a young couple to be man and wife, adding: "Have a nice day." Telephone companies instruct operators to say it in a smiling voice, and the message is printed on doormats. Heatedly, *The Watertown* (N.Y.) *Daily Times* editorialized: "We've found it on greeting cards, on cocktail napkins, on matchbooks, on menus, on ball-point pens, and even in church bulletins. We absolutely promise, vow and affirm that we will do our best to have a nice day each and every day forevermore, if people will only stop telling us to do so."

Obviously, the H.A.N.D. backlash is upon us. Rejoinders sent in by irate readers include "Thank you, but I have other plans" (first recorded by columnist Herb Caen in 1971); a plaintive "Too late"; a cynical "How much does one cost?" and an imaginative "I'll try, considering I have brain surgery this afternoon." An unnecessarily aggressive "How dare you tell me to do that" is heard from people who rebelled early in life at parental commands to a similarly well-intentioned imperative "Enjoy your meal."

Where did America's favorite farewell begin? Etymologist Peter Tamony credits Roland Dickison of California State University at Sacramento with unearthing the earliest use in English. In 1387, Chaucer wrote in *The Canterbury Tales:* "And hoom wente every man the righte way, there was na-moore but "Fare wel, have a good day.' "

Five and a half centuries later, in 1956, adman Ralph Carson of the Carson/Roberts agency in Los Angeles gave Chaucer a slight twist: "Have a happy day" became the agency's signature. "Our phone was answered, 'Good morning, Carson/Roberts, have a happy day," recalls Mr. Carson, now a lecturer at the University of Southern California. "We used the salutation on all letters, tie tacks, cuff buttons, beach towels, blazer crests, the works." Soon after, that phrase was popularized in the East by WCBS meteorologist (then called a "weathergirl") Carol Reed, who waved goodbye with "Have a happy."

Then, in the 1960's, "Have a good day" had a resurgence, replacing the

HAVE A NICE DAY

hapless "happy day." CBS correspondent Marvin Kalb concluded his radio reports with the "good" word. In 1971, on CBS Radio's "Spectrum," John K. Jessup commented: " 'Have a good day,' I very much fear, is becoming permanently entrenched in the American language. Since it can't be objected to on grounds of taste or grammar, I will merely warn you what it's going to turn into. Until four or five hundred years ago, when Englishmen split, their parting greeting was 'God be with you.' To save time, they gradually shortened it to goodbye. . . . But what about the comparable contraction that will inevitably overtake 'Have a good day'? It will come out something like 'Hagady,' which sounds like . . . a health-nut's breakfast gruel. . . ."

Although both "happy" and "good" are still heard, "nice" is shouldering them aside as Americans part. "Have a nice city" was a San Francisco mayoralty slogan in 1970. "Have a nice day"—its earliest appearance, according to my citations, in a 1948 Kirk Douglas film, *A Letter to Three Wives*—is a linguistic phenomenon of the 70's.

Why are so many people now finding such a nice expression so offensive? " 'Have a nice day' grates," writes Jean Braucher of Madison, Wis., "because it pretends to be more than the perfunctory verbal punctuation mark that it is. Because it comes close to real conversation, it sounds insincere, while a simple 'Thank you' does not."

The distinction is this: When H.A.N.D. is spoken with sincerity and eye contact, it is a social asset and a note of civility in a hurried world; but when it is spoken automatically, in the same tone as "Get lost," it comes across with a resounding clank of falsity.

Jack Sheehan, news director of WKRT in Cortland, N.Y., recounts an episode that took place in a local courtroom, as a judge sentenced a man recently convicted of robbery: "The judge committed the man to the Auburn State Prison for a term of seven to ten years. As the weight of his words sank in, the judge fired the parting shot: 'You are hereby remanded to the custody of the sheriff's department for delivery to the custody of state officials. Have a nice day.' The man almost sank to his knees. The phrase had worked its magic."

Dear Mr. Safire:

Your supposedly scholarly sources have done Chaucer wrong in regard to "Have a good day." The meter of the lines you quote is a tip-off that something is false; even Chaucer would not normally have called "There was namoore but 'Fare wel, have a good day" a line of iambic pentameter. And sure enough, both of my editions of Chaucer (F. N. Robinson and Albert C. Baugh) give the line as "Ther was namoore but 'Fare wel, have good day' "—without the extra-metrical "a."

To my ear, "Have good day" is hearty and red-blooded. Intruding an "a" lowers the wish to something approaching 14th-century Mellowspeak.

The line, in case you want to check, is 2740 in both the cited editions. It is in The Knight's Tale, immediately following The General Prologue.

> Sincerely yours,
> Donald M. Williams
> Waco, Texas

---

having your cake, *see* eating your cake

---

head of household, *see* census-ese

---

heady stuff

A man who seems to be a relic of the 60's, unkempt and personsute, sits atop a waste-disposal receptacle (once the trash can) on the corner of Connecticut Avenue and 17th Street in the nation's capital, a stoned throw from the Washington bureau of *The New York Times.* In front of him is a card table laden with small pipes, hoses, papers, and other paraphernalia associated with the use of the cannabis plant.

"Our prices are lower, so you can get higher," he calls out in a rasping, stentorian voice (from Stentor, the herald with the loud voice in *The Iliad*). Then he uses the slogan I like best: "Everything you need for the head of the house."

That double meaning tells a lot about the transformation of "head." Time was, the main meaning of "head" was as leader, or chief—"head of the house," or "head of the class." The original meaning, as the part of the body above the neck, always remained in metaphoric use—from "head over heels" and "lose your head" to "get this through your head"—but "the head" was most often taken to be "the boss," and rarely substituted for "the mind." (In the United States Navy, lavatories were often placed near the bulkhead, and came to be known as "the head," but that and the unrelated use of the word as sexual slang are tangents we need not follow.)

Then came the drug culture, and "head" was its key word. "Hopheads" took dope; "potheads" smoked marijuana; "acidheads" dropped LSD. A place where the accouterments of drug taking were sold was called a "head shop." Singers urged listeners to "get your head together," and people who liked to pick up drug-culture lingo without necessarily participating talked of "where my head is at."

In that sense, the head was a personal citadel—a physical fortress, to guard the self from the world. The head implied feeling, in contrast to the mind, which usually connoted thought. The head was a fragile, sometimes aching, often enchanted, thing; in contrast, the mind was disciplined, or something one was forced to make up. In this period, "hardheaded" fell into disuse, replaced by "tough-minded."

The science of linguistics properly views all hunches with suspicion, but I have a hunch that the use of "head" to mean "citadel of awareness" is declining in common parlance, which could signal a general decline of self-indulgent inwardness. That's cause for optimism: I would hate to think of a new decade's writers and academics electing to pursue the life of the head.

Dear Bill,

Without intending to be overly nit-picky, I believe there is a bit more precise explanation for the nautical use of "head" for lavatory: In the days of the sailing ships the facilities were placed in the bows, or head of the ship, where natural action of the ship plunging through the waves exercised a bit of cleansing.

"Head" is generally archaic in present usage for the fore part of a ship, with bows, forecastle, etc. more used, but "down by the head" is still good terminology for a ship which has taken on water in the chain locker, and which is floating lower at the bows.

"Bulkhead," I believe, is a more modern term, not really connected to the "head," having come into general nautical usage with steam, and compart-

mented bulk carriers of coal, wheat, etc. "Head" is quite ancient, and pre-dates bulkhead.

> *Best regards,*
> *Gordon Eliot White*
> *Washington Correspondent*
> Deseret News
> *Alexandria, Virginia*

Dear Mr. Safire,
   "The head" in U.S. Navy terminology has nothing to do with the placing of the lavatories near bulkheads. It comes from the fact that in sailing ships there was no plumbing. The crew had to go forward to the head of the ship where they had to clamber over the bulwarks and use the nautical (and unenclosed) equivalent of the outhouse.
   If you examine authentic models of men of war in the Smithsonian or the Naval Academy museum, you can see the holes cut out near the bulwarks and bowsprit. The officers, incidentally, had their head in the after part of the vessel.

> *Sincerely,*
> *Wright Britton*
> *Delray Beach, Florida*

Dear Mr. Safire,
   The term head pre-dates inboard plumbing. The forward part of a ship is known as the head, and is where the headsails are flown. The shrouds and stays supporting the bowsprit form a convenient maze of rigging in which the ancient mariner could find reasonable privacy and safety while pumping his personal bilges. As the seaman or non-com in charge of the sails on the mizzen-mast was called the "captain of the mizzen," so was the man in charge of the headsails called the "captain of the head"—a term which has carried forward to a slightly less dignified occupation in the modern navy.
   I might as well throw in another derivation for your collection—scuttlebutt, meaning gossip. In the absence of a drinking fountain the sailor's thirst was assuaged by providing one of the water barrels, or butts, with a ladle, or scuttle. This "scuttlebutt" performed not only its primary function but also the same secondary function as the office water cooler. Hence scuttlebutt.

> *A. J. W. Murphy*
> *New York, New York*

Dear Mr. Safire:
   In the interest of parallelism, should you not have spelled the new word in your column "pirsonsute"?

> *Sincerely,*
> *Jerome H. Taylor*
> *New Hyde Park, New York*

   I was playing on "hirsute," and played myself out.—W.S.

W. S.—
   Re heady stuff:
   We have also had, for quite some time now:

   heady
   pinheads
   hot heads
   boneheads
   fatheads
   pigheads
   draycups
   meatheads
   blockheads
   jugheads
   hopheads

   citadels of awareness all.

                                        Cordially,
                                        M.P. [Martin Panzer]
                                        New York, New York

Dear Mr. Safire:
   In your article "Heady Stuff" in yesterday's New York Times Magazine
you wrote of "the slogan I like best." Although I have no reason to doubt your
prowess as a sloganophile, I suspect that you meant most rather than best.
   One normally discusses only the quantity of one's affections, for fear that one
may misjudge their quality, to one's subsequent chagrin.
   Suppose, in this particular example, that the slogan in question had found
your technique lacking. She might tell her friends "If that was the best job of
liking that he could manage, then I certainly feel sorry for his favorite speech."

Dear Mr. Safire :

May I express our enjoyment of your Op-Ed columns, and your New York Times Magazine pages on language... In the magazine section entitled "Heady Stuff", we find much to the point, however one item needs consideration.

Therefore I must submit that, in dealing as you did with the "head", "head over heels", etc. you dealt not well in your mention of "the head" in regard to U.S. Navy lavatories... For regardless of U.S. Navy nomenclature, which often strays from time-honored naval usage, the great tradition and location of "the head" is indeed, the ship's head.

Originally an external feature, and since enclosure is ever with us, it was brought in board and put below. Of course the classic receptacle was the wooden bucket of ancient times. 'Twas emptied to leeward from the "head", beak-head, fo'c'stle head, billet-head, etc. into the flushing action of the salt bow wash.

Herewith sketches of an 18th century ship's head. (Imagine the facilities of the "Great Harry" of 1514 ?) This shows the arrangement of the crews' head of an American frigate of 1780. In most vessels the rails of her bow scroll-work provided seating enough. The lowest rating told-off to attend "the head" was referred to as "captain of the Head" (U.S. Navy jargon)

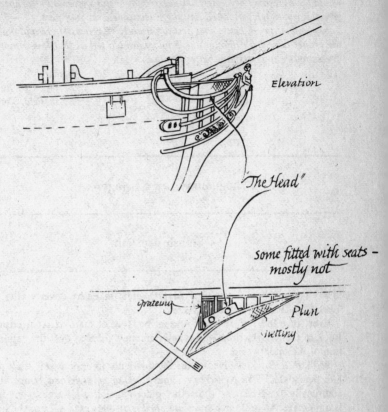

Elevation

"The Head"

some fitted with seats — mostly not

grating →

netting

Plan

with much appreciation
of your good pages
over the years . . . .

Sincerely

Samuel H. Bryant

Marblehead, Mass.^tts

How much better for you had you said that you liked the slogan most—you would have elevated her above her peers, and for this she would have cherished you and willingly overlooked any slight clumsiness on your part.

Remember: good, better and best are usually adjectives; more and most are the proper adverbs. Although the Bauhaus would tell us that less is more, no one seriously suggests that better is more.

Sincerely,
Roderick G. Bates
Springfield, Vermont

hegemony, *see* Kissingerese

hellish decision

"Feel like hell?" goes a snappy advertisement taken by Beverly Sills' New York City Opera. "Come see Faust."

Ever since the Fall (not the season, but that of man, as reported in the Book of Genesis), writers and typesetters have puzzled over the capitalization of the underworld.

William F. Buckley always puts the first letter in uppercase: "It's a place, like Scarsdale." *The New York Times Manual of Style and Usage* almost completely disagrees: "As the nether-place name, it is lowercase, but *Hades* is uppercase. As profanity and slang, *hell* is also lowercase." For the hell of it, the manual adds: "It is also best avoided as common and tiresome."

When I write a stylebook, sometime after I learn to spell, here's how I'll handle that nether-nether land: in all secondary usages, lowercase: *hell's bells, what the hell, the hell with it, hell-raising, hell-bent for election, come hell or high water.* But in all cases where the sense of place is clear and primary, I'll capitalize it—like Scarsdale—as deserving of a place name: *You've made my life Hell. Hell hath no fury like a woman called a "girl."* ("Go to hell" and "To hell with you," though they originally referred to Hell as a place, have lost that specific meaning. "Damn it to Hell," though common and tiresome to some, is explicit enough with its reference to damnation to cause Hell to be treated as a place.)

This is the evenhanded way. One can exclaim "Good heavens!" and describe a godsend as "heaven-sent," but when you use that word to mean a specific, angelic place, you thank Heaven.

Help! but

"You might have a go at ridding the world of 'cannot help but,'" writes Barbara Bernstein of Rockville Centre, N.Y.

Easy. "Cannot help but" confuses two different idioms: "I cannot but do it," and "I cannot help doing it." In the first, the "but" means "other than"—"I cannot but do it" means "I cannot do otherwise." In the second, the "help" means "help myself from," or "stop myself"—thus, "I cannot help doing it" means "I cannot stop myself from doing it."

What, then, does "I cannot help but do it" mean? Jacques Barzun, editor of the current edition of Wilson Follett's *Modern American Usage,* says: "It means that one does not know the existence of two distinct idioms."

"Cannot help but" is confusing, redundant, and sloppy. I hope today's kick in its mouth will curtail its use, though I can't help but think that this diatribe won't rid the world of the squared idiom.

hembra, *see* macho for women

heyday

If we were to back down on our Iranian sanctions, opined a Washington editorialist, "Soviet propagandists . . . would have a heyday."

That did not have the right ring; I think the writer meant "field day."

A "field day," as might be supposed, is a day spent in the fields—a class outing, especially connected with sports, its metaphoric meaning rooted in winning the competition of that day. To have a field day is to win, gloriously, in any field of endeavor, indoors or out.

A "heyday"—probably from "high day"—implies a longer period, a time of life rather than a single momentous occasion. We can expect the word to come into vogue as a result of its use by Dore Schary as the title of his memoirs, and by Linda DuBreuil as the title of her paperback novel. Schary, the former screenwriter and movie-studio head, cites lexicographer Samuel Johnson's definition: "an expression of frolic and exultation, and sometimes wonder." That shouted expression—a predecessor of Willie Mays' "Say, hey"—turned into the noun used by Shakespeare in *Hamlet:* "At your age the heyday in the blood is tame, it's humble."

Keep your eye on the article that precedes the noun: It is usually *a* field day, and *the* heyday. Remember: One field day does not the heyday make.

Dear Mr. Safire:

Time out o' mind farmers have been at the mercy of the weather for the critical task of making hay in spring and summer. When a day came with just the right combination—sunshine, warm, dry air and a gentle breeze—every member of the family worked furiously to put up the largest possible amount of the best quality hay. A day like that was called a "real hay-day."

In the dairy country in upstate New York (and I suppose elsewhere too) the term is still commonly used in that sense, but it also is used as slang to indicate a particularly good day or era.

Incidentally, although it's mechanized, haying still goes on in the same spirit too.

I suspect that the term was ancient when Francis Bacon used it in Hamlet.

> *Regards,*
> *Harold C Bennett*
> *Syracuse, New York*

hit parade

In the continuing saga of the slang term "hit," a man who identifies himself as "a semiretired coke dealer" writes to bring us up to date on some venal vernacular.

"Although 'Do you want a hit?' is perfectly acceptable," he advises, "much more common or fashionable are 'Do a toot?' 'Do a blow?' " He speculates that the origin of "toot" is "because you toot your horn after doing it—in other words, your head is lifted like the top of a boat whistle."

As a slang noun, "hit" is not limited to a dose of cocaine: Any "motivational aid" qualifies. You can not only get a hit of coke, but a hit of dope (marijuana) and a hit of Scotch. Sometimes "off" is added on: "Let me have a hit off your beer."

Our pedagogic pusher adds a point of interest to linguists: Among the names for cocaine ("nose candy," "toots," "lady," "pearl") is "blort." Just as in "Jabberwocky" Lewis Carroll combined "chuckle" and "snort" to create "chortle," today's underworld wordsniffs combined "blow" and "snort" to come up with "blort."

In narcotics lingo, the impact-laden word was used in the 40's as a verb to describe the onrush of reaction to a heroin injection: "It hit the heart like a runaway locomotive," wrote Nelson Algren in *The Man with the Golden Arm.* "It hit like a falling wall." In the 60's, "hit" turned to a noun, with one definition curiously close to the original Old Norse of a thousand years before: Stuart Berg Flexner gave one meaning in the latest Dictionary of American Slang as "an appointment or meeting related to illegal business or contraband; the time, place, person or operation from which one obtains contraband, usually narcotic drugs. . . ."

In the 70's, a "hit" became associated with cocaine, a white powder that is laid out in a one-inch "line" and sniffed; in 1971, Harold Schmeck of *The New York Times* wrote "The current price of cocaine was about $10 'a hit.' " The current slang meaning is "a single dose."

In all discussions of accusations, our judicial system's traditional presumption of innocence ought to be remembered. "The charges are ridiculous," snorted one White House spokesman.

hit parade II

Mike Wallace, on CBS, bored in on a political fat cat: At a Beverly Hills party, Wallace asked, did Hamilton Jordan ask for "a hit"? A few weeks before, a couple of disco tycoons, at Studio 54 in Manhattan, wanted the world to know that a group of White House aides, including Chief of Staff Jordan (rhymes with burden), had arranged for "a hit."

Whence "hit"? This is one of those short, powerful words, taken from Old Norse, which originally meant "to meet with." As it mingled with Anglo-Saxon, it took on the sense of a fist meeting with a jaw, and came to connote "striking with violence."

In slang, the word offers a smorgasbord of meanings: "Hit me," says the poker player, asking for another card; "He's set up for a hit," says the gangland leader to his murderous "hit man"; "Can I hit you for a C?" asks the hundred-dollar borrower; "I think we have a hit," says the producer to the angel.

Dear Mr. Safire,

It's interesting to hear of the origin of "hit"—more so because it sheds light on a perplexing usage common among younger people these days. When someone looks to "score" sexually with someone (else, since few onanists have claimed scores after doing their thing) they speak of "hitting on" the person. I always considered the allusion to be somewhat violent. Now I wonder what linguistic intuition has given us this true-to-roots colloquialism. Now, "hit" does in fact seem more sexual to me than a more literal translation. After all, how intriguing or exciting could it be to look forward "to meeting with" an alluring member of the opposite—or one's own—sex?

Art Gatti
New York, New York

Mr. Safire:
   There is a further use of "hit" loose in the land.
   Within IBM, hit has come to mean impact or conflict.
   For example, during a planning session, a proposal for action can be described as "having a hit" on a current project or a proposed one.
   Or, when there is no impact, a plan has "no hits."

An industrial writer

Hobson-Jobson, *see* Mondegreens: "I led the pigeons to the flag"

Hobson objects

Some people whose view of history is slightly askew use "Hobson's choice" as a synonym for "dilemma." Earlier this month, at a White House briefing to explain the easing of clean-air rules, Douglas Costle, administrator of the Environmental Protection Agency, agonized over the difficult choice he faced between the risk of more hydrocarbons in the air and the risk of destroying catalytic converters by using leaded gasoline. "It's an environmental Hobson's choice," he declared in a front-page article of *The New York Times.*

It was not. A Hobson's choice is neither a dilemma nor a difficult decision: It is no choice at all. Thomas Hobson (1544–1631) ran a rent-a-hackney-horse agency in Cambridge, England. "When a man came for a horse," wrote Sir Richard Steele in the *Spectator,* No. 509 (1712), "he was led into the stable, where there was great choice, but he obliged him to take the horse which stood next to the stable door; so that every customer was alike well served according to his chance, and every horse ridden with the same justice. From whence it became a proverb, when what ought to be your election was forced upon you, to say Hobson's choice."

A take-it-or-leave-it proposition was all Mr. Hobson offered. It befuzzes a good figure of speech to use his name to describe a dilemma in which the choice of either alternative is bad: "A strong dilemma in a desperate case," wrote Jonathan Swift. "To act with infamy, or quit the place." (That was pre-Vietnam.)

Our environmental administrator is hereby placed on report for attempted mopery; if he chooses to continue to take Hobson's name in vain, he will be cited for linguistic pollution.

Dear Mr. Safire:

Today, I think you are being too hard on Douglas Costle, Environmental Protection Agency, by holding him to the original definition of Hobson's choice. This term has taken on a somewhat broader and more useful meaning through general usage as indicated in Webster's Third New International Dictionary: "The necessity of accepting one of two or more equally objectionable things."

It would appear Mr. Costle's comment re an environmental Hobson's choice was most fitting.

> *Sincerely Yours*
> *Jerome S. Blumberg*
> *Fair Lawn, New Jersey*

In its most recent Collegiate edition, Merriam-Webster went back to the old way. They had to—it was that choice or none.—W.S.

Dear Mr. Safire:

Buridan's ass is what people should be thinking of when they mistakenly invoke "Hobson's choice." The animal in question starved to death between two haystacks, unable to decide which to attack first. Buridan, of course, was the medieval Schoolman.

> *Sincerely,*
> *Lionel Landry*
> *Executive Vice President*
> *The Asia Society, Inc.*
> *New York, New York*

Dear Mr. Safire:

Your reference to mopery is in egregious error. Mopery is a misdemeanor and, as any veteran New York cop can tell you, it consists of indecent exposure before a blind woman. We had numerous such cases, in the old days, at Kings County Hospital.

> *Very truly yours,*
> *Sylvanus Peters*
> *Sun City, Arizona*

homonyms, *see* Mondegreens: "I led the pigeons to the flag"

hopefully

Evidently, the word "hopefully" has become the litmus test to determine whether one is a language snob or a language slob.

Angrily, traditionalists hold that the word is an adverb, usually intended to modify a verb. In the sentence "He will look at me hopefully" the verb "to look" is modified by "hopefully," to mean that the look will contain hope. Purists reject "Hopefully, he will look at me" because it is confusing. Does it mean "with hope in his eyes" or "I hope he will look at me"? They argue that when you mean to say "it is hoped" or "I hope," you should come out and say those words, and not cloak your hopes in a fuzzy "hopefully" that can be misinterpreted.

Additionally, the anti-dangling-adverb crowd insists that "ly" has a use in helping understanding and should not be corrupted. For example, if you say "Close the door tight," the adjective "tight" modifies the noun "door," thus describing accurately the desired condition of the door; but if you say "Close the door tightly," the adverb "tightly" modifies the verb "close," and does not describe the door.

Coolly, and against all that good sense, the language slob replies: "What most people use becomes 'correct,' and most people use 'hopefully' to mean 'one hopes.' To wrinkle your nose at common usage is to be a language snob."

Fortunately, we do not have to choose up sides on the basis of slob versus snob, descriptive versus prescriptive linguistics, to deal with "hopefully."

Importantly, the editor of Webster's New World Dictionary, David Guralnik, agrees: "Happily, there are many precedents for such a usage," he writes. "Presumably, purists howled when each one first appeared. Probably time will take care of 'hopefully' as well."

Doubtlessly, my deliberate decision to adopt "hopefully" in its sentence-coloring sense, and to defend it vigorously as structurally correct rather than to accept it listlessly as common sloppy usage, will be attacked by people who get their kicks out of hanging out on old ramparts. But while they're knocking "hopefully," they'll have to deal with the deliberately dangling adverbs that begin every new paragraph in this entry.

ily cannot get together on whether to hyphenate top management, it suffers from stylistic schizophrenia.

So do I. One day, feeling bloodyminded (no hyphen), I wrote about a politician's rising "Dracula-like" from the body politic; *The Times*'s copy editor killed the hyphen. That is because the suffix "like" is glued to the word it turns into an adjective, according to *Times* (and A.P.) style: as, "the phoenixlike Mr. Deng." The only exception permitted is for words ending in double-l, as in "bell-like," because three "l's" together look funny.

I think the rule should be modified. In a lifelike, businesslike way, the hyphen can be dropped when "like" is attached to ordinary nouns, but when it comes to proper nouns, I stand—bulldoglike and Horatio-like—at the bridge.* Why? Because "Draculalike" just doesn't look right. "Dracula-like" looks right. In the correct use of hyphens, looks count.

Hyphens should be used mainly when not using them causes confusion. As Fowler wrote in his *Modern English Usage:* "A little used car is not necessarily the same as a little-used car." Hypheneticist Maxwell Lehman adds: "An old-world city is not the same as an old world city. A full-grown man refers to one who has reached adulthood, but a full grown man might be one who, already adult, has had enough to eat." Similarly, a small-business man could be a huge fellow who runs a mom-and-pop enterprise, but a small businessman is always a runt.

Hyphens should not be used when avoidance of them does not cause confusion—for example, "newly elected officials," "freshly painted faces," "the then Secretary of State," "fellow Democrats," "the Watergate coverup."

Ah, now we've come to the puzzler: When does a compound word lose its hyphen? "To cover up," or conceal evidence, was made a noun in the 20's. Raymond Chandler used "cover-up" in *Black Mask* magazine in 1935—and the compound word was immortalized in the mid-70's. Just this year, I decided to drop the hyphen, on the theory that once a compound word has been impregnated with a life of its own, it no longer deserves the hyphen that marks nonce words and tryout words.

If you think a word has made it—then it's solidarity forever. If you think a word is compounded only for the time being, hyphenate: "life-style" has begun to fade, embarrassing those who prematurely embraced "life style" (*Time*-style for "life-style" uses a hyphen).

What of "hyphenated Americans"? Mexican-Americans, Polish-Americans, etc., keep their hyphens because the first part of the compound is a kind of prefix, denoting origin; however, "French Canadian" is not hyphenated because the first word is an adjective denoting not origin but current membership in a discrete society—French Canada. Same with "Latin American."

Clear? No? When in doubt, leave it out, unless it looks funny. Go with

---

* *Horatio should have been Horatius, as nine readers pointed out—sometimes even Virgil nodded.—W.S.*

Winston Churchill: "One must regard the hyphen as a blemish to be avoided wherever possible." He had a cold-war mentality.

Dear Sir:

Your recent article on hyphens was a disappointment to me, in its failure to take up the most egregious nonhyphenation favored by The Times *itself. I trust this was due to oversight, not pusillanimity. I refer to your society pages pet headline word, "rewed," as in, "Mrs. Smith Rewed." When I first noticed this word, many years ago, there was an awful instant when I truly did not know what was meant, and I still never fail to find it startling. It leads to meditations along the line of, "She rewed the day she met him," or "Why was he so rewed to her?" . . .*

For a complete change of subject, this query: are you able to pass one of those stores with a sign reading "organic foods" without speculating on what an inorganic food might be?

> *Very truly yours,*
> *R. W. Tucker*
> *Philadelphia, Pennsylvania*

> *Owed to Punctilio*
> *or*
> *(We been waitin for ya, Willie)*

> *In language Safire's a dick*
> *In tracing abuses that stick:*
> *Like colons and dashes—*
> *and hyphen mish-mashes;*
> *He writes permissable (sic)!!!*

> *Mike Leifer*
> *Long Island City, New York*

I declare

A new American art form is emerging: the formal declaration of candidacy for President of the United States. In English classes across the country, students are being given the assignment "Write a 500-word declaration of your candidacy for President, including your vision for America and the reason you are uniquely qualified to lead us into the 80's. Try to avoid the word 'leadership' and the phrase 'prayerful consideration.' "

Grading on the basis of uplift, brevity, catchiness, and evocation of past greatness—sorry, substantive ideas are out of place in this exercise—here is how a few of the recent submissions have rated.

Howard Baker uplifted nicely with "a new generation of confidence," though that seemed to bottom on "a full generation of peace" slogan by a former President who is not ordinarily quoted. The Baker declaration was not short; the minority leader is conscious of his shortness and comes to grips with that by pledging to "stand tall" against Soviet threats. He offered a catchy jibe at President Carter, calling on voters to "judge me," a deliberate contrast to the "trust me" theme of the Carter 1976 campaign.

Ted Kennedy's Boston kickoff was lengthy for an "I declare," but he was willing to linger over the evocation of historic figures and places. His speechwriter, Richard Goodwin, specializes in giving speeches a "sense of place"—the calm, 1970 election-eve address by Edmund Muskie from the rock-ribbed coast of Maine was a Goodwinner—and Kennedy's Faneuil Hall setting made natural the warmly familiar reference to founding father Samuel Adams as "Sam Adams."

The key Kennedy words were chosen with care. In recalling his work in the Senate, he said: "I have learned the necessary ways of persuasion and conciliation." Not "compromise"—that's nothing to claim—but "conciliation," which in this case means compromise but is soothing and has no unprincipled overtones.

On the issue of defense, the pledge (never "promise," which is political, while "pledge" carries solemnity) is "sufficiency," which sounds slightly better than the dull "parity," or the jingoistic "superiority": ". . . our defense will always be sufficient beyond doubt. . . ." The intensifying "beyond

doubt" gives the present policy a satisfying shove, the way "second to none" seems to toughen "tied for first."

In political declarations, a myth is as good as a mile: Kennedy's was "The only thing that paralyzes us today is the myth that we cannot move." That was an evocation of F.D.R.'s "The only thing we have to fear is fear itself," used earlier by Epictetus, Cicero, Sir Francis Bacon, Burke, Thoreau, and others.

Jerry Brown's entry was trimmed to the size of the Gettysburg Address, but also used an evocative construction: However, Lincoln's "The dogmas of the quiet past are inadequate to the stormy present" lost something in the translation to Brown's "The economic and political doctrines that propelled us into such success after World War II are simply inadequate for the world we now inhabit."

Governor Brown gets the highest grade for statement of theme ("My principles are simple: protect the earth, serve the people, and explore the universe"), and the subsequent three-paragraph follow-up to each principle was tightly constructed. He used the with-it "caring" instead of Kennedy's outdated "compassionate."

But then Brown went overboard: ". . . at last we begin to sense our unity in the spirit on this small speck of universal time." Our unity "in" the spirit—or did he mean "of" the spirit? "On" this speck of time—or "in" this speck of time?

"Speck" is a good word, if humility is the object, and the earth is often considered to be only a speck in the universe—but at what cosmic subway stop do you get "on this small speck of universal time"? It may be unkind to flyspeck, but Governor Brown invited a close reading of his rhetoric with his opening sentence: "The language of politics today is debased."

---

idiom, see meta-fore!

---

impact attenuators, see prettifiers

---

inappropriate

"No comment"—a phrase that Winston Churchill claimed to have picked up from diplomat Sumner Welles—is no longer used by political and corporate biggies as a door-slammer.

Instead, the favored word to turn aside questions is "inappropriate." The rebuff takes this form: "It would be inappropriate for me to say anything at this time. . . ."

The word has gained a slightly accusatory quality; spokesmen who use it seem to suggest that questioners are demanding something improper, even wrong, and certainly against the public interest.

What does this new shield word mean? The most frequent dictionary synonym of "appropriate" is "fitting"—as Lincoln used that word to describe the ceremonies at Gettysburg as "fitting and proper." Thus, "inappropriate" would be "not fitting," "unsuitable," and, taking it a step further, "improper."

The root is "proper"—"belonging to one's self, as property"—and the evasive spokesman uses "inappropriate" to mean that such blatant truth-blurting would not be suitable to him. But he is reluctant to say "It would not be suitable to comment," because that does not seem strong enough—nearly as weak as "But that would be indiscreet."

And so we have "inappropriate," which means "jarring," "unsuitable," "out of character," or "not like me," all of which may be excuses for ducking an answer, but are not ordinarily reasons for any public official to refuse to make public comment. The only reason implicit in the word is "improper"—an ethical judgment—"wrong," which is a spokesman's hint that the reason for the refusal places him on the side of goodness and right.

Too few questioners insist that interviewers give the reasons for inappropriateness. If the meaning intended is "in bad taste," "untimely," "violates privacy rights," "unethical," or even "diplomatically embarrassing," let the spokesman speak it plain. "Not fitting for the occasion" should not do.

A longer tirade against this pretentious and offensive form of stonewalling would be inappropriate in a newspaper with the slogan "All the News That's Fit to Print."

indicated, *see* nouvelle vague

infix, *see* Nother's Day

insidious, *see* Kratz family

The Intriguers

Two weeks ago, this column promised to examine "the intriguing roots" of words. A *Times* colleague, Arthur Gelb, remarked he hoped I had used "intriguing" correctly—not as merely "fascinating" but as "mysterious; illicit; baffling."

The trouble was I had meant "fascinating." Glumly, I looked it up in Merriam-Webster's Second Unabridged (the Third is too permissive for me). Sure enough, "intriguing" has the same Latin root as "intricate," and its meanings were spread over "complicated," "beguiling," and "arousing curiosity." But wait—in the current Webster's New World, as well as in Merriam-Webster's Eighth Collegiate, the primary meaning is given as "fascinating."

The American Heritage Dictionary gives the reason for this problem: *"Intrigue,* as a transitive verb in the sense of arousing interest or curiosity, has been established on a popular level since the 1920's. It has been resisted by writers on usage, however, usually on the ground that it tends to displace words that would convey the desired sense more sharply."

Turning to a favorite "writer on usage," I find Theodore Bernstein explaining that he frowned on using "intrigue" as only "interesting" or "fascinating" because "first, it is an erroneous borrowing from French, in which the word means 'puzzle'; second, 'intrigue' has become a kind of fuzzy, all-purpose word to express meanings for which there are already precise words like 'mystify,' 'enchant,' 'interest,' 'pique' and 'excite.' "

That was a worthwhile usage defense, but the dictionaries say the fight is lost. Although, as a verb, "to intrigue" still means "to plot," or "to make intricate and mysterious plans," as a participle, "intriguing" has come to mean "fascinating."

When informed of the usage change, editor Gelb caught up with the times in a lightning reaction: "Really? That's intriguing."

My dear William Safire,

In the thirties I was one of a fast-disappearing breed. I was at Harvard doing classics. One of the last of Harvard's giants was still teaching—Greek. And I recall vividly our first meeting, at Seaver Hall, with the grand old man. He sat at his desk and looked at us through metal-rimmed glasses, the great Carl Newell Jackson, and these are the first words he uttered: "Gentlemen, when you write for me, I wish to admonish you regarding the use of a word I find not only meaningless, but also repulsive: 'intriguing.' Please avoid its use. You may say Clytemnestra had had an 'intrigue' with her lover, but you must not say that you find that situation 'intriguing.' And you cannot be 'intrigued' by it." Then, as if to deliver a coup de grace, he added, after clearing his venerable throat: " 'Intriguing' is a word which I find women have made popular. Remember, therefore, that the word connotes effeminacy. . . . For forty years I taught: for forty years I allowed no student of mine, to stoop to the 'intrigue' solecism. On my tombstone the legend will read: 'He never spoke the word "intriguing." ' "

Thank you for bringing to my ears the sound of that grand old classicist's voice. Thank you for fighting the only fight we should join: the fight that one inevitably loses. Glory! How many of those fights I've been involved in: the "like-as," the "who-whom," the "if I was-if I were," the "shall-will," etc., etc. It's been a marvelous war. Every battle lost.

Yrs., etc.
John Joseph
Shelburne, Massachusetts

---

invasion, *see* transgression

---

investigative reporter

Word has filtered down from wherever these decisions are made that *The New York Times* will no longer use the term "investigative reporter" to describe any of its reporters, each one of whom is expected to be investigative to some degree. A "noninvestigative reporter" is a contradiction in terms, if the reporter is doing what a reporter's job requires; the dramatic adjective "investigative" derogates all other reporters not so deliciously titled.

Over to you, academe: How about the highfalutin title "distinguished professor"? Doesn't that adjective lessen the prestige of "professor"? Who will be the first dissident to proclaim himself "undistinguished professor"?

June bugs

"Windfall" is a 400-year-old word that means an unexpected benefit, graphically describing the good fortune that falls to a passer-by when a piece of fruit is blown off a tree. The word was born again in politics in 1936, when the Supreme Court struck down a portion of the Agricultural Adjustment Act, and President Franklin Roosevelt moved to intercept what he said was "what may well be termed a 'windfall' received by certain taxpayers."

When President Carter announced his intention to decontrol oil prices recently, he laced an otherwise colorless speech with a denunciation of the oil industry and a call for a tax on the "windfall profits" that he feared the end of controls might bring. Even with that injection of populist fervor, and its evocation of Roosevelt's war on "economic royalists," the Carter speech contained little to make it memorable.

A few days later, however, the President used a down-home figure of speech to enliven his prediction that the oil companies would vigorously oppose the imposition of a new tax. He warned that an oil lobby "would be all over Capitol Hill like a chicken on a June bug."

City dwellers were confused: Since chickens are bigger than bugs, didn't he mean bugs on a chicken?

Not at all. Farmers and Southern-speaking lexicographers were familiar with the image: A June bug is an inch-long, scarablike beetle, brown or green, that appears in the South in the late spring. A Virginia farmer reports: "June bugs are too large and too tough for a chicken to make a meal of easily, so the chicken will run around pecking and scratching at it for quite a while, sometimes to no avail."

The word-picture has citations dating back more than a century in the Dictionary of Americanisms. Augustus Longstreet, in his 1835 book *Georgia Scenes,* wrote: "You'll see me down upon him like a duck upon a June bug." In the past century, the pursuing duck has changed to a chicken, but the tough bug hangs in there; in the dull vocabulary of oil decontrol, the vivid metaphor has provided us with a windfall.

Dear Mr. Safire,

We lived on an oil lease outside of Morris, Oklahoma, prior to WW-II. As was common in those days, we had a flare to burn off the excess natural gas, and, in our case, the torch was in the chicken yard. The June bugs, attracted by the two-foot flame, flew right through it—burning off their internal wings—and spun down as a toasted, and tasty, windfall for a hundred or so hungry birds. While the season lasted, the chickens stayed up all night, eating themselves bowlegged. The laying hens, particularly, refused to give up until they tipped over on their beaks. This position made the collection of their eggs, which they dropped wherever they happened to be, a simple chore.

The oil companies didn't mind the natural gas being burned off in this fashion, but they did object to the use of cold-weather condensate from the gas lines as fuel for our automobiles. My father's expression for this disapproval was "that oil company man will get on you like a dirty shirt if he catches you burning that drip-gas in your Whippet." Oddly enough, "chicken on a June bug" was not part of the language in that area. . . .

> Thank you,
> John McCleary
> Chappaqua, New York

Dear Mr. Safire:

Did you really mean that a windfall is a "piece of fruit" blown off a tree? This would make a windfall a part of an orange, apple, pear, or other fruit. Didn't you really mean "a fruit"? Piece of fruit is a line from Clifford Odet's "Awake & Sing" or one of his other plays, I believe; it is not English, but probably a translation from Yiddish. In any case, it's imprecise.

Sincerely,
Walter S. Ross
New York, New York

Kissingerese

In *Henry Kissinger White House Years*—I presume that's the title; there is no colon after the name, and the byline is placed on top of what would ordinarily be the title—all the doubts are "grave" and all the misgivings are "serious." Never a mild doubt or a lighthearted misgiving.

Worse, he writes of "opening gambits," a redundency*—in chess, a gambit is an opening move. And worst of all, on page 580, the man who was national security adviser from 1969 to 1975 makes the stupefying mistake of spelling adviser with an "o." (Yes, that's how to spell "stupefy"—not "stupify," a blunder perpetrated in this space recently.)

With those minor nits picked, let us examine the vivid Kissingerese, the vocabulary of the modern superdiplomat, as set forth by the only Secretary of State to have had two Presidents working for him.

Démarche. "Ambassador Rabin . . . presented a démarche from Golda Meir. . . ." "I found Vorontsov's démarche encouraging." This French word (originally meaning "to trample underfoot") means "move" or "line of action," and in diplolingo has come to mean a political or international maneuver. With enough démarches, a country could achieve détente, or go to war.

Condominium. "We would not participate in a Soviet-American condominium. . . ." "We would give no encouragement to visions of condominium, and we would resist any attempts by Moscow to achieve hegemony over China or elsewhere." The Latin word *dominium* means "lordship"; "condominium" means "joint rule or sovereignty," and was popularized by German political writers in the 18th century.

---

* *The correct spelling is "redundancy," as forty-seven gleeful wiseguys reminded me.*
—W.S.

A "Sino-Soviet condominium" is a tenant-owned apartment house in the Black Sea with a Chinese restaurant downstairs.

Hegemony. With the preferred pronunciation accenting the "gem," soft "g," this word—meaning "dominance"—comes from the Greek *hegemon,* or "leader." According to Kissinger: "Though this later became a hallowed Chinese word, it actually was introduced by us." As an etymologist, he's a better statesman; the dirty word for leadership was used a generation ago in the translation of Mao's "dig tunnels deep, store grain and never seek hegemony."

People. This seemingly ordinary word has a special meaning of "not a government" in Kissingerese. "Tass employed some strange language. It noted that the Soviet 'people' (that is, not the government) 'associates itself' with the struggle. The Soviet 'people' would continue to give the Vietnamese people 'the necessary support' (not 'increased' support, as Hanoi asked)." Mr. Kissinger does not point out a refinement required by Presidential speechwriters: to use the word "peoples," plural, when writing about the Soviet Union, in order to cover different ethnic groups.

Modalities. In the White House Situation Room (which could as easily have been named the "What's New Room," since "situation" is as vague as it is voguish), an assistant secretary of state urged: "I think we should not offer to discuss with the Chinese modalities of a meeting, such as communications, personnel, timing, security, etc. . . . Our discussion of such modalities will be interpreted as a firm commitment to a higher-level meeting. . . ." This venerable word, having to do with form rather than substance, has been snapped up by the foreign policy bureaucracy: In medicine, it is a method of treatment, and in diplomacy, it denotes conditions under which agreements take effect as well as the trappings of negotiation.

Interlocutor. "This unsolicited comment did not utterly mystify my interlocutors. . . ." "Brezhnev, who had physical magnetism, crowded his interlocutor." This is a useful word, meaning "someone who engages in conversation or dialogue," from the Latin for "to speak between," the same root as "locution" and "loquacious." In American usage, the word calls up a vision of a master of ceremonies at a minstrel show: "Mis-tuh Interlokkiter" is the straight man, in the middle, who questions the end men. As a result, "interlocutor," in the United States, came to mean "questioner" or "interpreter." But in Kissingerese, the usage is broadened to "one who engages in discourse." This is a useful stretch of meaning, since no other single word covers the other person engaged in a colloquy.

Oral note. This oxymoron is defined by Kissinger as "a written but unsigned communication whose status is that of the spoken word and which can therefore be more easily disavowed." Example: "When Dobrynin balked at being asked to pass on a threat, I had the offending paragraph typed on a separate sheet of paper and called it an 'oral note.' Dobrynin . . . accepted it in this form. Such are the little victories."

Backchannel. "At the end of the day Rush backchanneled with justifiable pride." This is the verb form of the noun "back channel," which means "secret communication"—or, more specifically, "unknown, thank God, to those untrustworthy, leaking miscreants of the State Department."

Chutzpah. "With amazing chutzpah, Brezhnev's letter argued that the Soviet departure from Egypt was in part an implementation of the troop withdrawal proposal. . . ." This Hebrew term, which has come to us via Yiddish, means "effrontery, impudence, brass" and has been enshrined by Mr. Kissinger in diplomatic usage on matters dealing with Middle East "intransigence" (an unpronounceable word rooted in "unwilling to transact business in a negotiation").

Neuralgic. "Cuba was a neuralgic problem for Nixon." To the Soviets, "Peking was a 'neuralgic' point." Apparently this is a new vogue term in diplomacy, taken from the severe pain along a nerve, meaning "more than usually distressing" and requiring fast fast fast relief.

Up to now, we have been dealing with standard diplolingo; however, Kissingerese has also adopted certain substandard forms for informal use:

Chivy. "Opponents deliberately chivied the Administration until harassed officials . . ." "Chivy," pronounced with the *ch* as in "chin," is an ancient slang verb meaning "to chase, hound, harry, pursue" and has an interesting background: Cheviot Hills, called Chevy Chase, was the scene of the Battle of Otterburn in 1388. The losers were said to have been "chevied," or "chivied"—perhaps from the local hunting cry—and the word now means "to subject to vexations, petty maneuverings that annoy and confuse an opponent." Much of this takes place among Washington officials who live in suburban Chevy Chase, Md.

Loose change. "Brezhnev, never able to forgo the temptation to pick up some loose change, proposed a bombing halt. . . ." "The Shah . . . could have . . . striven . . . to pick up whatever loose change could be found by manipulating the rivalry of the superpowers for short-term ends." This colorful locution seems to mean "unworthy diversion," or "insignificant and temporary advantage," as in the rifling of pants pockets for a few coins when an entire wallet filled with cash could be lifted by a skilled negotiator.

Thus, *Henry Kissinger White House Years,* if that is indeed its title, or *Henry Kissinger/White House Years* (there is a line separating the name from the "time frame" on the title page, though not on the cover), provides the student of diplolingo with a feast of neologisms and a guide to current Foggy Bottom usage.

The one-starred tome even hints at new coinages in its sequel: "This was coupled with the proposal of 'proximity talks,' a procedure by which an American diplomat would shuttle between the two delegations housed in nearby hotel rooms." We all know that was the predecessor phrase for "shuttle diplomacy," which we will read about in *Henry Kissinger State Department Years,* or *Henry Kissinger After the Fall,* or *Henry Kissinger Henry Kissinger* or . . .

good advice

Some ornery orthographers have objected to the correction here of former National Security Adviser Henry Kissinger's spelling of "advisor," contending that some dictionaries find the "o" permissible as an alternate form of "adviser," and, besides, what about "supervisor"? I don't buy that: Spelling "adviser" with an "o" is as plainly a mistake as the misbegotten "relevent" and "permissable." In a generation, the repeated mistaken usage may make the mistake correct, but let the alternative form work at it for a while.

Dear Mr. Safire:

Your "On Language" feature in today's Times *identifies a "Sino-Soviet condominium" as "a tenant-owned apartment house." A "co-operative" apartment house would have been closer to the mark.*

A "co-op" features ownership of stock in a corporation having title to the real estate plus a lease of the apartment itself.

A purchaser of a condominium unit takes title to the dwelling unit itself, together with an undivided percentage interest, with all other unit owners, in the common elements of the condominium (land, stairways, halls, heating boilers, parking areas, etc.)

There is a good possibility that "condominium" has, as one of its roots, not "dominium" but "domus," since it originally referred to people living together rather than ruling together.

The most common error is something like this—"Linda Moviequeen recently purchased a condominium in Hawaii," for the fact—". . . purchased a condominium unit (or apartment) . . ."

> Paul J. Le Vine
> Counselor at Law
> Spring Valley, New York

Dear Mr. Safire,

"Opening gambits" is indeed a redundancy (not "redundency"). "Gambit" alone, however, is even more often misused to mean any opening move. Not all opening moves are gambits, though all gambits are opening moves.

> Yours truly,
> Lewis W. Beck
> Rochester, New York

knee jerk

The phrase "knee jerk" suggests a slavish following or automatic response. The charming story about the word's origin in medicine was given by Sir Ernest Gowers, author of *Plain Words* and editor of the second edition of Fowler's *Modern English Usage*. Wrote Sir Ernest in 1948:

> Some 70 years ago a promising young neurologist made a discovery that necessitated the addition of a new word to the English vocabulary. He insisted that this should be 'knee jerk,' and 'knee jerk' it has remained, in spite of the effort of 'patellar reflex' to dislodge it. He was my father; so perhaps I have inherited a prejudice in favor of home-made words.

kooks, *see* flakes and kooks

Kratz family

I once imagined a family named Kratz running a huge spaceship: the paternal Demo Kratz as commander, with his protective son, Buro, as fighter pilot, his other son, Techno, running the computers, and his snooty daughter, Aristo, lollygagging around.

Demo Kratz has other relatives—uncle Pluto provides rich breakfasts for aunt Auto—but the black sheep of the family is cousin Kakisto. This patron saint of kakistocracy was recalled by N. Jean Dorman of Madison, Wis., who drove me to an unabridged dictionary for the word meaning "government by the worst men." A useful term; should be in collegiate editions.

She also zaps me for using "insidious" ("sly," "lying in wait for," rooted in the Latin word for "ambush") when I meant "invidious" ("offensive," with the same root as "envy"). I used to have a mnemonic to help me remember the difference between "invidious" and "insidious," as well as "stalagmite" and "stalactite," but I keep forgetting how to spell "mnemonic."

language arts, *see* Experience counts

languajoke

When asked: "Is sloppiness in speech caused by ignorance or apathy?" an English teacher replied: "I don't know and I don't care."

Latin lovers

Nothing beats a good Latin riposte.

At the winter dinner of the Gridiron Club in Washington, Dudley W. Dudley—a woman whose name echoes in New Hampshire as a top Kennedy organizer—reported that Governor Jerry Brown had begun a speech in her state with a quotation in Latin. "We don't have a very large Latin-speaking constituency in New Hampshire," Dudley Dudley derided derisively.

Brown's father, former Governor Edmund (Pat) Brown—a man who knows that there is no arguing about taste—rose to speak next and remarked, ad libitum: *"De gustibus non disputandum est."*

Less is more, not fewer

"It's time you did a paragraph on 'less-fewer,'" writes slanguist Stuart Berg Flexner. "The new 'Lite' beers claim to have 'less calories' (though anyone who spells 'light' as 'lite' can't be expected to know too much about usage—I hope their beer is purer than their language). I'm sure the admen sat around debating whether they should use *fewer* because it was correct or *less* because it might sound more familiar, or relaxed, to the listeners, or even seem macho to make the mistake."

Carol Klein of New York agrees: "These beers can have less body, less foam, less taste, less color, and they can be less filling, less fattening and less expensive, but they can have only *fewer* calories." "Less" deals with quantity; "few" with number. "Much" goes with "less"; "many" goes with "fewer."

Because I enjoy thin beer, and even like simplified spelling, I was prepared to let the "lite" guys get away with it. But along came an advertisement for a car promising "less gallons" of gas, and then another for a laundry product that cost "less dollars" than the usual soap and bleach. Now comes American Airlines with a plan for checking in at either the front counter or the departure gate, hawking "one less line!"

That does it. If American—doing what it does worst—keeps undermining our grammar, Texas International will gobble them up and there'll be one less airline.

Dear Mr. Safire:

I can't resist telling you that a high government official spoke in Stamford last week of "less people per capita."

I envision the evolution of two-headed persons. . . .

Sincerely yours
Tessa Ried
Stamford, Connecticut

Dear Mr. Safire:

I read with interest your discussion of "less" and "fewer," and I agree with you that failure to mark the distinction seems barbarous. But why should that be so? In contrast, we can make do with the single word "more": "more soldiers" and "more time." Why should decrease rate the increased linguistic refinement?

Sincerely yours,
Prof. Timothy Stroup
Philosophy
John Jay College of Criminal Justice
New York, New York

Dear Mr. Safire:

A much, much better rule for less-fewer *than the one you gave in the* Times *last Sunday is that* less *is used to modify a singular noun &* fewer *a plural noun.*

This rule *always works; there are no exceptions. For example:* less *money,* fewer *books....*

Yours,
Lionel Chagrin
Brooklyn, New York

Dear Mr. Safire:

... "If American [Airlines]—doing what it does worst—keeps undermining our grammar, Texas International will gobble them up and there'll be one less airline." (Emphasis supplied.) As you correctly realized at first, American Airlines being a corporation takes singular verbs and pronouns. Unfortunately, you then shifted into the plural "them" at the conclusion of your sentence....

Sincerely,
Michael L. Richmond
Assistant Professor of Law
Nova University
Fort Lauderdale, Florida

---

literally illiterate

If you get a ladder, climb up to within reach of the top of the room and smash your fist into the ceiling, then—and only then—can you be "literally hitting the ceiling."

If, however, you explode in anger, then you are "figuratively hitting the ceiling."

"Literal" means "actual," without exaggeration, no fooling with metaphors. But for more than a century, it has also been misused to mean just the opposite; now, "literally" is reaching a critical mass, when it will become a Humpty Dumpty word, meaning whatever the speaker chooses it to mean.

"You are literally pushing money out the door with a wheelbarrow," complained former Treasury Secretary Michael Blumenthal this summer. Donald Goldsmith, of Berkeley, Calif., protests: "This is literally murdering the English language." What Mr. Blumenthal (who was figuratively pushed out of the Carter Cabinet Room door in a wheelbarrow) meant was "metaphorically," or "virtually," or "practically" (not synonyms, but all far from "literally").

You can literally drop dead on the spot, but you cannot literally jump out of your skin. Why the confusion? This is what probably happened: The word was first used for emphasis, to mean "no kidding." "I am literally broke: not a dime to my name." The penniless speaker, still well-dressed, then went on to use a metaphor, but kept the adverb as a modifier, even though it directly contradicted its own meaning: "I am literally in rags."

From that mistake came the debasement of the word. The total destruction of its meaning came when it was coupled with its opposite as a re-emphasizer: "I was literally and figuratively sweating blood."

"Literally" is not the only word that has lost touch with reality: Look at "really." That word also was meant to describe a state of reality, or literalness. Even as a substitute for "Is that so?" the word asked: "Is that true, or real?" Nowadays, one guy goes "I literally flew off the handle," and the other guy goes "Really." It's a grunt, meaning, "I'm still here." (One does not "say" anymore; one "goes," as if to say "He goes, 'Crazy!'")

Is "literally"—meaning "actually"—worth fighting for? Some of us think so. Really.

Dear Mr. Safire:

Your comments re "Illiterate Literates" brought to mind one of my favorite quotes. Several years ago a seaman writing in The National Fisherman *was describing a storm: "The waves were 10 feet high—not literally, but actually!"*

Another possible reason for the confusion about the meaning of "literally" may be that it is associated with the word "literary," which in turn suggests freedom from the restraints of exactitude, of exaggeration to produce a desired emotional response, of "poetic license."

Sincerely,
George E. Hall
Mount Holyoke College
South Hadley, Massachusetts

"Practically" for "virtually"? Oh, Mr. Safire, how could you?

What is the world coming to anyway?

First you concede on hopefully and now this. How much more of this do you think I can stand?

What is happening to you?

Don't you realize that now that Bernstein is gone we're counting on the few of you who are left to carry the banner?

Please pull yourself together and hang in. We're behind you and we need you.

> Respectfully,
> Renee Lord
> New York, New York

---

loop, *see* White House-ese

---

macho for women

Clare Boothe Luce recently predicted that a new adjective would have to be coined, on the analogy of "macho," to stand for "exaggerated female pride." She suggested "facho." But that seemed too derivative, like Adam's rib, and might lead to the noun "fachism." I wrote: "Readers of this space are urged to send in suggestions."

The first letter on this subject began "Although I am reasonably literate, I have never learned how to read a space." Thanks; I needed that. That is the kind of spaced-out reader who reads what is written in this space. Now to the process of coinage:

"Macha" was frequently suggested, as a Spanish feminine form of "macho." This was topped by "femacha," "femacho," and "feminisma"; and, to get away from Spanish, "femo." The "o" ending called forth "womo," "nowcho," "busto," "she'smo," "vergo," "msmo," "fexo," "wacho," and "bellacho." An offbeat suggestion was "eggsy."

Though most of the ideas came from feminist women (that's not redundant—men can be feminists, too), many male readers participated. A few were antifeminist—one male baseball fan grumbled that, to him, E.R.A. would always stand for Earned Run Average—but the winner, in my book, was Paul Beckerman of Boston, who wrote:

"Your call for a feminine analogue to the word 'macho' made me recall a line from a Mexican film called *La Generala*. In this film, the actress Maria Felix—tall, slender, fascinatingly beautiful—plays a woman who takes up

arms to avenge the death of her brother at the hands of a tyrannical army officer. . . . She arranges matters so that the officer in question thinks that he is seducing her. At one point in this scene the officer, rather inebriated, tells her (as best as I can recall it), '*Yo soy muy macho, pero tú eres muy hembra.*' ('I am very *macho,* but you are very *hembra.*')

"The Spanish word *macho* is simply an adjective applied to a male animal (other than human in 'polite' usage). *Hembra* is the female counterpart, and perhaps it is just the word that you seek."

So it is. Hembra, or hembrista, for the adjective, and hembrismo for the noun. Aspirate the 'h' to make it American. (That's what my linguistic head tells me, but my heart is with "eggsy.") Someone will point out that "hembra" is sometimes used to refer to female dogs, but that sense would be applied only by someone who uses "macho" to refer to male dogs, and the progress of language cannot be stopped by catering to extremists.

Now to use the new adjective and noun in contrasting sentences. When Edward Kennedy announced his candidacy for President, he used a quotation that he said was taken from Thomas Wolfe to soar into his peroration: "So, then, to all persons their chance to work, to be themselves. . . . This, seeker, is the promise of America." An alert editorialist for *The St. Petersburg* (Fla.) *Times* found the original line in *You Can't Go Home Again:* "So, then, to every man his chance . . . to work, to be himself. . . ."

That substitution of "person" for "man," seeker, is an example of hembra speechwriting.

Contrariwise, Senator Kennedy's oratory (used for examples here because it is more vivid than the prosaic prose of most other politicians) frequently makes use of the fig-leaf metaphor. The fig leaf was used in classic statuary to preserve male modesty. Since it was such an obvious and artificial device to avoid offense, the use of a fig leaf is easily seen through—a coverup that is transparent. The device, not the fig leaf itself, is transparent; however, in an unfortunate display of metaphoria, the Senator recently denounced the reduced windfall tax on oil-company revenues as "no more than a transparent fig leaf over the industry's enormous profits."

That, seeker, is an example of speechwriting that cries out for editing. Where was his *hembrismo* when he needed it?

Dear Mr. Safire:

There are several possibilities which come to mind for the female equivalent of "macho."

Should one desire to refer to such a female who also obtains of the mammillarian proportions of Dolly Parton: mamacho.

Or of the characteristic of an Irma LaDouce: cracho.

Or of the Steinhem crowd: eracho.

Or of the pulchritudinous Raquel Welch: pulacho.

Or of the sisters of Sappho: lesbacho.

In borrowing from the Spanish, the purist, of course would insist these minted adjectives should end with an "a" rather than an "o."

> *Sincerely,*
> *Bruce Stoner*
> *Oxon Hill, Maryland*

Dear Mr. Safire:

Up here in southern Vermont we have been happily using "macha" as the female version of "macho" for years, knowing full well that it is an improperly invented form, but enjoying the irony of stealing a word thought to be exclusively "male" in order to describe a trait once thought—pre-women's lib—to be the exclusive burden of males as well.

Keep up the good wordswork!

> *Yours truly,*
> *Londa Weisman*
> *North Bennington, Vermont*

Dear Mr. Safire:

After your readers have whetted their word coinage appetites on a satisfactory female equivalent of "macho," perhaps they would like to turn their attention to "horny." Webster's New Collegiate Dictionary *derives this state of sexual excitement from "horn (erect penis) + -y." Surely, no self-respecting "facho" woman would feel comfortable admitting to such male-rooted feelings!*

> *Sincerely,*
> *Linda R. W. Jones*
> *New Rochelle, New York*

Dear Mr. Safire:

I think it would have been best for you to leave out any reference whatsoever to Spanish. It is a tremendous "filet of solecism" to write "mucho macho feminists." An elementary knowledge of the most basic Spanish would have let you know that the correct expression could only be "muchas machas feminists."

I also thought that you would like to know that in Uruguay and Argentina, "facho" would be taken to mean "male fascist" by a leftist person.

I remain,

> *Yours sincerely,*
> *Emilio E. Falco*
> *Cambridge, Massachusetts*

---

masterly inactivity, *see* standing busily by

---

media/medium, *see* plural of "um"

---

meta-fore!

Senator Howard Baker called President Carter's response to the Soviet combat brigade in Cuba "inadequate" and added: "In a toe-to-toe confrontation, we blinked."

No. Toes may be used metaphorically in testing the water, or in being alert, or even in a slugfest, but toes do not blink.

The phrase that the minority leader had in mind was "eyeball-to-eyeball confrontation," which blazed across the political sky in the Cuban missile crisis of 1962. The words used by Secretary of State Dean Rusk to ABC newsman John Scali were: "Remember, when you report this, that, eyeball to eyeball, they blinked first." The phrase was fixed in the lexicon by columnists Charles Bartlett and Stewart Alsop as "We're eyeball to eyeball and the other fellow just blinked."

The image is so well known it rates parody: Columnist Joseph Kraft described an argument between Secretary of State Cyrus Vance and Israeli Foreign Minister Moshe Dayan as "eyeball to eye patch."

Where did it come from? According to General Harold Johnson, Army Chief of Staff in the mid-60's, the phrase originated in the military and is a contribution of black English. The 24th Infantry Regiment, before integration in the armed services, was all black; in November 1950 it bore the brunt of a counterattack in Korea. When General MacArthur's headquarters sent an inquiry to the 24th regiment—"Do you have contact with the enemy?"—the reply, widely reported at the time, was "We is eyeball to eyeball."

The Senator blinked his toe on that one.

Dear Mr. Safire:

As a linguist who worries about both idioms and metaphors, I would like to suggest that you used the latter term where the former was appropriate.

Most of us, I suspect, use the term idiom *to refer to those phrases whose meaning has become fixed; for example, phrases such as "kick the bucket," "burn one's bridges" and your "keep on one's toes." Indeed, these phrases were once in the realm of metaphor but through time, a meaning became conventionally associated with the phrase. Metaphors, on the other hand, arise when the speaker says one thing (which may or may not be grammatically acceptable) and means another. The speaker who says that "Cigarettes are time bombs" is speaking metaphorically, and the hearer must calculate what is intended using the context and cultural background. Idiomatic meaning is found in dictionaries; metaphorical meaning is not.*

A final comment on metaphor: When I asked my teenage son "What's a metaphor?" he quickly replied, "To graze cows in." So much for the use of native informants.

> Yours truly,
> Bruce Fraser
> Professor of Linguistics
> Boston University
> Boston, Massachusetts

---

mindful, *see* watersheds

minimal: de minimis

Hot new word is "minimal." Comes from art world, now in fashion in Fashion, voguish at Vogue. Calvin Klein advertisement: "His hallmark: simplicity . . . the fashion line that's pared down, beautifully basic. . . . He made it easy. Minimal."

"More of Less" headlines *Time* magazine re California's Governor Edmund G. Brown Jr. "Our minimum goal is to have enough delegates to play a role in drafting the Democratic platform," says candidate's manager. Subhead: "Jerry Brown: Minimalist."

Enough. Strike modifiers, articles, conjunctions. Cut item short. Modern man is minimal animal.

Dear Mr. Safire:
De minimis non curat lex.
As I'm sure you know, the above means: The law does not concern itself with trifles.
It may be of interest to you to learn that through the years law students have found that its meaning is best exemplified and remembered by the following limerick:

> *There was a young man named Rex*
> *Born with a diminutive organ of sex*
> *When charged with exposure*
> *He replied with composure*
> *"De minimis non curat lex."*

Cordially,
Simon A. Lubow
New York, New York

miscreant

Alfred E. Kahn, chairman of the Council on Wage and Price Stability, still grimly referred to as "the nation's chief inflation fighter," may not be slowing inflation but he continues to enrich the political vocabulary.

He recently threatened businessmen who do not respect the President's wage and price guidelines that he would "identify the miscreants publicly." There's a word from the pages of Finley Peter Dunne's Mr. Dooley: "miscreants," which Mr. Dooley would pronounce "miscreents."

A miscreant is a villain, but the word is especially apt since it is rooted in "disbelief"—a miscreant is an unbeliever, thus a heretic, thus a villain. Businessmen who do not obey the guidelines do not give credence to the anti-inflation program, and are well-labeled "miscreants."

Mr. Kahn, the banana republican, went on to denounce "the predations of the international oil cartel." The seldom-used "predations" means "plundering," as by a predatory bird preying on a flock of fat pigeons. The more frequently used word "depredations" also means "plundering," but seems to me to mean "robberies" in general rather than the booty that miscreants grab during their marauding predations. So goes life among the double digits.

mnemonic, *see* Kratz family

modalities, *see* Kissingerese

mogulese

In The Industry (formerly The Business, which replaced Hollywood, once called Movieland), a jargon has been developed that offers a sentence like this: "He packaged a world-class director and a bankable gross player, aimed at rolling it out to Yumpsville in 60 situations, was greenlighted after he took a meeting—but another element was a mouth-breather, and the writer phoned it in, and suddenly it was Tisha b'Av Nellie-time."

That vivid argot is "Movie Mogulese," and was analyzed for linguistic Javerts by producer Daniel Melnick, screenwriter David Z. Goodman and Warner Communications executive Edward Bleier.

First take a fix on suffixes: Mogulese requires an addition to words that quickly describe, and exaggerate, trends or conditions. *-Ville* was the preferred form of the 50's, and still exists—"Splitsville" is the state of getting divorced—and was followed by *-arama,* popularized by Cinerama and later seen on seafood restaurants named "Fisherama." The Anglicization of *-ville* brought on *City,* as in "Fat City"—a state of euphoria. The preferred suffix at the moment—*time*—harks back to early radio days, in shows directed at children before "sleepytime." Thus, a movie that loses money— once called "Disasterville," then "Bombarama," then "Flop City"—is now "Tisha b'Av Nellie-time."

(Tisha b'Av is a Jewish fast day marking the destruction of the Temple in Jerusalem, and its association with disaster is obvious, but the addition by moguls of "Nellie" is, as lexicographers say, obscure.)

Talent—not quality, but a person on the "creative side"—can be *bankable* if his name commands ready investment. Novelist Linda Palmer notes *high-Q* as a component of bankability, a play on "I.Q." but rooted in "TV-Q," a rating of actors' recognition by television viewers. *Casting* is respectable, but a calibration below: I'd guess that Barbra Streisand is bankable; Jane Fonda is casting.

A superstar like Robert Redford is a *gross player,* who gets a percentage of gross revenues—*points.* A poor actor is a *mouth-breather.*

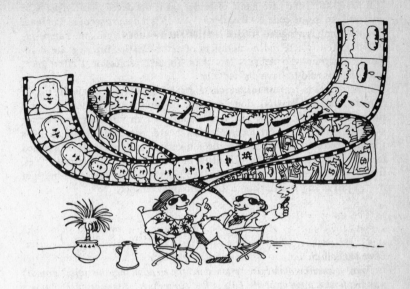

Newest category: *Crossover star,* one who can bridge the troubled waters separating special audiences, as Dolly Parton does with both country and pop singing, and as Diana Ross does with blacks and whites.

In Mogulese, these people are *elements* of a *package* that may do *good numbers* or achieve a *breakthrough,* as *Jaws* did. Producers *greenlight* or *no-go* a deal—which, if weighted with too many "points," will *never fly.* When moguls gather, they *take a meeting.* Nobody meets, has a meeting, or convenes a group of colleagues: The omnipresent verb is to "take" a meeting, as if to snatch its minutes from the jaws of time or industry sharks.

Frenetic optimism is expressed by clichés like "the crew applauded after the dailies" and "the cards were great." ("The audience-reaction cards at previews are always 'great,' " sighed one producer.) A "hot" property or idea is one that has not yet been exposed to public view, or to another producer—its definition is "not yet successful."

If a mogul wishes to protect himself against word of mouth, he *opens broad* on a thousand *screens* in 500 *situations*—which have replaced "movie houses" or "theaters." The opposite of "opening broad" is *rolling out,* as in waves, which should not be confused with *the rolling break-even,* a technique by which moguls keep adding advertising costs until point players complain. As industry spokesman Jack Valenti informs me, sometimes a movie *loses its legs* after the *first runs* and flops in the *nabes* (neighborhood situations) and the *ozoners* (drive-ins).

No deal is ever "turned down" or "rejected": The universal euphemism is

"I'll pass," from the card game of bridge, as if the decision can always be reviewed; an inside code is "Pasadena." A flop is a *bomb* except in England, where a bomb is a big hit. A *buck* is $100,000, 10 bucks a million. *Yumpsville* is Yahooland, where *macho* admirers of actor Charles Bronson are derogated. A writer who delivers less than his best professional effort on a screenplay is said to have *phoned it in*.

In jargon, as in real language, meanings change. *On spec* originally meant "on speculation," or work done in hopes of being accepted but without a prior commitment; now it has a connotation of an unnecessary effort or waste of time. When producer Melnick heard, some years ago, that his friend screenwriter Goodman had been taken to the hospital, he telephoned to ask: "Did you really have a heart attack?" The writer gasped: "Yes, they're putting me in intensive care," and the producer said: "I'll be right over. I just didn't want to come to the hospital on spec."

Dear William Safire:

Your researchers must have "phoned in" the erratum that the suffix "arama" was first foisted upon us in the '50's. A flack and show biz term its inception was a decade earlier as witness Futurama, Norman Bel Geddes great GM exhibit at the 1939–1940 N.Y. World's Fair, all too soon to be followed by Kosherama, a nearby Flushing butcher and Striperama on the marquee of Minskys and other burlesque houses. Significant history warrants meticulous research! All best wishes.

Sincerely,
Alfred Stern
New York, New York

Dear William Safire:

I think that Messrs. Melnick and Company pulled the wool over your eyes with such alleged expressions as Tisha b'Av Nellie-time. But rather than suggest that your acumen in this field is below the superior level of your political acumen, I prefer to add some colorful, and I assure you ubiquitous, expressions which you omitted.

1. *Turnaround. A turnaround occurs literally when a studio abandons a project and in so doing gives the producer a fixed period of time (usually one year) to find another buyer for it. The expression is, "Columbia has just put project X in turnaround." One studio executive, when asked of his marital status, replied, "I put my wife in turnaround."*

2. *Pay or play. Pay or play literally means that a studio has an obligation to pay someone for his services (usually a director or star) whether or not the movie is actually made. Thus, "Joe is pay or play on project X." This, too, has its metaphoric uses.*

3. *Masturbatory metaphors. Many people in Hollywood liberally sprinkle their speech with such expressions as, "The studio is jerking me off," "It's down to the short strokes," and so forth.*

4. *Turn-down. This is synonymous with pass, Pasadena, and even El Paso, as in, "We've gotten a turn-down at Paramount, now let's go to Fox." This is a noun, rarely a verb.*

5. *Up front/back end. These terms are used to refer to when monies are paid in a deal, as in, "The up front terms are fine, but we need more points at the back end."*

6. Pari passu. *People say this when they mean* pro rata.

7. *Touch base with. You never call a client, for example, you touch base with him. I hate this expression. And after having called several people about setting up a deal, you say, "I've touched all the bases." I hate this expression, too.*

I hope you, in turn, are entertained by these supplements. All are guaranteed genuine.

> Sincerely yours,
> Robert Bookman
> Los Angeles, California

Molasses Delivery Systems

Systems analysis led me to "Anytime Delivery Systems" and "Archer Courier Systems" of New York, and "Choice Courier Systems" of Washington, D.C. We are now dealing with the terminology of speedy delivery.

In New York, private delivery services usually call themselves "messengers," though some have changed to the more elite-sounding "courier," such as "Big Apple Courier." In Washington, probably because of the local tradition of "diplomatic courier" (with attaché case chained to his wrist), the word "messenger" is less often used—the preference is for "couriers" and "delivery systems," with an occasional "express."

In Washington, the names of these services reflect a bureaucratic stodginess: "All State Air Courier," "Dependable Courier," "Dulles Delivery," "National Courier."

In New York City, however, the accent is on speed: "ABC Comet Messenger" streaks alongside "Dash Messenger," and "Charger Messenger" is best for San Juan Hill; "Flash Messenger" vies with "Instant Courier," "Dash Messenger," and "Rocket Messenger Service." Is "Spurt Messenger" faster than "Bullet Courier Systems" or "On the Double Messenger"? What special edge do "Orbit Messenger," "Supersonic Messenger," and "ESP Messenger Service" provide?

If I were starting a private delivery service and wanted to stand out from the pack, I would choose something like "Lethargic Couriers," or "What's the Big Rush? Delivery Systems," or "Dawdling Messenger." Only one agency now in business approaches that idea: the "En Route Messenger Service." ("Where the hell is your man? I called an hour ago!" "He's en route.")

Dear Mr. Safire:

We appreciate the mention of our company.

You certainly are right about Washington, D.C. They don't like the word "messenger" there at all. When adapting the New York literature for Washington, we kept the word "messenger" and they were not happy with it. We'll have to edit it out for the next printing.

We'd be most gratified if you'd use us in New York or Washington or elsewhere in the country or, for that matter, around the world.

We're very fast. No kidding!

> *Sincerely,*
> *Stanley Katz*
> *President*
> *Archer Courier Systems Inc.*
> *New York, New York*

---

mole, *see* spookspeak

Mondegreens: "I led the pigeons to the flag"

The most saluted man in America is Richard Stans. Legions of schoolchildren place their hands over their hearts to pledge allegiance to the flag, "and to the republic for Richard Stans."

With all due patriotic fervor, the same kids salute "one nation, under guard." Some begin with "I pledge a legion to the flag," others with "I led the pigeons to the flag."

This is not a new phenomenon. When they come to "one nation, indivisible," this generation is as likely to say "One naked individual" as a previous generation was to murmur "One nation in a dirigible," or "One nation and a vegetable."

"The Stars Bangled Banger" is a great source for these creative mishearings: "the Donzerly light," "oh, the ramrods we washed," "grapefruit through the night" that our flag was still there.

Then there is the good Mrs. Shirley Murphy of the 23rd Psalm: "Shirley, good Mrs. Murphy, shall follow me all the days of my life." (Surely, goodness and mercy would not lead us into Penn Station.)

We all hear the same sounds. But until we are directed by the written word to the intended meaning, we may give free rein to our imagination to invent our own meanings. ("Free rein" has to do with letting horses run; some people are changing the metaphor to government, spelling it "free reign.") Children make sounds fit the sense in their own heads. In "God

Bless America," the misheard line "Through the night with a light from a bulb" makes more practical sense than "a light from above." Writes David Thomas of Maine: "In Sunday school I used to sing, 'I will follow Henry Joyce,' part of a hymn. Who Henry Joyce was didn't concern me—I was following him at the top of my lungs. When I learned to read, I found the words were 'I will follow and rejoice.'"

Sometimes that awakening never takes place. "To all intents and purposes," a nice old phrase, is sometimes spoken as—and written as—"for all intensive purposes." With the onset of adulthood, correction should not be taken for granted—or "taken for granite." In the song "Lucy in the Sky With Diamonds" (its title subliminally plugging LSD), the phrase "the girl with kaleidoscope eyes" came across to one grandmother as "the girl with colitis goes by."

What is this mistaken hearing called? In a query in this space recently, I remembered that I had called bandleader Guy Lombardo "Guylum Bardo," and asked for other examples of "false homonyms." That was a slight misnomer; homonyms are words pronounced the same, but with different meanings. Along with the other examples sent in—crooner Victor Moan, actress Sophie Aloran, musician "Big Spider" Beck, pro-football back Frank O'Harris, novelist Gorvey Doll—came instruction from linguists too mentionable to numerate. In each category, childlike translation can lead to semantic change.

(1) The Guylum Bardo syndrome—the simple misdivision of words—is called *metanalysis*. Many of the words we use correctly today are mistaken divisions of the past: A "napron" in Middle English became an "apron"—the "n" slid over to the left; an "ekename" of six centuries ago became a "nickname"—the "n" slid to the right.

In a future century, some of today's metanalyses (for "wrong cuttings") may become accepted English. An exorbitant charge is called "a nominal egg," perhaps committed by a "next-store neighbor"; some runners, poised at the starting line, hear "On your market—set—go!" Millions of children consider the letter of the alphabet between "k" and "p" to be "ellemeno." Meteorologists on television who speak of "a patchy fog" do not realize that many creative viewers take that to be "Apache fog," which comes in on little cat feet to scalp the unsettled settler. Affiants seeking official witness go to a land called "Notar Republic," and Danny Boy, hero of "The Londonderry Air," casts a backward glance at what is often thought of as "The London Derrière." Future historians may wonder why chicken-hearted journalists coveted "the Pullet Surprise."

(2) The "José, can you see?" syndrome—the transmutation of words when they pass through different cultures or languages—is known to linguists as the *Law of Hobson-Jobson*. British soldiers in India heard the Mohammedan cry *"Ya-Hasan, ya-Husain!"* and called it "hobson-jobson." Noel Perrin at Dartmouth College reports that American soldiers in Japan transmuted a popular Japanese song, *"Shi-i-na-na Yaru,"* into "She Ain't Got No Yo-

Yo." Similarly, *"O Tannenbaum"* is sometimes rendered "Oh, atom bomb."

(3) Semantic change can come from *malapropisms,* named after Mrs. Malaprop, a character in *The Rivals,* a 1775 play by Richard Sheridan. More people than you suspect read and pronounce "misled" as "mizzled," and the verb "to misle" will one day challenge "to mislead." Others hum what they call "the bronze lullaby," though it must spin Brahms in his grave. One fascinating malapropism is "to hold in escarole," which combines the escrow function with the slang metaphor of money as lettuce.

(4) *Folk etymology* is the term for the creation of new words by mistake or misunderstanding or mispronunciation. "Tawdry," for example, came from Saint Audrey's, a place where cheap merchandise was sold. In today's language, "harebrained" is often giddily and irresponsibly misspelled "hairbrained," perhaps on the notion that the hair is near the brain.

The slurred "and" is one of the prolific changers of phrases. When "hard and fast" is spoken quickly, it becomes "hard 'n' fast," which sometimes gets transformed to "harden-fast rules." In the same way, the old "whole kit 'n' caboodle" is occasionally written as "kitten caboodle," a good name for a satchel in which to carry a cat. ("Up and atom!" is not a member of this group; it belongs with those Christmas carolers singing "Oh, atom bomb.")

Lest you think that such mistakes can never permanently implant themselves in the language, consider "spit 'n' image." One longtime meaning of "spit" is "perfect likeness"—a child can be the very spit of his father. But some writers have mistaken the first two words in the phrase to mean "spitting," or ejection from the mouth, and prissily added the mistaken "g" to the sound of "spitt'n'." Novelist Paul Theroux entitled a chapter of *Picture Palace* "A Spitting Image." From such a respected writer, one expectorates more.

What all-inclusive term can we use to encompass the changes that our brains make in the intended meaning of what we hear? Linguists suggest "homophone," "unwitting paronomasia," and "agnominatio," but those terms sound like fancified dirty words to me.

I prefer "mondegreen." This is a word coined in a 1954 *Harper's* magazine article, "The Death of Lady Mondegreen" by Sylvia Wright, which reported on the doings of "Gladly, the cross-eyed bear" (the way many children hear "Gladly the Cross I'd bear"), and other sound-alikes. Miss Wright recalled a Scottish ballad, "The Bonny Earl of Murray" from Thomas Percy's *Reliques of Ancient English Poetry,* which sounded to her like this:

> Ye Highlands and ye Lowlands,
> Oh, where hae ye been?
> They hae slain the Earl Amurray,
> And Lady Mondegreen.

She envisioned the bonny Earl holding the beautiful Lady Mondegreen's hand, both bleeding profusely, but faithful unto death. "By now," Miss

Wright wrote, "several of you more alert readers are jumping up and down in your impatience to interrupt and point out that, according to the poem, after they killed the Earl of Murray, they *laid him on the green*. I know about this, but I won't give in to it. Leaving him to die all alone without even anyone to hold his hand—I won't have it."

Thanks to responsive readers, I have a column on sound defects and a whole closetful of mondegreens. But a nuff is a nuff.

Dear Mr. Safire,

Not only napron, but also norange—Sanskirt nāranza, Spanish naranja. "Orange" was aided by the House of Orange (Oranien or Oranje), the royal house of Holland, also William III of England (William of Orange).

> Arthur J. Morgan
> New York, New York

Dear Mr. Safire:

My favorite example of the false homonym concerns the grade-school theatrical effort at enacting portions of MacBeth. During the witches scene, the aspiring young harpies were heard to say "Double, double, toilet trouble."

I am writing, however, to point out a minor inaccuracy in the column. Noel Perrin was a much-respected professor of mine at Dartmouth, but I fear he gave you some slightly incorrect information. The popular Japanese song he refers to is not "Shi-i-na-na yaru," which would translate roughly as "four-seven does it" to the extent that it makes any sense at all, but "Shina no Yoru," meaning "China Nights."

When sung, the first syllable "shi" is read as two because it has two notes, in the same sense that the "O" in "O, say can you see" is sung as two syllables. "Shina" is a Japanization of the English word for China which was used during the 1930's and 1940's. "No" is the possessive particle, and "Yoru" means "night" or "Evening." The song is a melancholy love ballad dating back to the early days of World War II. A young soldier in his garrison reminisces about a glorious evening's dalliance with a bar hostess he met while on leave in Hong Kong. It is sort of a Japanese version of "I Left My Heart in San Francisco."

> *Sincerely,*
> *Ernest J. Notar*
> *(Yes, this is my real name.*
> *No, I am not from the Notar Republic.)*
> *San Francisco, California*

Dear Mr. Safire,

Regarding your recent query about false homonyms. . . .

A few years ago, I was working as an ersatz nurse in a rather small city in

Mexico. One of the doctors, a Haitian who spoke several languages with a varying degree of fluency, came into the clinic one morning looking perplexed. Seems he had encountered some old American friends in a café. What, he wanted to know, was the meaning of this English expression, "having sex." I explained, rather abashed, that it referred to sexual intercourse, making love. "And that's all?" he asked, obviously bewildered. "Then why do you say that to people when you're surprised to see them?" Now I was confused. "You know," he reminded me, "you say, 'oh, for having sex, it's good to see you again.'"

And I, for heaven's sake, had had it wrong for years. . . .

> *Best regards,*
> *Deborah Miller*
> *Minneapolis, Minnesota*

Dear Mr. Safire:

There never was any such person called "The Earl of Murray." It's a Scots ballad called "The bonnie Earl of Morey," *pronounced Murray. Ye ken am in the recht aboot that, freen, since I have the recording by Richard Dyer-Bennet afore m' eyes.*

It's a problem you anglo-saxons have with us Celts, which, of course, is pronounced Kelts, by Celts, and not Seltz. Just as the port at Dublin Bay is Dun Laoghaire, pronounced Dun Leery. Just as the Prime Minister of Ireland is the Taoiseach, pronounced Tee-Shuck, see? In Dublin, people call him, "Air Tee-Shuck." And the people of Ireland are not represented by elected officials, they are "REE-presented," which is a damn site more accurate than we poor fools who are "REPresented, especially when the accent is on "resented." . . .

> *Best,*
> *Edward Langley*
> *Flushing, New York*

Mondegreens II

The human ear hears words in its own way, not necessarily the way the human voice intends. This results in "mondegreens," inspired by "Lady Mondegreen," a phrase of ancient poetry that was originally "laid him on the green."

Sometimes sound-alikes are easily spotted as errors. In "Winners & Sinners," an occasional roundup of sparklers and duds put out from the news desk of *The New York Times,* a few were recently identified: "Joan Blondell was eulogized yesterday as a 'real trooper'. . . ." The correction was *trouper,* a French variant that puts a troop into showbiz. "The fact that there was no model home to look at did not phase Charles and Martha Papa." The correction was *faze,* a variant of "feeze." Finally: "I honestly don't think that Joan Kennedy has to be put through the ringer" was corrected to *wringer,* because the "wring" has an etymology meaning "bend" and is also the root of "worm." (Without a "W," "ringer" in slang use is a horse clandestinely substituted for another in a race; a second use might be by a person who says

"Why don't you get your husband to throw his hat in the ring, Mrs. Kennedy?")

When far from an office, I dictate my copy over the telephone to a machine in the recording room of *The Times;* a human transcriber of uncanny accuracy then takes my shouted transmission from Nanjing or wherever and types it into the computer that sets type. Mondegreens can be expected, but occasionally human error is creative enough to produce neologisms.

While rapping President Carter's rhetorical activism in the face of his "demonstrated pacifism," I was stunned to see "pacifism" appear as "passive-ism." Since that word better expressed my thought, and appeared to be a brilliant play on "pacifism," I said nothing and continued to use the mondegreen as my own invention.

Months later, I yelled "foolhardily" into a bad connection, and next day read the word "foolheartedly" in my column. Before I could grumble, a colleague who has never been one of my fans came by to say he admired the portmanteau coinage—"the way you combined 'foolhardy' with 'wholeheartedly.' " Right; not for me to foolheartedly complain.

---

munching out, *see* gorilla

Names: So long, Mary

In the 20's, the most popular boys' names were: Robert, John, William, James, Charles, Richard, George, Donald, Joseph, Edward. By the early 50's, the preferences had changed, but not radically: John, Robert, James, Michael, David, Steven, William, Richard, Thomas, Mark. But in the mid-70's, it was goombye Charlie to many of the old familiars, as the most frequently reported names in birth announcements became Michael, Jason, Matthew, Brian, Christopher, David, John, James, Jeffrey, Daniel. (Richard, for a reason too painful to explain, has plummeted to 25th on the list.)

"Jason is probably No. 1 today," says Dr. Kelise Harder of the American Name Society, the nominal headquarters at the State University College at Potsdam, N.Y., "perhaps influenced by the legend of Jason and the golden fleece, which appears now in many children's books." Dr. Harder notices a certain crispness in the names that are in fashion at the moment: "New names for boys that have been appearing in large numbers are Todd, Duane, Scott and Brad—one-syllable names with a snappy sound." Toughness is the feeling—linebackers' names.

Girls' names a half century ago were Mary, Barbara, Dorothy, Betty, Ruth, Margaret, Helen, Elizabeth and Jean. Mary held her own through 1950, reports Leslie Alan Dunkling in *First Names First,* but by 1975 had fallen from grace. (Grace, along with Phyllis, had fallen down the list at about the time Karen and Linda got hot.) The mid-70's baby girl was most often named Jennifer or Amy, with the biblical Sarah a surprise entry, followed by Michelle, Kimberly, Heather, Rebecca, Catherine, Kelly, and Elizabeth.

Curiously, at a time when many women resent the idea of Adam's ribbing, girls' names of the 80's are often derived from boys' names. "Danielle and Stacy are very high on the birth announcements these days," reports Dr. Harder. The top name among gurgling female infants today? "Michelle."

Neither is correct

Potato, Potahto,
Tomato, Tomahto,
*Let's call the whole thing off!**

That 1937 Ira Gershwin lyric played on the notion that differences in pronunciation between lovers could lead to a demand for a dissolution of the relationship. If that song were among the "Top 40" today, its trickiest line would be

Eether, eyether,
Neether, nyther,
*Let's call the whole thing off!**

According to I. Willis Russell, dean of American word-watchers, the "ee" pronunciation—preferred by Americans—is now being challenged in the United States by the "eye" pronunciation, preferred in Great Britain. He cites the "eye-ther" use by ABC anchorman Max Robinson and on the soap opera *As the World Turns.*

Which is correct? Both, of course; the question about pronunciation is better posed as "Which is preferred?" The answer: "ee-ther," with "eye-ther" coming up fast; in this case, the "preferred" form may be changing.

"Covert" is marked in the dictionaries with the preferred pronunciation rhyming with "lover" and "cover" without a "t." But the great majority of people who inveigh against the C.I.A.'s covert operations say "koh-vert," rhyming with the opposite, "overt." That means "koh" is preferred over "kuh," and the dictionaries are still zigging while the population has zagged.

And try "schism." The preferred pronunciation is "sizzem"; the mispronunciation, which has crept up by usage into an alternate pronunciation, is "skizzem." A few months ago, a reporter for *The Atlanta Constitution* asked the President in a televised press conference: "Do you sense . . . a widening schism in the Democratic Party between yourself and Senator Kennedy?" President Carter picked up the reporter's pronunciation—with a "k"—and replied: "I don't consider there is a schism, a growing schism, in the Democratic Party at all." (This Kennedy-Carter nonschism, pronounced with a "k," has developed into a chasm, also pronounced with a "k.")

Does the foregoing suggest that languaslobs, in great number and full cry, can turn any garbled pronunciation into the "correct" way to say a word?

No (pronounced "gneaux"). Some mispronunciations will never (well, not for a generation at least) become right by sustained error. "Zoology" is "zoe-ology," and will not become "zoo-ology." A zoological garden was jocularly called a "zoo" and the shortening stuck. Similarly, "nuclear" will not become "nuke-u-lar" no matter how Walter Mondale mispronounces it.

The most heinous (pronounced "hay-nes," rooted in "hatred"; "hi-ness" is flat wrong) mispronunciation sweeping the country today is "nego-see-ation." At Foggy Bottom, all you can hear (after the unpronounceable "intransigent") is the mispronounced "negotiation," which has been picked up and disseminated by State Department correspondents. The only correct way to say the word is "nego-she-ation"—"she," not "see." Adherence to "she" would be appreciated.

As for "acumen"—a-KEW-men or ACK-umen—the first-mentioned pronunciation is preferred by lexicographers, the second is preferred by most people. My choice: Either. (How did you say that?)

Dear Mr. Safire:
I recall from my childhood the tale of the Irishman to whom the eether-eyether dispute was referred. He declared, "Ayther will do."
Sincerely yours,
Laura H. Moseley
Pompano Beach, Florida

Aha, Safire. So you recently exposed your heel of Achilles (ah-kill-ees, not ah-shill-ese).

At your leisure (l-eye-sure, of course) you and perhaps eight (eye-t) of your staff might have taken the trouble to trace to its source the mispronunciation of either—called eye-ther by pretentious prigs who indulge in such affectations.

Queen Victoria married Prince Albert. He was from Germany. In the language of that country, "ei" is pronounced "eye" (as in eius). Members of the Court, apparently as a fawning gesture, adopted this and other mispronunciations. This mispronunciation continues to this day—over there but not over here except among those previously identified.

Another probably apocryphal example of Germanified pretentions is that oldie about the American who used the word schedule (skedule) in the presence of a Britisher who asked "Where did you learn to say 'skedule' for the word 'shedule'?" The American replied, "In shool!"

So let us continue with our own language. Let us say "ee-ther" and "nee-ther" and let the pretentious prigs expose their own ignorance.
Edward M. Perrin
Sunnyside, New York

Dear William Safire,
One quibble and one I hope will amuse you:
1. In regard to "You say potato, I say potahto" there is a joke that when this unusual song was sung in English theater auditions, nobody got it because the singers invariably sang it:

"You say potahto and I say potahto
You say tomahto and I say tomahto . . ."

But when I was at the University of Texas, we had our own linguistic joke that went like this:

"You say potato and I say pertayter,
You say tomato and I say termayter!"

2. I'm wondering about "schism." Isn't it really pronounced accurately SKISSEM? After all you don't say schizophrenic without the K. . . . The Greek is "schizein" or "schisma."

I didn't really understand whether you preferred the "preferred pronunciation" or the "alternate."

I guess your life is now mostly summed up in the old joke EXPLAIN YOURSELF!

> Regards,
> Liz Smith
> Daily News
> New York, New York

Dear Mr. Safire:
  Is it Sayfire or Saphire?

> Cordially yours,
> John P. Rugh
> Executive Director
> St. Luke's Hospital
> Newburgh, New York

Sapphire.—W.S.

Dear Mr. Safire,
  Regarding your article last week about words and their pronunciations, I think that perhaps the most mispronounced words in the English Language are:

flaccid	secretive	inexplicable	grievous
dour	precedence	lamentable	inherent
grimaced	genealogy	irreparable	acumen
conversant	demise	domicile	consummate
mineralogy	vagary	impious	
culinary	incognito	err	

However, as Clarence Darrow said, ". . . Even if you do learn to speak correct English, whom are you going to speak it to?"

> Very truly yours,
> Marc A. Feigen
> Bronx, New York

Dear Mr. Safire:
  I was happy to see you concern yourself with pronunciations in your column. But have you thought of the sounds some Americans, even professionals, can no longer make?

  Channel 4 News brings us a young lady from California talking about the DC-Tin—sounds pretty flimsy, doesn't it?—and its equine injun mounts. Evidently Southern California has lost the short E so completely that lack of it is no longer an impediment to a broadcasting career. The sports broadcasters were the camel's nose in this case; Charlie Jones and Frank Gifford have been getting by without the short E for years.

Many New Yorkers, unable to say "million" or "Williams," make do with "Meehan" and "Weeyums." And does that disability preclude a broadcasting career? Not at all. Listen to Marv Albert (Alpert?)—sports again, but there are others—when the Knicks play the Sonics.

Most Americans have lost their broad A. They think they don't need it. But then when a diphthong or the long I requires it they too are lost. Nothing to worry about, though. No professional need to be concerned that his "1000 lines" comes out "thayosand loins." They are like the witness in the Irish court case. "Now, on your oath," the incredulous judge inquired, "is the testimony you are giving the truth?" "On my oath, your Worship," the witness replied, "it's very close to it."

We have a whole young generation advertising and buying shampoos and deodorants because they are gennle (ginnle, of course, in Southern California) or wearing one-hunnert-percent cotton shirts that require no ironing.

Sometimes the disability is psychological, since the faulty pronunciation includes the correct one: any actor who can say "teeyewthpaste" can say "toothpaste" if he puts his back into it. Perhaps we are determined to go out with a whimpering beeyewm. It's so refined.

> *Sincerely,*
> *William F. O'Connor*
> *New York, New York*

---

no comment, *see* inappropriate

---

no-name nomenclature

I'm thinking of getting an XF-70, but the 300-TD is tempting; wish I could afford an SX-1280.

A "nomenclator," in ancient Rome, was the slave who called out the names of arriving guests; today, it is the person who dreams up the scientific-sounding labels for automobiles, stereo sets, cameras, and airplanes.

Time was, Americans liked to humanize technology, calling a flying machine the "Enola Gay," and a racy auto the "Bearcat." Today, the trend is in the opposite direction; a combination of numbers and letters, anti-acronymic and often requiring prodigious feats of memory, is the fashion in nomenclature.

One reason is the need to create internationalese, a lingua franca that will sell Japanese cameras in New York and American aircraft in Yemen. A stronger reason is that numbers and letters in often meaningless sequence have gained a pseudotechnical cachet of great delight to aficionados of technology who like to rave about the intricacies of their newest ski equipment to the bewilderment of fireside-loving snow bunnies.

Sometimes the lettering-numbering has a rationale. In Mercedes autos, the letter in the "280 E" stands for *"einspritz,"* or "fuel-injection," gasoline engine; the number relates to the engine's displacement, the measurement in cubic centimeters of the space within the cylinders. The 450 SEL is the *"super einspritz lang,"* with a long wheel base, and costs a gebundle. More often, the nomenclature is meaningless. At U.S. Pioneer Electronic Corporation, here's how the SX-1980 receiver breaks down: The "S" comes from "stereo amplifier," the "X" from the old TX tuner, but the 1980 has no relation to the year.

Cameras may or may not be coded to anything in reality. Kodak's X15-F was born, it is claimed, with the "X" lifted from the mark on top of the self-firing "magicube"; the number "15" from the product's place in the sales line; and the "F" from the "flip-flash" that replaced the magicube, which lost its magic but left its "X." At Polaroid, the SX-70 has no such real or imagined pedigree: the corporation's spokesman claims that "SX-70" was the drawer that contained the plans for instant photography. Funny name for a drawer.

The glamorization of equipment through letter-numeral designations is rooted, I think, in an attempt to emulate the excitement of experimental aviation. In the Air Force, the letter prefix has a meaning—"FB" is "fighter-bomber," "SR" is "search and reconnaissance," "H" is "helicopter," "C" is "cargo"—and the number is the design number. When the numbers get too big, as in the F-111, the Air Force goes back to square one:

That's why, with B-52's getting old in the air, we're arguing about developing the B-1.

When a design is in an experimental stage, aviation designers add the letter "X" to the front. That's why so many cameras and sports cars and stereo sets have an X to mark their spots: The X contains a sense of adventure, of test pilots bailing out heroically as wings fall off some avant-garde design. (There's no telling what they had in the SX-70 drawer.)

The next logical step in nomenclature—naming people with symbols—has already been hinted at in the movie *Star Wars,* with R2D2 the name of the anthropomorphic little robot. We will soon have a human star, perhaps an electric guitarist, with a name like RP-78. The time is ripening for a sultry love object named SX-342434—maybe the woman who stars in the movie *10.*

Okay, I've decided: I'll get a 300-XP. The only thing I don't know is whether I'll drive it, fly it, shoot it, or make love to it.

Dear Mr. Safire,

I thought you might like to know (in view of your explanation of the etymology of the "SX-70" camera) that the robot R2D2 in Star Wars obtained its name from a box containing edited film and soundtrack to American Graffiti *that was sitting in front of George Lucas as he was writing a draft of the sci-fi film (Reel 2, Dialogue 2).*

> *Very truly yours,*
> *Robert Kugel*
> *New York, New York*

---

nonce words

For those with a taste for the freshest in clichés—who take their bromides with Perrier and lime, and feel the need to make sense out of nonce words—here is a guide to those currently "in" phrases that make up our transient-talk.

Clearly (a term that has replaced *obviously,* which long ago replaced *manifestly*) anyone who has not been *tracking* (a term that has replaced *monitoring,* which long ago replaced *following*) fashionable lingo is in *big trouble.*

Basically (which has replaced *I mean, uh,* and is akin to the British throat-clearing *actually*), the great slang spawning grounds of the past—the

music and drug-culture worlds—have failed us in the last year, popularizing merely *punk* (a stylish *kitsch*) and *angel dust* (a toxic hallucinogen first used to sedate primates). Instead, the new foundations of argot are the media, kids' talk, diplomacy, and sports.

From the media comes *biggie*—as in "ad biggie" or "Hollywood biggie"—which has taken over for American Indian expressions like *sachem* or *himuckeymuck* (from the Algonquin "has plenty food"), or last year's fading superstar. "Biggies" make *big bucks,* sometimes *megabucks,* for turning on the *hype* that sells books that used to be called *page-turners* but are now referred to as books *with legs,* presumably because they seem to walk off the shelves.

The advertising branch of the media has dispensed with designations like "plain" or "regular" for *natural;* though "plain" may be a put-down, "natural" has unspoiled environmental overtones. In gasoline, "regular" has changed from meaning "without tetraethyl lead" to its opposite—"with lead"—while "premium" has changed from its former "with lead" to "unleaded, high octane."

Advertising's "lead-free" phrase has led to a new licentiousness in *-free* usages. The absence of what had formerly been desirable is now proudly advertised: not only lead-free gas, but salt-free diets and sugar-free soft drinks. Soviet propaganda biggies could capitalize on dissent by asserting their system to be "freedom-free."

Kids' talk, spread by television, has not been delinquent in coinages. *Cool,* that product of the 40's, continues unabated, but *dynamite* as an adjective has fizzled, as have *beautiful* and *terrific;* the new word for excellence is, unbelievably, *excellent.*

The summarized continuation, or indication of a continued series, has long been a staple of kids' talk: *Etcetera-etcetera* was followed by *blah-blah-blah,* and more recently by *and all that stuff* or *and like that;* the current locution *is y'know what I'm saying.* An old slang term, *narc,* has been revived for *tattletale,* and *suave* kids enter the room with *"What's the rave?"*

For an explanation of the rampant use of the term *turkey,* for the old *drip* or *jerk,* let us turn to David Guralnik, editor of Webster's New World Dictionary: " 'Turkey' is obviously a pejorative that is much in use, but its current provenance is uncertain. In earlier slang, it meant 'a coward.' It has also been used in the illicit drug trade for a fake capsule containing only sugar or chalk. And, of course, there's the theatrical use for a flop. Whether the current use retains some of these connotations or is a total reinvention based on the accepted stupidity of the bird is hard to say. Seems to me, I first heard it as a piece of black street slang."

Diplomacy, which not long ago brought up *step-by-step* and the unpronounceable *intransigent,* has been unusually productive of clichés lately: *Constraint* was used by President Carter six times in a single press conference, and interest in the Cuban African corps has revived *quagmire, confrontation, mercenary,* and the big favorite, *adventurism.* In terrorism, shooting at victims' legs has been termed *kneecapping.* Not-so-good neighbors have become *front-line states,* and *rejectionist* is finding acceptability.

Other regions of government have had a luckluster year, after the heyday of Watergate coinages. *Koreagate* was derivative; *clout* has been replaced by *juice,* and *The System* is now *the process.* With the demise of Vietnamization, the *-ize* have had it, excepting only *trivialize,* of which much is being made.

An appendage of government, the Washington press corps, has popularized *burned,* to mean scooped or seriously embarrassed, probably from "once burned, twice shy"; in that *community's* subdivision of television, the most feared pejoration, *controversial,* has been replaced by *abrasive.*

Sports metaphors have not been letting down the side, especially in providing coinages. *Welcome to the N.F.L.* is a phrase used to point to unexpectedly rough treatment; a *full-court press* is a basketball term now taken to mean all-out effort. The skiing term *hang a left* is used generally to mean to take a left turn; jogging has contributed terms like *ball of the foot* and *footstrike* which have not yet outstripped their special meanings.

The layered understatements of fashion lingo have kept changing with the fashions: *Blouson* is the word this year, a French word meaning "sport or military clothing that stops at the hips." *Frye-boot chic* was swept aside as *big-top* looks became *slimdown* looks, and pants lost its plural: The *trouser pant* seems redundant, but is used to mark a contrast with the tapered or bloused pant. Or so say the formerly *beautiful people,* once the *jet set,* now called the *glitterati,* which appears to be a combination of literati, or illuminati, with a glittering generality.

A surprise source of vogue words is the academic community. The "in" discipline is *bioethics.* The new title is *Distinguished Professor* of whatever, thereby imputing a lack of distinction to all other professors. Much thinking is described as *seminal,* and all wisdom—once "received"—is now *perceived.* Among reviewers, the favored adjectives of the past—*trenchant* and *ironic* for books, *taut, pert,* and *luminous* for theatrical productions—have been overtaken by *sentimental,* which is modified either by "sloppily" or by "unabashedly," depending on the sentiments of the writer.

This was not a big year for euphemisms. Political scientists unduly influenced by macroeconomics started calling voters *microdecisionmakers.* "Basement" became a word to be shunned: Macy's offered its bargains in a new *cellar,* giving it a winey rather than a cheap tone, and hotels started calling their subbasement and other dungeon space *lower levels.*

Life-styles (a term coined in 1929 by psychologist Alfred Adler to be snapped up two generations later by journalists) are a petri dish for neologisms. Anne Soukhanov, associate editor of Merriam-Webster (dictionary-makers unsurpassed in citation-gathering), points to the *-mania* construction: *Discomania* in nightclubbing and *condomania* in housing. *Skateparks* accommodate the life-style of skateboarders, and the *CB'ers* have a language that's *10-4* with them. The *-happy* suffix, which originated in "slap-happy" and was popularized by "trigger-happy," has been replaced by the *-aholic* suffix, from "alcoholic," now used in *workaholic, chocoholic,* and *bookaholic.*

The derivation of some vogue phrases is a mystery: Why does *out of pocket,* which used to mean "not yet reimbursed," now mean "out of touch"? What visual need caused the unforgettable "whatsisname" to become *whatsisface?* Why, at death's door, have we replaced "kick the bucket" with *buy the farm?* And the most expert gamblers are at a loss to explain the metaphoric origin of *bargaining chip.*

Other vogue-word etymologies can be traced. Lexicographers have been certain that *glitch,* the relatively new word for *snafu,* is rooted in the German-Yiddish *glitschen* (to slip), and was probably first used by NASA's German space scientists to mean "electronic error" or to shrug at a gremlin in the rocket works.

Word-watchers, like bird-watchers, must get their vigilant act together and come on like *Gangbusters:* Somebody has to figure out why drinkers who used to order "soda on the side" now say *soda back,* and why whisky "straight" has to be ordered *straight up* rather than *neat.*

Clearly, the biggies of the Word Mafia—with their abrasive lust for megabucks—have been burned by the speedy trivialization of the language by the glitterati. Only by tracking our bromides can wordaholics impose any kind of constraints and make our excellent lingo vogue-word free. Y'know what I'm saying.

---

no outlet, *see* prettifiers

Nother's Day

"That's a whole nother ball game."

The "whole nother" construction currently in vogue has caused head-scratching among readers and scholars: Whence comes this phrase? ("Whence" means "from where"; it is a redundancy to write "from whence," as I did recently; might as well make a dent in the shame-on-you file.)

This rampant usage just might be the rarest of the rare: a printable American infix. Look up "infix" in any big dictionary: It is a letter or syllable inserted, or implanted, inside a word. The examples usually given are in Latin or Sanskrit; English words often have additions at beginning or end (prefixes and suffixes) but are otherwise impregnable to infixes.

Only slang can split the atom of the English word. The Britishism "absobloodylutely" is a mild example; in the United States, a participle form of a vulgarism is occasionally inserted for emphasis, as with "infuckincredible."

According to Richard Lederer, chairman of the English Department of St. Paul's School in Concord, N.H., "a whole nother" can be explained as an infix: "Some languages, such as Filipino," he writes, "are quite rich in infixes, but, in English, infixes appear to occur primarily in a few idiomatic expressions involving taboo words. . . . It seems to me that 'a whole nother ball game' qualifies as a bona fide and printable example of the rare infix construction."

An infix must not be confused with a "quick fix," the derogation by politicians of a simplistic remedy, rooted in drug lingo; that, as people used to say colorlessly, is an entirely different situation.

Dear Mr. Safire:

Richard Lederer is utterly wrong when he says that "'nother" in "That's a whole 'nother ball game" is an infix. As indicated by the definition you quote, an infix is a letter or syllable, not an entire word. And it is implanted in a word, not a sentence. If "'nother" is an infix, then so is "only" in the sentences you give as examples earlier in the same column.

In technical terms, an infix is a morphological phenomenon, not a grammatical one.

"'Nother" is merely a shortened form of "another" (which is why you should write it with a preceding apostrophe). It is an adjective modifying "ball game." "Whole" is an adjective used incorrectly as an adverb (instead of the correct "wholly") to modify "'nother."

The peculiar locution is the result of confusion in the speaker's mind between two common constructions with the same meaning: "That's a whole different ball game" (again using "whole" instead of the correct "wholly") and "That's wholly another ball game." The speaker unconsciously drops the "a" from "another" because he or she remembers having inserted it before "whole."

Confused constructions of this sort, resulting from simultaneous recollection of two different ways of saying the same thing, are common in language. Often the speaker tries to straighten things out as he or she goes along (e.g., by dropping the "a" from "another"), but only succeeds in making things worse.

Another example in English is "These kinds of problems occur . . ." when the speaker means "Problems of this kind occur . . ." (there are several problems, but only one kind of them). Once off on the wrong foot, the speaker feels a plural verb coming up and thus pluralizes "this kind."

The philologists tell us that the French word "haut" ("high" or "height") resulted when the Latin "altum" and the German "hoh" came simultaneously to the minds of the bilingual Franks.

Sincerely,
Lee Levitt
New York, New York

Notion: How deep is it?

"Why is it," inquires Sondra Mayer of Great Neck, N.Y., "that no one has any idea, concept or thought anymore? It is now always a 'notion.' It always makes me feel that is the teeniest of ideas."

True; one cannot buy a big idea at a notion counter. That is because the lexicon of what goes on inside the mind is rapidly changing.

For a time, *idea* had its day. It was the word the Greeks used for "appearance rather than reality." Bright political plans of generations ago were dubbed "the Wisconsin idea" or "the Ohio idea," because the word had more excitement than "plan" or "program." To this day, "idea" remains the encompassing word for imaginative activity, but the luster seems gone; it's just another thought.

A *thought* is a brief idea, usually modestly derogated as "just a thought," but deserving of respect because of its contrast with a mere "feeling."

A *concept* is an idea with big ideas. Of late, academics who had a good thought, or even the makings of an extensive idea, dressed it up as "a concept," or even as part of "a conceptual framework." (Card-carrying members of the Conceptual Frameworkers Union abound in the National Security Council.)

A *notion,* originally from the Latin verb for "to know," is an idea that has been kicked in the head. The word is now used in attacks on opinions: "The notion that the budget can be balanced" uses the term "notion" to mean "crackbrained idea" or "cockamamie thought."

"Notion" has always been the stepchild of intellect. The element of whim or caprice was long associated with the word, and a product based on a cute or catchy idea became a notion to be sold at a "notions counter." In the product sense, a notion is a knickknack (some word coiner had the notion of making up a word with four k's).

Today, as Sondra Mayer points out, "notion" is in vogue, but it should not be used as a synonym for idea, thought, or concept. It's a sneer word, meant to be applied to the quirky noodling that goes on in unthinking minds.

Dear Mr. Safire;
   Allow me to offer some thoughts on "notion," suggested by the comments of Sondra Mayer (no relation).
   James Boswell, discussing Samuel Johnson's tireless battle against "infractions upon the genuine English language" and especially "colloquial barbarisms," remarks:

> *He was particularly indignant against the almost universal use of the word* idea *in the sense of* notion *or* opinion, *when it is clear that* idea *can only signify something of which an image can be formed in the mind. We may have an* idea *or* image *of a mountain, a tree, a building; but we cannot surely have an* idea *or* image *of an* argument *or* proposition.
> *(23 Sept. 1777; p. 873 of my copy of the* Life—Oxford Standard Authors, *1953 edition.)*

Note the distinction Johnson makes. The underlying sense of abstractness ex-

plains "notion" 's derogatory implication: abstractness suggests vagueness and triviality.

Has it occurred to Ms. Mayer that perhaps people really don't have ideas (in this strict sense) anymore? Surely by today's standards "the Wisconsin idea," for example, was a fully imagined goal; its supporters had a far clearer vision of their social and political ideal than do the proponents of more recent programs of reform, which are truly notional. "Notion" replaces "idea" in our speech as notions replace ideas in our minds—perhaps.

On the other hand, I can report that "notion" is frequently used without derogatory implications by social scientists and other academic types who think there's nothing wrong with being abstract (or, for that matter, "academic"). A notion, in these circles, is sort of a less pretentious concept—which may explain why the usage is not prevalent around the National Security Council.

Even in academia, however, "notion" may be a sneer word. When Beardsley Ruml left the University of Chicago to become treasurer of Macy's, the wife of a colleague remarked that he had "abandoned ideas for notions." (This is an approximate quotation—I've seen this in print recently, but can't find the reference.)

In any case, we may take some comfort from the thought that, in this one instance, we seem to be abandoning (two-hundred-year-old) "modern cant" and returning to Johnsonian purity of language.

Sincerely
André Mayer
Boston, Massachusetts

Dear Mr. Safire:

I was very puzzled by your reference to "idea" being used by the Greeks for "appearance rather than reality." At least one Greek, Plato, used "idea" in the opposite meaning:

The Ideas ought rather to be treated by us as an attempt to convey Plato's conviction that there was a truth unrealized beyond sense, which could only be grasped by the mind when freed from the thralldom of body.

(From Jowett's introduction to the dialogue Parmenides in Jowett's edition of the Works of Plato, Volume IV, p. 312, Tudor Publishing Co., N.Y.C.)

Very truly yours,
Dr. Burton Cohen
Asst. Professor of Education
The Jewish Theological Seminary of America
New York, New York

not un-

Double negatives do not a positive make. To be "not unhappy" is not the same as to be happy; in that case, the "not un-" construction is a useful, if lazy, device to describe a feeling along the happy-unhappy scale.

On the other hand, I am not unmindful (actually, I'm mindful) of the confusion caused by the convoluted "not un-" construction. Most often "not un-" is effete affectation used by people who know what they are not but are uncertain about what they are.

Secretary of Defense Harold Brown, discussing the costs to the United States of the Egyptian-Israeli treaty, wanted to say something like "Peace and security are not cheap, but war and insecurity cost more." But what came out of his mouth was "Peace and security are not inexpensive, but war and insecurity are even more so." Think about that: War is even more "not inexpensive" than peace. Those who are against unsimplicity will find that not inoffensive.

Dear Mr. Safire:

. . . The "not un-" construction is not a double negative, but rather an example of the rhetorical device known as litotes.

And so, since "Sincerely" without the concomitant "Yours" has no meaning whatever,* I am,

> *Your columnistship's most humble and obedient servant,*
> *Paul Randall Mize*
> *New York, New York*

Dear Mr. Safire:

Apropos of "Not Un," please allow me to recount a distant memory of an incident that occurred on my father's farm at Olney, Maryland, somewhat more than sixty years ago.

The hands were blasting out some rocks. When the fuse was ignited, the men were supposed to run away to a safe distance. But one man ran two or three times the distance considered safe by the rest. The group guyed him for being timorous. He shouted out, "Nobody can't tell me no damn nothin'." We two supercilious boys were delighted with the grammar, and decided that his four negatives had made a positive. The other miserable pedant retired some years ago as a four-star general. The writer retired about the same number of years ago as a professor of English. Naturally, you will say!

As I write this, another incident comes to mind, which I have used in univer-

* See "salutations."—*W.S.*

sity classes to illustrate how wrong supercilious boys can be. We were in the old Model-T visiting the battlefield of Gettysburg. We had a favorite guide, an old man who was excellent. But we were particularly delighted when he referred to the soldiers who had been wounded in the battle. He pronounced wounded *as we say the* ou *in* founded (*i.e.,* confounded). *Of course we assumed that the old guide was simply illiterate, but we liked our own superiority. Many years later, when I was trying to understand the ins and outs of Old English and Middle English, I learned that many words passed through stages from* sund (*pronounced* soond) *to* sound. *Hence it was historically correct to say* wounded— *indeed they were* wound *up in their winding sheets.*

Your articles entertain this old pedant very much.

> *Sincerely yours,*
> *Rudolf Kirk*
> *San Marcos, Texas*

It is incorrect to end a letter "Sincerely." You should add the "yours."

Dear Mr. Safire:

You rightly criticized the mis-users of the double negative who wish to express a positive. I hope, though, that your characterization of this device as an "effete affection" will not prevent good writers from carefully using the ancient and honorable figure of litotes (λιτότης, assertion by means of understatement). To the Romans, for example, there was a slight but meaningful exaggeration and a rhetorical irony contained in the words "non ignoro" that could not be conveyed by "scio."

This figure of speech is useful, as in the following sentence:

> *The services of Rich Gossage thus curtailed, the appearance of Ron Guidry in the Yankee bullpen was, to the fans and to his teammates, not unwelcome.*

The emphasis expressed by the words "not unwelcome" would be all but lost with the simple positive "welcome." There being so few rhetorical figures from antiquity that still survive in our prose, it would be unfortunate to lose this one, too.

> *Very truly yours,*
> *Philip Winters*
> *New York, New York*

All right, hail Saf!

. . . Apropos of double-negatives. Somebody—not you—has claimed that a double negative may be a positive, but there is no double positive which may be a negative. To which a voice in the back surlily responded, "Yeah, yeah."

> *Ave atque vale?*
> *Franklin Drucker, M.D.*
> *Los Angeles, California*

Nouvelle vague

A new wave of vagueness is in vogue. "Rain" is dead; the television meteorologist (remember "the weather girl"?) now speaks imprecisely of "precipitation activity," a foggy locution covering everything from a fine mist to a biblical 40-day-and-40-night downpour.

One reason for the new fuzziness may be rooted in legal advice: A witness is better off saying "he indicated" than "he said," because "indicated" could range in meaning from an explicit statement to a rolling of the eyes. They can't get you for perjury as easily on "he indicated."

Another reason is deliberate loophole leaving. Say a White House spokesman is asked "Does the President plan to go to China?" If the answer is "We have no present plans to do so," the spokesman is hinting that newsmen should be on the lookout for "future plans" to pose for pictures in front of a long wall. The follow-up question is another exercise in vagueness: "Do you have a time frame?" This has replaced the oafishly specific "When?"

Airplanes never land in a definite place anymore. "Welcome to the New York *area.*" This gives the navigator an alibi in case he mistakes La Guardia Airport for the facility at Newark.

On occasion, this soft-focus language can be creative. *People* magazine discussed "split-speak," the vocabulary of separation, quoting Hollywood composer David Shire about his "very positive and loving separation" from his wife, Talia. She explained: "We're going to rotate the house and we even rotate the cars. We've been separated for four months, and it's a growing experience."

He moved out, and has not moved back in a year. Her nouvelle-vague way of coping linguistically with this definitive indecision: "We're into distancing."

Now hear this

At this point in time, let us examine what is happening to "now."

Because of its bluntness and immediacy, the word is scorned by circumlocutionists. Instead, they prefer *currently,* which evokes a picture of a person watching the current of events flow by, or *presently,* which incites to confusion. "Presently" was coined to mean "at present," but centuries ago came to mean *soon, shortly, in a little while,* and *momentarily;* now it means both "now" and "soon," and is a word that is best forgotten, at least for the time being.

Meanwhile, the rejected little "now" is making its appearance in farewells: "Bye, now." What does that mean? "Goodbye for now" is as meaningless as "Goodbye for later." Perhaps the speaker is trying to soften the impact of "goodbye," using the modifier in the same way "now" is used to soothe—"Now, now, everything's going to be all right."

More about language presently. Take care, now.

Dear Bill—
  I think Goodbye [for] now is to be distinguished from Goodbye forever.
                    Best—
                    Monroe
                    (Monroe Freedman
                    Dean, Hofstra University School of Law)
                    Hempstead, New York

---

number of

A number of letters have crossed my desk (and when my desk is crossed, it retaliates with a furious memo) about a meaningless phrase, used by lazy writers, which is enjoying a boom. The phrase is "a number of."

Complainants zero in on the number of times "a number of" is used in *The New York Times.* In a piece about editor Roy E. Larsen's retirement: "Mr. Larsen, who held a number of titles . . ." In a financial story: "A growing number of other major bank holding companies . . ." In a dispatch from overseas: "Pretoria had ordered the expulsion of a number of American embassy personnel . . ." An irate editorial: "What is unseemly, however, is how a number of United Way chapters . . ."

What is unseemly is the way this locution fails to answer the simple question "How many?" If the writer does not know, and has no time to find out, several more specific fudges are available: "Several" is one; "a few" is another; "many" and "scores" are available as well, and then we're off into "a whole bunch," and on up to the Greek "myriad," which means 10,000.

The best way to break ourselves of this habit is to think of phrases that might have wound up as "the face that launched a number of ships," "through the valley of death charged a number of soldiers," "a number of years ago, our fathers brought forth on this continent . . ." Newsmen in biblical times might begin their stories "Moses descended from Mount Sinai with a number of commandments," or "It rained for a number of days and a number of nights."

How many? Give us readers a hint; "a number of" is too broad to mean anything. Therefore, change the opening of this entry to read "Five letters have crossed my easily irritated desk," all from one man, Alex W. Burger of New Rochelle, N.Y., who gets all worked up at writers who do a number on him.

Dear Mr. Safire:

I'm afraid I was a bit confused by your argument against the expression "a number of."

Do you mean that "a number of" is unacceptable simply because it fails to distinguish among "several," "a few," "many," "scores" and so forth? If so, you would also want to attack "some" (which to a logician means anything between none and all).

It doesn't seem quite fair to suppose that laziness is the only reason for the phrase. Reliable reckonings are hard to come by. "A number of" is more timid than the alternatives you suggest, but also more cautious.

> *In vague security,*
> *Mike Shenefelt*
> *New York, New York*

P.S. Perhaps "a growing number of" was included in your list of offending expressions by accident. Growing numbers, unlike big and little numbers, don't take a fixed hat size.

---

numbers in slogans

The habit of marrying a place to a number, and thereby describing a group of people under attack, was popularized in the 50's with The Hollywood 10; this was followed by The Chicago 7 and more recently by The Wilmington 10. The verb used to create a short slogan supporting these groups has customarily been "free."

This sloganeering suffered a blow after a recent action by the Federal Aviation Administration when broadcaster Daniel Schorr suggested that a bumper sticker be carried to read "Free the DC-10."

---

ochlocracy, *see* crisis crisis

---

one-word sentence

The hottest item in advertising copy is the one-word sentence. Putting a period after a single word graphically suggests what the spoken word—"period"—says: "I mean it. No nonsense. I've had enough. Period." A comma is for sissies.

Senator Howard Baker has the toughest-looking press-release stationery of any candidate. The Baker Committee strips the word "BAKER," all caps, across the top, and across the bottom are these three sentences: "Tough. Honest. Right for the 80's." The last sentence is underlined in red.

Those of us who read political tea leaves know who is the target of each of those three quick shots. "Tough" is intended to contrast with George Bush; "honest" is not a word that John Connally uses in his literature, and "right for the 80's" is evidently a wave of fond farewell to Ron Reagan, who was on the right during the 60's and may have been right for the 70's, according to the Baker adman, but that's in the past.

The Senator and his admen will claim this intense scrutiny is going from the subliminal to the ridiculous—reading far more into the phrases than they intended.

Sure.

---

on line/in line

In a dissertation on the letter "q" and its abandonment by the formerly faithful "u," I wrote that "in months to come, we will be getting on line to use the 17th letter of our alphabet in a different way."* This was an example of the once-removed pun, a play on a word deliberately not used ("queuing," for "getting in line"). Nobody got it; like President Carter, I am a little disappointed in all of you.

However, several readers were moved to ask about "in" and "on." Do you

* See "Q"— there's no "U."—W. S.

"get in line" or "get on line"—"stand in line" or "stand on line"?

Across the country, "in" is in. Just as an executive hopes he is *"in"* line for promotion," he gets *in* line for a movie. But not in New York: A New Yorker who will also say "in line for promotion" (perhaps because of the use of "in" in "in the line of fire") departs from national usage when it comes to a queue.

In New York, you stand "on" line, or so I have been led to believe by folksy etymologists. To determine the accuracy of this old husband's tale, as well as to discover the origin of "to wait on" rather than "to wait for," I queried University of Wisconsin Professor Frederic G. Cassidy, the director-editor of DARE, the Dictionary of American Regional English.

"Standing *on line* to buy tickets [English *queuing up*] is definitely New York City and its area," reports Professor Cassidy. "Of course, New Yorkers carry it all over the place into the *in line* area, which is the rest of the world, but are probably not imitated by adults. On the other hand, I know of a New York Catholic nun who has been posted to teach school in Wisconsin and who tells her children to *stand on line*—and they take it home. Whether it will survive beyond her influence is the question, but changes in language generally come about through the younger people."

Just as a Southerner will look askance at a New Yorker who says "on line," a New Yorker will askance him right back when the Southerner says impatiently "I'm still waiting on you." In the North, "to wait on" means to serve, as waiters do; in the South, it can also mean "to hang around until the other person is ready"—an inaction that Northerners describe as "to wait *for*."

"*Wait for* and *wait on* are a very different kettle of fish," reports Cassidy, "which has been on the boil in schoolrooms for a long time. [We lexicographers enjoy metaphors.] *Wait on,* meaning 'attend' or 'delay until someone else is ready,' was once used throughout the country, and, as our maps show, still is to some extent, though the concentration is definitely in the South and South midland.

"This is clearly due to the concomitant factors of Southern conservatism and Northern schoolmarming. About the middle of the 19th century, someone drew the distinction between *wait on,* do a service for, and *wait for,* attend till another person is ready. It was taken up in schools and became a standard entry in books of correct usage.

"Our maps," concludes the man from DARE, "show *wait for* solid throughout the North, pretty strong in the Atlantic states generally, and, surprisingly, stronger in southern than in northern California. Evidently the schools have made some headway. I remember my high school teacher insisting on the distinction."

Though the differentiation began early on, Southerners have clung to their regionalism just as New Yorkers grimly stand *on* line. (Wait up—why early *on?*)

Dear Mr. Safire:

I perceive a difference in connotation between "getting in line" and "getting on line." When a crowd of people suddenly form a line, they are getting "in" line. When someone arrives at an already formed line and gets on the end of it, he is getting "on" line. What it probably means is that in New York City someone cannot take part in forming a line unless he arrives at 1 A.M. with a sleeping bag!

Incidentally, I got your queuing pun but didn't consider it worth writing home about. Sorry.

Regards,
Marilyn H. Shenton (Mrs.)
Stamford, Connecticut

Dear Mr. Safire,

Sometimes one wonders.

I am in line ⎱ *i.e. at a certain place. "In" implies a conceptual place, in a*
I am on line ⎰ *table of organization, "on" a specific physical spot.*

As a consequence, I would probably say, "Get in line," whenever I would then be "standing on line." But the reverse would be equally acceptable if in my mind I meant to place myself in a physical position rather than a conceptual order. One could just as well tell someone to get over there, i.e. "get on line," so he would then be "standing in line," in a conceptual order (or standing "on line," in a given spot.)

I don't know about the general public, or the etymologists, but the difference between "in" and "on" is perfectly clear to me. (Nobody in any part of the country would say, "He's on line to be the next vice-president." The image is clearly one of someone waiting outside the office door.) If there is an area difference in their usage in the sense of queuing up, it rather clearly stems from the New York sense of being in a specific kind of location being opposed to the broader American sense of making oneself entitled by inserting one's self in a conceptual table of organization.

The difference does exist, and the etymologists really ought to check the N.Y. nun in Wisconsin for her context. Does she mean that her students should get into a purely physical location and gestalt, or is there a concept of organization and entitlement by order? Since either possibility could exist, does she mean just stay put, or you'll get yours one by one?

My own impression is that articulate New Yorkers expect to be able to get things, that elsewhere they know they must deserve it by their actions. But even outside of New York, I haven't really noticed any real confusion of the concepts involved. "Get in line" has a completely different moral connotation than the ethically more neutral "Get on line." "In" would be used by persons standing on their rights, "on" in itself has no ethical meaning.

Wait on and *wait for* are of course a completely different kettle of fish; the operative word there is *wait.*

> Sincerely,
> John T. Boyt
> New York, New York

Dear Mr. Safire:

I was born in NYC, went to public school and high school here and live here now, and what I remember about elementary school—and also, I think, about lining up nowadays for movies and such events—is that "getting on line" meant either joining a line that was already in existence (what always happens by the time I arrive at the movie theatre) or forming a line out of the sort of messy crowd that has gathered. But "getting in line" meant straightening out the line one already was on—it seems to me I can still recall my grade-school-teacher's voice as we lined up to go into assembly, telling us to "get in line"—we were on line, but rather raggedy, with people bulging out here and there, and she wanted us neatly one-behind-the-other in either one or two rows.

Perhaps it's that Americans aren't very good at lining up at all: I remember being amazed in London to see that the people who lined (queued?) up for the buses did so facing into the direction the bus was coming from, which is very sensible. Over here, we form lines in the same direction the bus goes, so that in order to see whether the bus is coming, we have to look back over our shoulders. That is, when we bother to line up at all—mostly we seem to loiter and then charge, the devil take the hindmost. . . .

> Sincerely,
> Carol Brener
> New York, New York

Bill . . .

For years and years I stood in line. At least when lines stood between me and my desires. (In England, of course, I queued.)

Recently, however, I've noticed that Americans have abandoned both these tiresome necessities. Nowadays they stand—and wait—on line. Last week a Queens man was shot while waiting on line for gasoline service. I suppose he was killed on line of gasoline. If fallen in combat for his country, would he have been killed on line of duty?

Standing on line at New York movie houses is now commonplace. I've seen no explanation of why Americans got out of line and on it instead. I recently stood on line for a movie and didn't feel a bit better than I did when using the old in-line approach.

> Yrs,
> Russ
> [Russell Baker
> The New York Times
> New York, New York]

only the lonely

The adverb *only* has slipped its moorings, and now drifts anywhere in a sentence. Arthur Isler writes from Mexico: "Why do most people say, ' I only have eyes for you,' when they really mean, 'I have eyes only for you'?"

Only the other day I was humming that golden oldie, and it never occurred to me that the sentence would gain emphasis if the *only* moved closer to the *eyes.* Frederick Mish, editorial director of the G. & C. Merriam Company, says: "More often than not, *only* qualifies the whole idea of a sentence, and in that use most naturally precedes the verb." But the songwriter could have written three other versions: "I have eyes only for you," "I have eyes for only you," or "I have eyes for you only."

"Most people would understand all four versions to mean essentially the same thing," notes lexicographer Mish, but he adds that the lonely *only* must not be allowed to float too far: "They would immediately recognize that 'only I have eyes for you' means something very different and less flattering."

We are talking here about the order of words in a sentence, a subject that transforms grammarians. My correspondent in Mexico takes the question a step further: "Why do people say, 'I don't think I'll go' when they really mean, 'I think I will not go'?"

I think I will not answer that, because I don't think there is a good answer in logic or grammar. I will only say: "An idiom is its own excuse for being." (I will say only? I only will say? Only I will say?)

Dear Mr. Safire:

Whether or not you have eyes only, only have eyes, or eyes for only you, the fact is that "I Only Have Eyes For You" was written by Mr. Al Dubin, the lyricist.

When you refer to a songwriter, *I believe you mean the venerable Mr. Harry Warren, who is alive and well, and who sat at his piano and wrote the melodic da-da-da-da-da-da-da which lies so well beneath Mr. Dubin's lyrics.*

> *Yours in precision,*
> *Max Wilk*
> *Westport, Connecticut*

opt/choose—Pick 'em

"CARTER OPTS FOR BUILDING BIG MISSILE" was a banner head-line announcing the President's decision to develop and produce the "Missile Experimental" designated "MX."

The verb was ill chosen. "Opt" is a trendy new verb, clipped from the formerly trendy noun "option," which was in favor as some sort of improvement over "choice" or "alternative." But "opt" was a useful verb because it carried the connotation of an impulsive choice—a lunge to decision that one makes at a checkout counter surrounded by impulse items.

Most dictionaries now define "opt" as a synonym for "choose" without that nice distinction. That's a pity, since the word is now used merely for its "in" feeling or (in headlines) for its shortness. Perhaps, with the help of discerning decision-makers, the verb can regain its narrow definition that gave it a reason for being. Bergen Evans, in *Comfortable Words,* split the hair precisely: "Confronted with a choice between *choose* and *opt,* my impulse is to opt for *choose.*"

Dear Sir,

Although your excellent article in the Times Magazine, *"On Language," is both well written and informative, I must take exception to your description of the verb "to opt" as "a trendy new verb, clipped form the formerly trendy noun 'option.'" Nonsense. The O.E.D. tells us that it was borrowed from the French "opter" and exported to England in 1877 in an article by the Paris correspondent for the London* Times *about Alsatians "opting" between France and Germany.*

The French acquired the word in 1552 by gallicizing the Latin verb "optare" (to choose) thus creating the same confusion between "opter" and "choisir" that we now have in English. If anyone "clipped" the word, it was the old Romans who also had a noun "optio" from which both French and English derive the word "option."

Oddly enough, the French "opter" and the English "opt" have retained the same definition in modern usage, a rare phenomenon among cognates, cf. the following definitions, the first from Le Petit Robert, *the second from the* O.E.D.

opter: *Faire un choix, prendre parti entre deux ou plusieurs choses qu'on ne peut avoir ou faire ensemble.*

opt: *To choose, make a choice (between alternatives); to decide (for one or other of two alternatives)*

Warren L. Wellman
West Oneonta, New York

oral note, *see* Kissingerese

orient, *see* ate-haters

oscillate

The most pointed early barb of the 1980 Presidential campaign was delivered by Republican candidate George Bush, the former everything. He described President Carter's foreign policy as "splendid oscillation."

"Oscillate"—from the Latin for "swinging back and forth"—is a double-entendred attack word because it sounds like a Southern pronunciation of "isolate." Thus, when Mr. Bush applies the handy label of "oscillationist," it means "head-in-the-sand" down South and "indecisive" up North. Eyes are being peeled for a stinging statement on "the new oscillationism."

ostentatious rejection

The useful rhetorical technique of ostentatious rejection is back with us.

Government staffers know the trick of "Option Three," which presents the boss with a series of choices, called options, in such a way as to dictate the only sensible choice: For example, Option One could be "abject surrender," and Option Five "nuclear holocaust," steering the decision maker toward Option Three, which is the staffer's preferred course.

By rejecting extremes, the speaker puts himself in the mainstream and invites his listeners to join him there. In a recent foreign policy speech, President Carter set up a few "myths" to reject, placing himself—and his audience—on the side of reality. And on his successful Middle East shuttle, before achieving what was universally dubbed a "breakthrough," he turned to the classic middle-way speech:

"For the past 24 hours I have been writing different versions of this speech. I have discarded the speech of despair; I have discarded the speech of glad tidings and celebration; I have decided to deliver the speech of concern and caution and hope."

It was not hard to empathize with the speechwriter who submitted all three drafts. In my own speechwriting days, it was my job to go into the Oval Office and say: "Mr. President, take the easy way. Do the popular thing." This enabled me to submit a draft that included: "Some of my advisers have suggested I take the easy way, and do the popular thing. I have rejected that advice. . . ."

---

parameters

"Most vogue terms are fun to watch come and go," I expostulated to a friend recently, "but 'exacerbate' rubs me the wrong way, and 'parameter' is the limit."

The friend was Daniel Bell, the Harvard sociologist, whose interest in words led him to be the first to apply "charisma" to an American public figure (John L. Lewis, in a 1949 *Fortune* article). " 'Parameter' is a good word," he expostulated right back, "which has been getting a bad press. Don't join the pack."

He had a point: "Parameter" is a word that has been used by academics and engineers with great glee in the past few years, usually fuzzily as in "the parameters of the problem." But just because it has been snapped up by jargoneers does not mean that the word cannot become a useful addition to the language.

A parameter (accent on the "ram") is not a perimeter, nor is it a man who leaps out of an airplane to check your gas reading. In mathematics, a parameter is "a constant whose value may vary," but we're more interested in the word's present metaphoric use as a tool we can measure other things by. A parameter is some specific yardstick we can use to help us judge the unknown quantity nearby.

Unhappy with my own definition, and unsatisfied by the two mathematical definitions in dictionaries, I asked Dan Bell for one good, solid example of parameter.

"Sixteen thousand miles an hour," he replied unhesitatingly. "That's as fast as anything can go on earth. You go one mile an hour faster and you're in orbit. So, 16,000 m.p.h. is a parameter you work with if you're dealing in transportation. Now—what's the highest potential black vote if you're a Republican candidate?"

That I knew: "In New York State," I calculated, "if you were Rocky or

Javits and having a good year, maybe you could get 35 percent of the black vote to pull the Republican lever, instead of the average 20 percent."

"So the parameter of the black vote for Republicans is 35 percent."

A parameter, then—leaving the dictionaries to catch up with us—is not merely a "constant," but a "limit," an outer reach, that helps shape, characterize, or define the scope of an idea or a problem. In that way, "parameter" is similar to "perimeter," the edge with which it is confused; but a "parameter" has more of a meaning of "criterion" or "standard" to help it give shape to the idea in its field.

A parameter is a ball park in which we play; it is a measurement that gives a character to anything we want to compare it with. The best definition for "parameter" would be "that which gives definition"—but what kind of definition is that? The best one-word synonym, in its new meaning—which the dictionaries need to get moving on—is "limit."

Mr. Safire: (*to whom it may concern*)

Last week, you used the word "jargoneer." My copy of Webster's Seventh New Collegiate Dictionary (a gift from my Uncle Ben and Aunt Irene when I graduated from high school in 1966!) contains "jargonistic" and "jargonize," but not "jargoneer." In any event, I prefer the neologism "jargonaut," which implies exploration of the uncharted seas of English usage.

> *Yr. faithful reader,*
> *Daniel J. Fink*
> *Philadelphia, Pennsylvania*

Dear Mr. Safire:

Not too many years ago, the word perimeter *was used only by mathematical people. It was (and still is) the technical term for "the distance around" some flat region being discussed; for example, a certain triangle might have a perimeter of 217 feet. Over the years,* perimeter *came to be used by others not just for the* length *of a boundary, but for the boundary itself. Thus, for example, a general might speak of the "perimeter of our defenses." Indeed, this "boundary itself" meaning for perimeter has found its way into our usual dictionaries. The cultural jump (or passage) to this meaning wasn't very great, to be sure.*

On the other hand, if you pick up a copy of some fairly recent good dictionaries, you will not *find the word* parameters, *another word which started with mathematicians—who are very careful with words. Parameters now finds itself being used to mean something very much different from its original meaning. The cultural jump is much greater than the one experienced by our friend, perimeter. Most mathematicians cringe when they now hear "parameters" used to mean something like "limits" or "upper bounds," even though they will defend* most strenuously your right (and theirs) to have a word mean whatever you want it to mean. [They do just want you to be clear about your definitions, though, and to use your words with care and consistency. They realize, too, that time does sometimes corrupt and sometimes improve on original meanings of terms.]

Why do they then cringe? Well, because this change in meaning has taken a bad turn. A good meaning for the word and many careful uses for it have been lost forever to the land of imprecision.

The original meaning for "parameters" is nicely given by "shape determiners," certain numbers, often very few in number, which determine the shape of some mathematical object being studied. For example, consider the family of all possible ellipses, those simple, closed curves which are "cousins" to circles. A choice of just two numbers will specify the shape of that one ellipse you wish to select. (For example, you may want one which is very big, lies on its side, and is very thin. Or you may want one that is about the size of a football field and is nearly circular.) Those two numbers are the parameters of that family. Picking specific values for the parameters determines the shape of the member you wish to deal with. [An ellipse is given by $(\frac{x}{a})^2 + (\frac{y}{b})^2 = 1$. The parameters here are the numbers a and b.]

Similarly, imagine an irregular, somewhat wave-like, horizontal curve. For many families of such curves, the parameters—the "shape determiners"—may be very small in number. [Such a curve—with parameters a, b, c, d—might be this one: $y = ax^3 + bx^2 + cx + d$.] A family made up of "very wiggly" curves of this sort usually has very many parameters; to pick a particular member of that family, you must choose specific values for quite a few "shape determiners."

Here's another example: When considering a troublesome company problem, the boss seeks to learn the parameters of a solution. That is, what numbers determine the shape of a solution? His administrative role boils down to his having to choose the values of certain parameters, values which, in his judgment, will produce the solution which best fits the circumstances. These numbers may very well be "limits" in some sense, but they need not be.

For a final example now, what are the parameters of Mr. Safire's financial condition? What numbers related to this human family member help me answer? Well, numbers related to his salary, real-estate holdings, savings, other assets, blood pressure, insurance companies' charges for his life insurance, the number of his well-disposed rich relatives, etc.

Parameters is a useful word. If people want to say "limits," I wish they wouldn't use "parameters." I am quite sure many scientific people join me in that weary wish.

Sincerely,
L. H. Lange
Dean, School of Science
San José State University
San José, California

---

p's and q's, *see* apostrophe

---

partings, *see* Have a nice day

---

patellar reflex, *see* knee jerk

---

pet peeves

Readers have been sending in their "pet peeves."

Mrs. Frances Julius of London objects to the American use of "balmy" to mean "crazy." She points out that "balmy" best describes a calm and fragrant tropic breeze, and "balm to his soul" is just the opposite of agitation. The word, and spelling, intended for "crazy" is "barmy"—from barm, or yeast, which offers the proper picture of a wildly fermenting brain.

Ken Zahm of Portsmouth, R.I., is turned off by the way sportscasters use "waffled" to mean "acted indecisively." Be calm, Zahm—the verb has a fine pedigree, from "wave" in Scottish, or possibly "waff," to bark or yelp foolishly, and has nothing to do with the kind of waffles that come "drenched in maple-type syrup" and that are akin to wafers.

The pet peeve of Helen Landrim of Whiting, N.J., is the disappearin' "ing" sound. "Whatever has happened to 'ing,' as in 'going' or 'wanting'?" she asks. "These words have become almost invariably 'gonna' and 'wanna.' " She's right, and if we're gonna make a big deal out of the vanishin' "g," I wanna put in my objection to the ominous "Ommina" (for "I'm going to") and its New York variant "Ongana."

A few of my colleagues in the Washington press corps bridle at the phrase "press availability." According to a spokesman at Connally for President headquarters, here is the meaning: A "press conference" begins with a formal statement followed by questions; a "press availability," on the other hand, means that there will be no opening statement and the candidate will throw himself immediately on the mercy of the press for Q. & A.

Innumerable (that's better than "a number of," which in turn is better than having to say "only four") correspondents have complained of "shower activity" instead of "rain." (Whatever happened to "intermittent precipitation"?) Television-commercial-watcher Ida Marshall of New York City seethes at "Stops decay before it starts" and "The closer you get, the better she looks." ("He is standing still; she is moving toward him on TV.")

The Unicorn Hunters, a group of linguists at Lake Superior State College in Sault Sainte Marie, Mich., are reported to take umbrage (good word, "umbrage"—from "shady") at the term "self-addressed": "We banned 'self-addressed' some time ago," asserts Professor W. T. Rabe, "because that implies that the envelope wrote an address on itself."

Statistician James Hargan of Tampa, Fla., is miffed at my contention that because "datum" is pedantic, "data" can be used in the singular, as "The data is . . ." He writes: "Statisticians deal with sets of numbers, each number measuring some discrete individual person or object. 'Datum' refers to one of these individual measures, while 'data' refers to the set as a whole." Mr. Hargan is further peeved at the abuse of "statistic" to mean "datum": "A 'statistic' is a number which measures data, under the assumption that the data are a proper subset, called a 'sample.' A statistic cannot measure a datum. . . . This makes the cliché 'I am not a statistic' into a tautology: You are not a statistic; you are a datum." (I have been called worse by mathematicians infuriated by my layman's embrace of their beloved "parameter.")

My own pet peeve is the phrase "pet peeve." Doesn't anybody have any other kind of peeve? Alliteration is dandy—as the perpetrator of "nattering nabobs of negativism," I cannot denigrate alliterators—but can't we try "favorite fury" or "preferred provocation"?

One of these days, ongana get a dog and name him "Peeve," so I can introduce him to friends in the ecstasy of exasperation with "This is my pet, Peeve."

Dear Mr. Safire,
Regarding your article which, among other things, included "Ommina," I must say you did not include my favorite—"Yuzzada." This means "if yuzzada" did this—. (If you had done—)

Thanks—
Don C. Kunze
Roanoke, Virginia

Dear Mr. Safire,

In the introduction to a book of Frank Loesser songs, it is stated that he had wide-ranging interests, including techniques of 16th-century cabinet-making. On one occasion he constructed with great craftsmanship the corner (just the corner) of a Regency desk, inlaid and perfectly finished. He then sent it to John Steinbeck, a piece of note paper attached with the printed words "From the Desk of Frank Loesser."*

On a more recent note: The term "self-addressed" was already accepted by Webster's 2nd International and seems a perfectly acceptable, and more importantly, completely understandable term.

Grammatically I suppose you could say that "addressed" is the participle being used as an adjective with self modifying the adjective. However shady their reasoning, I don't intend to take the Unicorn Hunters to court to Sault Ste. Marie.

In my correspondence with you I fully expect to make many inadvertant errors with the expressed advertant ones.

> Barry Skeist
> Roosevelt Island, New York

Dear Mr. Safire:

The English lady who tells you that "balmy" should be "barmy" in British usage may be too young to have known this slang term in its youthful prime fifty or sixty years ago. We Americans borrowed it from the British, true, as "balmy," and that is not a distortion. For corroboration: In his SHADOWED! published in the late 1920s, Hilaire Belloc has a character known to her friends as "Balmy Jane"—and they meant she was off her rocker, gone round the bend. . . . And Heaven knows Belloc was impeccably and authentically British.

> Very truly yours,
> J. C. Furnas
> Lebanon, New Jersey

Dear Mr. Safire;

It was interesting to read your English contributor's explanation of "barmy." However, having spent over two years in England in the early nineteen-sixties, I was led to believe that "barmy" was a derivative of the name of the town Barming, in Kent County. At Barming, there is a rather extensive psychiatric hospital. It follows, naturally, that, over a period of time, the local blokes whittled Barming down to barmy to describe someone who is a bit "off" in the head. Or, as we might say, someone who is not hitting on all eight cylinders.

* See desks who write.—W. S.

I hope this sheds some linguistic light on a barmy use of the word.

> *Sincerely yours,*
> *Laurence A. Booker*
> *Computer Center Manager*
> *Addison County Vocational Center*
> *Middlebury, Vermont*

---

pettifogging

What's in an insult? Fun, if it uses an offbeat word.

Speaking for the Soviet bloc in the United Nations General Assembly, Leonid Dolguchits, chief delegate of the Byelorussian Soviet Socialist Republic, was roundly denouncing the "campaign of slander and lying" by the United States following the liberation of Afghanistan. After a few paragraphs of boilerplate condemnation, he zapped the "American-Chinese pettifogging complaint."

Pettifogging?

The Russian word used by Dolguchits is transliterated as *klauza,* pronounced "klow-oo-zah." "It is not a frequently used word," reports Stephen Pearl, the U.N. interpreter who chose "pettifogging" to translate *"klauza"* into English. He adds: "There is no obvious rendering," which is what my Brooklyn grandmother used to say as she reached for Rokeach's Nyafat. In 17 years at the U.N., the interpreter recalls encountering the word fewer than ten times.

Mr. Pearl helpfully passed along an example of a *klauza* given him by a Soviet colleague: "A Moscovite filing a complaint about a neighbor making too much noise—even though the neighbor was innocent—would be involved in a *klauza.* The complainant would be called a *klauznik.* The meaning is 'a petty complaint inspired by bad motives, and connected to the letter of the law.' "

In English, "pettifogging" is defined by most dictionaries as "malicious, underhanded," with a second meaning of "quibbling over insignificant details." The word is used to insult lawyers who use the letter of the law to subvert what the insulter considers to be the spirit of the law. In current American use, the connotation of trickery and deceit has been overwhelmed by the specific meaning of using technicalities to filibuster. "Pettifogging" is now as closely wedded to "delay" as "unmitigated" is to "gall."

The word sounds as if it came from a combination of "to befog the issue" with "petty details." Not so. Most dictionaries hold that the origin of "fogger" is obscure, but the Oxford English Dictionary suggests that the term probably comes from a family of German merchants and financiers renowned for their methods of cheating in the 15th and 16th centuries.

---

physical, *see* adverbial lapel-grabber

---

pinyin alphabet, *see* ZIP codes

---

plugged in

Since my friend Alonzo McDonald of the White House began to use the verb "interlink"—rather than the old-fashioned "connect" or even "link"— I have been on the lookout for electricity metaphors.

To "turn on," as in turning on a light, was originally drug-culture lingo, later gained sexual overtones, and now means "to excite, interest, or titillate"; one who is turned on, or "switched on," is hip, with it, an avant-gardian angel.

The latest version of this electrical connection is "plugged in." If you are still saying "turned on," you are not plugged in. (However, the opposite of "plugged in" is still "turned off," and not "unplugged," and certainly not "plugged out.")

A recent advertisement for Gloria Vanderbilt corduroy pants, prepared by Macy's, nicely extended the metaphor: "Fall Status Report: Gloria Vanderbilt switches to plugged-in cords." With "corduroy" clipped to "cords," the word gains in allusion to electrical cord, which plugs in to a neat fit.

By the way, the same advertisement used "punched up" to describe a color. Bruce Emra of Ramsey, N.J., wrote to ask: "A curious phrase, 'punched up brights.' What is implied by it? Is the language derived from computer lingo? I know I ask my stockbroker to 'punch in' a stock on his Quotron machine for an up-to-the-moment selling price of the stock. But 'punched up'?"

The creative director of Macy's, Tom Raney, explains that "punched up" went well with "plugged-in." He reports that "punched up" is fashionese for "made brighter"—"cobalt rather than navy, grape rather than burgundy." (Grape color does not have as black a base as burgundy, and is thus brighter.)

The combination of "plugged-in" and "punched up" would have propelled me into the store for the cords, but I was turned off by the inconsistency in hyphenation, and by the elitist touting of Mrs. Vanderbilt's monicker, beginning with "status report" and concluding with "the name to remember for status dressing." To my taste, status dressing is the oil and vinegar you pour over the heart of palm in "millionaire's salad."

Dear Mr. Safire,

Punched-up? Do you never hear the phrase used in the American TV industry? I was in British Television for ten years and we never asked vision mixers to 'put up' a picture or to 'switch on' a picture, inevitably the request was to 'punch up' a picture and I can only assume that the phrase derives from the action of pushing a button on a mixer desk. 'Push' is hardly dramatic enough for television folk. From TV to advertising seems a reasonable route for the phrase.

If I have your ear for a moment, may I offend it? An omelette fine urb eaten by a ooman being. Why is America dropping the initial 'h' from words like 'herb' and 'human'? 'Herb' seems a decent enough word, rather better, I think, than 'urb'; and to drop the 'h' from 'human' is to need to replace it with a kind of suppressed guttural. It sounds ugly, it seems to be an affectation rather than a natural sound change, so why do it? For the sake of euphony, Mr. Safire, use your influence to save the American 'h' from extinction.

> Yours sincerely,
> Bernard Wiggins
> Westfield, New Jersey

Dear Mr. Safire:

As a fan of your "On Language" column (if not always of your political views) I thought you might be interested to know that "punched up" is almost certainly derived from the language of theatrical lighting. It refers to bringing up the level of intensity of an instrument (i.e., a light) or grouping of lights (for instance, in a given area of the stage or of a given color). It also has the connotation, as opposed to "bringing up," of increasing intensity suddenly, though in technical rehearsals one may hear a lighting designer instruct the electrician at the dimmer boards to "punch that up a point and write it" (i.e., bring it up tenth of the total range and use that as the level of light for the given lighting cue). "Punching up" is therefore a particularly apt expression for use in colors. You might wish to check these usages with a professional lighting designer as I am a stage manager, not a designer.

> Yours truly,
> Bruce Conner
> New York, New York

Dear Mr. Safire:

Tom Raney of Macy's was unaware of exactly how well "punched up" went with "plugged in." "Punched up" may have been adopted by the fashion industry, but it originated in the theater—and fits in more comfortably than you may have been aware with an item on electrical metaphors.

Many early, and some more recent, theater lighting boards had vertical dimmer controls. When the lighting director wanted brighter lights, he would literally "punch up" the dimmer control.

> Sincerely,
> Joan B. Nagy
> New York, New York

Dear Mr. Safire:

I enjoyed your article in last week's edition, especially the paragraphs referring to the advertising hype in regard to Gloria Vanderbilt Jeans.

But I think your copy editors are sticking it to you. We all know about The

New York Times' *rather anachronistic convention that prevents writers from referring to women as "Ms." However, Gloria Vanderbilt cannot possibly be "Mrs." Vanderbilt as she was called in your column. She is the widow of a very nice man whose name was Wyatt Cooper. She was "Miss" Vanderbilt a couple of marriages ago. Therefore, because she chooses to keep her maiden name professionally, she should be referred to as Miss Vanderbilt or Mrs. Cooper.*

All of which would be avoided if The New York Times *could raze itself up from its Lazarus-like position of meaningless tradition and join the present generation.* Ms. *Vanderbilt would be perfectly suitable under any other masthead but yours. Nor would the use of it inspire the kind of confusion that sends copy editors, grammarians and even researchers back to their texts on proper English usage. Think of all the money* The Times *could save! Anyway, the incorporation of the very popular "Ms." before Gloria Vanderbilt's name would be a much easier way to write a few simple lines about the woman.*

> *Sincerely,*
> *Goldine Eismann Triantafyllou*
> *Ms. Eismann*
> *Mrs. Triantafyllou*
> *Ms. Triantafyllou (less preferred)*
> *Miss Eismann (definitely* **Verboten***)*
> *New York, New York*

Dear Mr. Safire:
I question the accuracy of the current expressions "turned off, turned on, plugged in." I find them misleading off and on. My new Cuisinart can be plugged in and still turned off till I engage the switch and we're both turned on.

If I didn't need to be punched up in spots, I would be happy to be plugged in to Gloria Vanderbilt's cords, but if they were a neat fit, would I not be well turned out as well as turned on?

> *Sincerely,*
> *(Mrs.) Matilda Komishane*
> *Elizabeth, New Jersey*

---

plural of "um"

"As an F.B.I. agent in the foreign counterintelligence field," writes James Tierney of New York City, "I frequently write intergovernmental memoranda (ums?). The Latin scholar in me insists on the former. However, the dictionary indicates that both forms are correct. In retrospect, the Latin plural might seem to be correct to a fault, or even something of an affectation. Any thoughts?"

When it comes to "um," I take firm positions all over the lot.

On the plural of "memorandum," you pays your money and you takes your choice. The "ums" ending has a four-century pedigree: In Shakespeare's *Henry IV*, Part I, Prince Henry upbraids Falstaff for carrying "memorandums of bawdy-houses" (best little bawdy-house in Stratford-on-Avon). On the other hand, I prefer "memoranda," not only because it is the correct Latin plural, but because it sounds right. The controversy can be avoided by dropping the "randum" entirely: The plural of "memo" is "memos."

On the plural of "medium," it's "media"—which means that you should keep the singular and plural separate. One newspaper is a medium of communication; two newspapers, or two television networks, are media. If you say "The media *is*," you're wrong; the correct construction is "The media *are.*" I have good reason for banging my spoon against the highchair on this; we should resist the notion that "the media" is one vast, amorphous lump. By preserving the plural form, we assert the diverse idea.

On the plural of "datum," it's "data"—but most people are using "data" for the singular, too. "The data shows" comes more readily to the tongue than "the data show." In *Dos, Don'ts and Maybes of English Usage,* Theodore M. Bernstein writes, ". . . the preference in good usage is to keep it a plural," but in reviewing that lucid and sensible book for *Verbatim, The Language Quarterly,* Laurence Urdang disagrees: " 'Data' used as a plural strikes me as a pedanticism."

I think "the data is" is widely accepted and "the data are" is passé; the word is a collective noun construed as singular, as referendums would show.

In sum: "Memorandums" is as correct as "memoranda," but both give way to "memos"; "mediums" is wrong, and "media" takes a plural verb; and "datums" is wrong—in fact, the singular "datum" is dying, and if you want to refer to a single part of the data, try a word like "fact."

"Do I contradict myself?" asked Walt Whitman in *Song of Myself.* "Very well, then, I contradict myself. . . ." It makes no sense to fight for Latin endings when the English language has changed, unless there is a good reason. (One item on a list is known by F.B.I. men and other Latin scholars to be an "agendum," but if you want to be understood, talk about "the first item on the agenda.")

When change does not obfuscate, don't fight it: Legend has it that *New York Tribune* editor Horace Greeley insisted that "news" was plural, and once wired a reporter: "Are there any news?" The prompt, if apocryphal, reply: "Not a new."

re Data is/are?

Dear Mr. Safire:

Here is a sensible resolution of the above debate.

H. J. Tichy (*professor at CUNY and business communications consultant*) believes that writers do conceive of data *sometimes in the singular and sometimes in the plural sense. In* Effective Writing for Engineers, Managers and Scientists *she offers these two sentences (p. 149):*

"This data supports my theory."
"These data are useful in a number of fields."

Professor Tichy *contends that the writer of the first sentence intends* data *to mean "information," whereas the writer of the second sentence intends* data *to mean "facts." Therefore, the simple mental substitution of "facts" or "information" for* data *will help the writer to avoid sentences using* data *with singular verbs and plural pronoun referents (which mixed numbers underscore the writer's ambivalence).*

A neat solution, wot?

Sincerely yours,
Anne M. Lange
Katonah, New York

Dear Mr. Safire:

As a faithful reader of your weekly column in The N.Y. Times Magazine, *I was distressed by your recent comments on the singular "datum." Although "data" used as a plural may strike some as a pedanticism, its singular, far from being moribund, continues to enjoy a well defined role in scientific communication. Furthermore, it will not do to substitute "fact" for "datum," as you suggest.*

The term "datum" *signifies neither more nor less than its literal meaning, a "given" of experience or observation, whereas "fact" carries the connotation of actuality and thus conveys a sense of "truth." The scientific literature abounds in examples of faulty observations due to human error or instrument malfunction (not to mention the occasional, if rare, example of outright fraud). Most of these (n.b.) reported* data *are eventually discovered to be non-facts. In short, to confuse "datum" with "fact" can have awkward consequences, and that's a fact!*

Although my remarks specifically refer to scientific writing, they are also applicable to less formalized usage.

Sincerely yours,
Kurt Mislow
Professor of Chemistry
Princeton University
Princeton, New Jersey

Dear Mr. Safire,
  I think the plural of medium is mediums when referring to 2 or more spiritualists.

Sincerely,
David Sinclair
New York, New York

---

plus, *see* Advertising: Belt the kids!

---

post haste

The Postal Service has a good stunt going which it calls "National Letter Writing Week." Postmaster General William F. Bolger writes: "The Postal Service is attempting to impress on the public that letter writing is a good way to sharpen writing skills, as well as a valuable form of communication."

That sentence does not work. Try it this way, General: "Letter writing is a good way to improve your writing, as well as a good way to communicate."

Whenever we see signs calling attention to National Letter Writing Week, we can do our bit for the cause of good English by inserting a hyphen between "Letter" and "Writing." We do not celebrate a Writing Week sponsored by the National Letter; the nation celebrates a week (a noun) dedicated to letter writing, a pair of words which, when modifying "week," becomes a compound adjective and requires a hyphen.

Have a successful promotion, General, and don't let the letter-writing nitpickers get you down.

---

preorgasmic, *see* prettifiers

---

pre-owner, *see* euphemism

---

presently, *see* Now hear this

---

prettifiers

Time for the 1979 Language Prettification and Avoidance of Ugly Reality Awards. The envelopes, please:

In merchandising: Here is a euphemism for "used" even more attractive than "pre-owned" in the selling of used cars—"experienced" cars. Runner-up is the Philadelphia secondhand dealer who advertised "pre-loved" Oriental carpets.

In the law: When governmental antitrust lawyers think they have discovered a conspiracy to fix prices, they have taken to referring to the practice as "conscious parallelism."

In union organizing: In the tradition of renaming garbagemen "sanitary engineers," people formerly called "maids" or "domestic servants" now do no heavy lifting in a category called "household technicians."

In high culture: Museum curators who hate to admit they have sold any work of art have come up with "deaccession." An accession is a noun that originally meant "a rise to power" and now denotes something purchased or required; as a verb, it means "to record an acquisition." To deaccession is to record the sale or to (yecch!) sell.

In politics: To Afghanistan's state radio goes this year's award for the announcement that President Noor Mohammed Taraki had resigned "for reasons of ill health"; it turned out his health was affected by 12 bullet holes in his body.

In government: Protecting reconstruction of New York's West Side Highway are bumpers which are not called bumpers but "impact attenuators." Candidates for office are now considering impact-attenuator stickers.

In natural monopolies: A singular kudos to the telephone company, which changed the name of "Information" to "Directory Assistance" because, as a phone-company official put it, "many of our subscribers were calling 'Information' for reasons other than to get directory listings."

In medicine: To the Sex Therapy Program at St. Luke's-Roosevelt Hospital in New York for its study of "preorgasmic women," which *The New York Times* reported meant "those who have never had an orgasm . . . and formerly were referred to as frigid."

In traffic-sign trafficking: To all those civic-prettification enthusiasts who have replaced the ominous "Dead End" signs with "No Outlet." (And here, to make the presentation, is "Expectoration," of "The No Outlet Kids.")

Dear Mr. Safire—

As an avid reader of your column in the Sunday Times, *I feel I must point out an error which you quoted today.*

Regarding the Sex Therapy Program at the St. Lukes-Roosevelt Hospital for its study of "preorgasmic women" which The N.Y. Times *reported meant "those who have never had an orgasm . . . and formerly were referred to as frigid."*

Preorgasmic means before or prior *to an orgasm. This could refer to women who usually or always have orgasms and are about to enjoy another one.*

Nonorgasmic or anorgasmic *would have been the proper term for that study, which is closer to the meaning of frigid.*

This from a gynecologist. Thanks for much enjoyment.

> *Yrs,*
> *Alex Charlton, M.D.*
> *Pelham Manor, New York*

Dear Mr. Safire:

Under the "1979 Language Prettification and Avoidance of Ugly Reality Awards," you listed the following:

> *In medicine: To the Sex Therapy Program at St. Luke's-Roosevelt Hospital in New York for its study of "preorgasmic women," which The New York Times reported meant "those who have never had an orgasm . . . and formerly were referred to as frigid."*

My first impulse is to chide you for being sexist, but I think your error is more one of insensitivity. The point of this study—and many others like it—is that so-called "frigid" women are indeed women who have not yet experienced an orgasm. But they may be very capable of warmth and sexual arousal; they have had inept male partners and are not necessarily "frigid" or repressed physically.

> *Ren Draya*
> *New York, New York*

Dear Mr. Safire,

You imply that antitrust lawyers prefer "conscious parallelism" to "conspiracy." This is not quite correct; anyone trying to convince a judge or jury that prices have been illegally fixed would try to prove a conspiracy.

The problem is that case law requires an actual agreement in proof of a conspiracy in violation of the antitrust laws. Where there was no actual agreement, antitrust lawyers try to prove that price-fixers pursued a common course of action without an actual agreement, because each made a rational decision that each other potential conspirator would make the same rational decision to take the lead in restricting output and raising prices, hoping others would follow.

While any plaintiff's lawyer would claim that there is no effective difference between "conscious parallelism" and "conspiracy," the terms are quite different from a legal point of view, since they require different kinds of evidence.

Your point is well taken, however. Some lawyers have recognized the inelegance of "conscious parallelism." They use "tacit collusion."

> *Sincerely yours,*
> *David Landman*
> *Class of 1981*
> *The University of Chicago, The Law School*
> *Chicago, Illinois*

Dear Mr. Safire:

. . . In Connecticut, at least, "No Outlet" is not a synonym or euphemism for "Dead End"; indeed, the sign represents an interesting case of a white lie. Let me explain: All real dead-end streets, cul-de-sacs etc. do indeed have signs at their entrance that say "Dead End." The "No Outlet" signs are posted at the entrance of streets that do lead to other streets (or sometimes back to the same street, having followed a semi-circular path). Why, then, such a misleading sign?

I believe it has to do with the status of the road as a "through" street. If the residents and/or the highway department want to prevent through (and hence lots of) traffic from using a street they post this sign. I offer this hypothesis based on the fact that the school where I live and work can be entered or exited by two roads. These two roads eventually connect (and, hence, are really one road) but since the roads traverse school (private) property and since the school is anxious to keep town traffic off its private roads whenever possible, I surmise that this is how we obtained such a sign.

Since I was as curious as you about the "No Outlet" sign, when I ran across some others I (somewhat defiantly, I thought) immediately turned down them, looking for outlets—and found them in each and every case. The pattern holds: the streets were windy, mostly semi-circular streets in residential areas that curve back to the street you left. Thus, perhaps "outlet" has more metaphysical connotations since you return to the street you left (albeit at a different place and time). Sounds like the myth of Sysyphus. In which case, the Highway Departments are even smarter than we thought; Sartre's No Exit, perhaps would have been better? . . .

> *Cheers,*
> *Grant Wiggins*
> *Chairperson*
> *Philosophy & Religion*
> *The Loomis Chaffee School*
> *Windsor, Connecticut*

pro-

A decade ago, people were "pro-abortion" or "anti-abortion." Now the debate is between people who are "pro-life" or "pro-choice." What brought about this double switch in sloganeering?

After the 1973 Supreme Court decision prohibiting states from making abortion illegal early in pregnancy, opponents of abortion reached for a handle that would not be considered negative. A good example was available in the generation-old movement to oppose the union shop, which called itself "right-to-work" rather than "anti-union." On that analogy, "anti-abortion" became "right-to-life," and later, to save valuable bumper-sticker space, "pro-life." (Nellie Gray, president of March for Life, popularized the latter; she has also been pushing "preborn" rather than "unborn" in order to state more positively the living nature of the unborn child, seeking the analogy of "prenatal.")

Supporters of the campaign to strike down laws prohibiting abortion were caught by surprise at the strong reaction to their court victory, and were flummoxed by the powerful "pro-life" slogan.

They could hardly march under banners proclaiming themselves to be "anti-life"; an even more negative and unacceptable alternative was "pro-death." How could people who were in favor of legal abortion put forward their position positively and punchily?

Here's how, as they say in the ad game: The Religious Coalition for Abortion Rights picked up the idea of "rights" from their opponents; they combined it with an old anti-integration slogan ("freedom of choice") and put forward "right-to-choose." The message in this slogan reached beyond those who already favored legal abortion and appealed to many who had not yet made up their minds. Then, as "right-to-life" became "pro-life," "right-to-choose" followed right along with "pro-choice."

So now we have two equally loaded phrases encapsulating the opposing views: "pro-life," which implicitly derogates all those who disagree as killers, and "pro-choice," which implicitly derogates all those who disagree as dictators. A matched pair of pistols for a bitter duel.

pro-active, *see* **stings and scams**

pronunciation of ee/eye, *see* **Neither is correct**

propertese

A house, courtesan Polly Adler assured us, is not a home. She was mistaken. Under the drumfire of real estate advertising, the word "house" has been replaced by "home."

No heap o' livin' was required. House—a cold word, meaning a structure—was rejected by copywriters a generation ago along with "development," another cold word for look-alike rows of houses. "Home"—a warm word, with nostalgic associations and connotations of family members gathered around a hearth—became the designation for domicile, along with "community."

Accordingly, when what used to be called "row houses"—attached houses—became economically desirable, they were at first called "town houses" and are now in the process of being renamed "town homes."

One real estate advertiser, unhappy with the sound of "town home," consulted his muse and came up with an English term: "mews." Originally, a mews was a stable for horses with living quarters for servants, usually around a courtyard near the manor or estate. Then it became a back street or alley for lower-middle-class tenants, and later a quiet place for city dwellers. Now the news is the new mews: a row of attached houses with a name redolent with chic.

"Manor" and "estate," as used above, are old hat to property salesmen. For single-family homes, today's home builders—let me start again. For single-family houses, builders of today's houses prefer "château"—this is a good year for the château country in the suburbs.

The hottest word in what used to be called "summer houses" (then "second homes," then "leisure homes") is "villa." This jet-set word for a seaside palace can also be applied to a lean-to on the beach.

Happily, abbreviations in the classified advertisements are coming into disfavor: The much-parodied "2 rms riv vu, wbfp" is now "an in-close efficiency with a glorious river view and a wood-burning fireplace for the ecology-minded apartment dweller."

In both houses and apartments, the number of rooms is no longer listed because it has lost all meaning. Rather than "12 rooms," the seller or renter will list "4 bedrooms, 2½ baths, family room, full dining room, library" and

whatever. The "finished basement," that phrase of opulence long ago, is now a "playroom," "wine celler," or "in-house family mortuary."

The kitchen, if large, is called a "country kitchen," and if it is equipped with a faucet that runs boiling water, is called a "gourmet kitchen." If small, it is not mentioned at all.

The real challenge to advertisers is the old, or previously owned, house. The favored way to attract buyers to an old house: "Antique Buffs Only." What if the house is in dire need of repair? "A Handyman Special." And what note of optimism can you insert into an advertisement for a cheap, ramshackle hut that would ruin the neighborhood of a slum? The answer can be found in the beginner's kit of every real estate salesman: "a starter home."

Isn't cellar still spelled cellar?!

> *xx*
> *Marjorie*
> *(Mrs. Donald Mayer)*
> *Asbury Park, New Jersey*

Dear Bill:
You referred to Polly Adler as a "Courtesan."
Would she not more properly be referred to as a "Madam"?
Or, do you know something about Polly that I don't?

Very truly yours,
Philip M. Schlussel
New York, New York

Dear Sir,
The word "Mews" is plural for mew, meaning a cage for hawks or falcons, especially when moulting. The confusion in use of the word came when the Royal Stables at Charing Cross was built on the site of the former royal hawk cages, or Mews. As a result, the word came in time to mean dwellings connected with stables.

Sincerely yours,
Lester Tuchman
Cos Cob, Connecticut

"Q"—there's no "U"

One of those bedrock rules that we always thought kept civilization tied to its moorings was that "q" is always followed by "u." You could be a terrible speller, but when you got to "q," you knew what the next letter was.

No longer. Martin and Lewis broke up; the Beatles separated; now that pervasive, modern fit to split is driving apart the most tightly bound letters of the English alphabet.

Qantas, the Australian airline, started it. That name, touted as "the only word in English where 'q' is not followed by 'u,' " is not a word but an acronym for "Queensland and Northern Territories Aerial Services." Perhaps they should have called it Ausways, or Downunder Airlines, or Thornbirds International, because Qantas—pronounced "kwantas," as if it contained a "u"—opened the floodgates of confusion.

Now we hear that the Ayatollah Khomeini has moved from Teheran to Qum, pronounced "hum" with a gutteral "h." Qum looks normal—its "q" is followed by "u"—but now we're getting reports from Qom (an alternative spelling of "Qum") as well as Qena in Egypt, Qataba in South Yemen, Qadima in Israel, Aqaba in Jordan, and muffled shouts from the Qasr prison in Teheran. All strictly non-"u."

Here's a Q. and A. on "q" and "u":

Q: Why drop the "u" after the "q" in the names of cities in the Middle East?

A: The Hebrew *koph* and the Arabic *gaf* are often not adequately described by the English letter "k." To pronounce some names in the Semitic world, we need a symbol for the sound we make when we are gathering up phlegm in the back of our throats—hence, the "q" without "u." Standing there nakedly, "q" is used to describe the final sound in "Yeccch!"

Q: Where does that leave "q" followed by "u"?

A: That combination stands for "kw," as in "quick" (which could also be spelled "kwik," but it's not).

Q: Does "q" followed by "u" always stand for "kw"?

A: No—in words we have taken directly from French, it stands only for "k." That is why it causes no pique to spell "antique," but it would be grotesque to spell Iraq "Iraque," since its final sound is not "k" but "ach."

Let's hear it, then, for the liberated "q," no longer slave to the queer querulous queries of questing questioners who believe only in the "qu" qua "kw."

For that necessary back-of-the-palate snarl, become a new you with the new "q." Try it on the radical leader of the Libyans, Colonel Qaddafi. Or try it on the Ayatollah himself, ensconced in Qum or Qom: The "kh" in "Khomeini" is another way of imitating that throat-clearing sound, and his name could be spelled "Qomeini."

In months to come, we'll be getting in line to use the 17th letter of our alphabet in a different way; for our new ability to handle the sounds of the Mideast, we can thanq . . .

Dear Mr. Safire,

I'm afraid I must taqe you to tasq.

There are two different Arabic letters with the sound "q," but khe *is not one of them.*

The letter qaf *is written like so:* ق *, and the letter* qein *like so:* ع

These have nearly the same sound—somewhere between the sound of k, q or g; a guttural rupture in the vocal plumbing. Westerners have great difficulty in pronouncing it, and usually settle for a simple hard k or hard g.

Speakers of Persian do not usually differentiate the sounds of qaf and qein; perhaps speakers of Arabic do. (Arabic also has three different 's,' three 'z' and two 't' sounds.)

Qaf and qein have also been transcribed "gh," as in the name "Afghanistan" (qein).

Khe (as in Khomeini) is written ح *, and is an entirely different sound in both*

Arabic and Persian. It has the sound of ch *in the Scottish* loch *and German* Buch.

So if the Ayatollah's name is Qomeini, then mine is Johann Sebastian Baq.

> *Sincerely yours,*
> *Dean Jonathan Askin*
> *Framingham, Massachusetts*

Dear Mr. Safire:

Your "Q-without-u" triggered memories of Du Pont's introduction of "Qiana" nylon in 1968.

This new fiber captures much of the esthetic character of silk while incorporating the performance properties of the man-made fibers. Our initial marketing objective was to challenge silk on its own ground by developing beautiful fabrics designed to be used in haute couture garments.

We needed a trademark that had an exotic sound, a word that would be unusual, memorable, carrying with it—in both sound and appearance—a feeling of elegance and luxury.

From a computer list of more than 5,000 words coined to our specifications of precise length and combinations of vowels and consonants, we winnowed out a handful that seemed to be likely candidates. After some testing and much subjective argument, we chose "Qiana," which was announced on June 27, 1968, in simultaneous press meetings in seven cities in Europe, Latin America and North America.

Anticipating pronunciation problems because of the absence of a "u," we included a phonetic spelling in our press releases and other materials (key-ahn-ah).

Shortly after disclosure of the trademark letters began to arrive from teachers, writers, lexicographers and others all of whom said, in effect, "you can't do that." The absence of a "u" after the "Q" bothered a great many traditionalists. We patiently explained that the word was coined, meant nothing, but was designed to symbolize beauty, elegance and luxury.

Since that time, "Qiana" has become a well-known fiber trademark. At least two children have been named "Qiana." But now and then a "u" still is sneaked into the word in newspapers and magazines, probably inserted by a typographer who is positive the writer erred.

I'm not certain whether "Qantas" or "Qiana" came to light first, but since the former is an acronym, it could be that "Qiana" deserves recognition as the first true Q-non-u word to enter the English language.

> *Sincerely,*
> *James Adshead Jr.*
> *Public Affairs Manager*
> *E. I. du Pont de Nemours & Company*
> *Wilmington, Delaware*

Dear Mr. Safire:

I was surprised to find two misspellings in yesterday's article.

Unless my dictionary is not up-to-date, there is only one way to spell "guttural," and only one way to spell "ensconce."

Very truly yours,
Robert H. Douglass
Chatham, New Jersey

Editor:

In "There's No U" William Safire incorrectly states that "Q" is used to describe the final sound in "Yeccch!" The grapheme "Q" is employed in most phonetic alphabets—and in the transcription of the Semitic words Mr. Safire listed—to describe not the voiceless velar fricative of "Yeccch!" but the voiceless uvular stop, which can best be described to English speakers as a "K" produced very far back in the throat. This sound is not "throat clearing," but rather comes across as a small explosion—as do the other stops.

Phyllis Lee
Department of Linguistics
Columbia University
New York, New York

Quebecker

This department wishes to secede from *The New York Times Manual of Style and Usage* on the subject of the name for residents of Quebec.

"*Quebecer* is preferred in news stories," directs the manual, "but *Québécois* (sing. and pl.) may be used in references to the distinctive French Canadian culture of Quebec; a *Québécois* novelist, or, '*Above all,*' the separatist leader said, '*I am proud to be a Québécois.*' Also: *Parti Québécois,* an exception to the general rule of translating the names of political parties."

To make exception to the exception: I see no more reason to write Canada's Quebecer Party as *Parti Québécois* than to write Germany's Christian Democrats as *Christlich Demokratische Union* or Israel's Labor Party as *Mifleget Poalei Yisrael (Mapai).* If we're going to speak English, let's put it in English. (What about Taiwan's Kuomintang? That's an exception.)

As for *Quebecer,* that spelling seems to call for a pronunciation of *Kwabeese-er.* When René Lévesque (pronounced without the "s," to rhyme with Quebec) recently visited Washington to explain to newsmen his plan for pulling his province out of Canada's federal-style constitutional monarchy, he spelled the word *Quebecker.* In my stylebook, he runs the *Quebecker*

Party, and if one wanted to derogate his supporters in fractured French, they would be *les secesh.* Premier Lévesque, a feisty and charming former newsman who is trilingual (French, Canadian, American), rejects Canada's offer of bilingualism. He does not want English translations on signs in French-speaking Quebec; as for Ottawa's proposals to carry bilingualism to the far reaches of the Yukon, he has a curiously un-Gallic response: "The rest of Canada needs French like a hole in the head."

William Safire:
    As a stickler for correct usage you should be ashamed of yesterday's piece on "Québecer," "Québecois," etc. Throughout the section you put a superfluous acute accent on the second "e."
    You don't need to know much French to know that the word so accented would be pronounced Kay-bay-kwah, a person who lives in Kay-bake.
    If you are correctly quoting the Times Style Book, you should have taken them to task for the error, but I suspect the style book leaves the second "e" accentless.

                                                    Van Vechten Trumbull
                                                    Washington, D.C.

Dear Mr. Trumbull,
    William Safire has passed me your note about the French spelling of Québécois.
    The New York Times Manual of Style and Usage *indeed prescribes both acute accents. Although that usage is not universal, it is preferred by the Canadian Government Bureau of Translation, which we consulted when editing the book.*

                                                    Sincerely,
                                                    Allan M. Siegal
                                                    News Editor
                                                    The New York Times
                                                    New York, New York

---

query

A word I find myself using often lately is "query." Why?
    The answer illustrates the value of "synonymy," as Samuel Johnson's close friend Mrs. Thrale called her study of the subtle differences in the

meaning of those words we lump together all too casually as "synonyms."

The verb "to question" now means "to doubt," or to ask a series of questions. "To query," on the other hand, has a brisk and businesslike air, as it goes above resolving a doubt from an authoritative source. "Query" is sharper than "ask," and—because of its frequent noun use, as in "send a query"—usually carries a connotation of written communication.

Such hair-splitting is considered at the highest levels. President Carter, when he wanted to assert strongly that he had asked the Soviets for an explanation on some provocation, chose the word "interrogate"—it was a step more forceful than "query," was much better than the hat-in-hand "ask," but stopped short of the harsh "cross-examine."

Thus, even as we search our heads in puzzlement, we can choose the precise, almost-perfect word to describe our action or express our wonder. Even when the prose is purple, it is helpful for all who paint with words to know when to pick lavender, mauve, or midnight blue. For example: Where does "to inquire" fit in the spectrum of information-seeking laid out here?

Don't ask me, or write a query. I resist questioning, resent interrogation, and offer cross-examiners a stone wall.

Quotation Demolishers, Inc.

"The only thing necessary for the triumph of evil," wrote Edmund Burke, "is for good men to do nothing."

I like that quotation. (I like the noun "quotation," too, better than "quote," but don't quotate me on that.) That widely known saying by the British political leader of the late 18th century is often used to revile eligible voters who fail to vote, and is used by activists to inveigh against passive-ists.

The trouble is that it may be a phony. When I used the "triumph of evil" quotation recently to condemn complacency, a man named Hamilton A. Long of Philadelphia wrote to ask where and when Burke had said it. I looked for Burke's aphorism in Bartlett's *Familiar Quotations*, 14th edition: There it was, page 454, cited in a letter from Burke to William Smith on January 9, 1795. Condescendingly, I dropped Mr. Long a note telling him to do his homework.

Then the quotation sleuth sprung his trap. "It's not in that letter," Mr. Long replied triumphantly. "Nor any other source quoted in the quotations books I've found. They are false sources." He enclosed a letter to himself from the Daughters of the American Revolution, whose president general, Mrs. Doris Pike White, had said in 1961: "The theme for this year is the old

adage, FOR EVIL TO TRIUMPH, GOOD MEN NEED ONLY DO NOTHING, made immortal by Edmund Burke." The D.A.R. historical researcher gave Mr. Long the correct quotation (apologizing for the "adage" version) and cited *The Great Quotations* by George Seldes as her source. Mr. Long scrawled across the copy: "Seldes admits he can't find correct reference." Plaintively, the D.A.R. researcher had added: "A penciled notation in the copy I consulted reads: 'From a letter to Thomas Mercer.' " Replied Mr. Long with scorn: "No good."

Putting the irritating Mr. Long in his place became important. I wrote the British Library* for the citation with which suitable uppance could be forthcoming. The representative of the Head of the Reading Room Information of the Department of Printed Books replied: "I have been unable to discover the source," and directed me to the Library of Congress—presumably because Burke was a noted friend of the colonials.

The Library of Congress phrase-detective crew has been down this trail before; George Seldes warned them about Mr. Long's challenge. They directed me to an eminent Burke authority at Amherst College, who turned out to be deceased; that was a dead end.

Meanwhile, over at Bartlett's, the editor working on the next edition came up with a speech Burke gave in Parliament on April 23, 1770, titled "Thoughts on the Cause of the Present Discontents." In that address, the British politician said: "When bad men combine, the good must associate; else they will fall one by one, an unpitied sacrifice in a contemptible struggle."

I am reluctant to send that almost-in-the-ball-park reference to Hamilton A. Long, who has moved to Windsor, Vt., since he began sending his persnickety postcards, because I can envision his probable response: "So what?

---

* Responded Gerry Loughran of Brooklyn: "I walked my corner store this morning, chatted the storekeeper. . . ." Okay. I wrote to the British Library. I thought I was pretty smart not writing the British Museum.—W.S.

Thousands of people have said something similar. Why are you and the Quotation Establishment attributing this to Burke? If you can't find a source—and I've read every page of his nine volumes of letters—then confess your ignorance and strike the quotation from all the reference books in the future. Stop perpetuating error!"

Let's face it: The collective wisdom of the Quotation Establishment is cringing in fearful confusion before the onslaught of Hamilton A. Long. Here is a man who evidently feels that he owes us, not his industry only, but his judgment; and he betrays instead of serving us if he sacrifices it to our opinion. (Did Burke say something like that to the electors of Bristol? Who can be sure?)

If Burke did not say the "triumph of evil" line, then who did? It's a great idea, cogently phrased: Somebody, somewhere—a parliamentary press agent, a quotation-book blurb writer—deserves great credit.

Seekers after truth, as well as doting quotesmen everywhere, must reluctantly salute the icon-busting Mr. Long. The only thing necessary for the triumph of misquotation is for wise guys to do nothing. Unless some Burkian scholar refutes him with the genuine citation, that chunk of concentrated wisdom directed to "good men" is declared counterfeit. Evil has triumphed; good guys need do nothing. You don't even have to vote this year.

Postmaster
Windsor, Vermont

Dear Sir:

The statement in yesterday's N.Y. Times Magazine, page 8, that I have "moved to Windsor, Vermont" is without any basis in fact and was simply dreamed up by the writer of that inexcusably careless assertion.

As a result, some of my friends and acquaintances nationwide may write me at Windsor by mistake. Please forward to me in Philadelphia, any such misdirected mail; and send the bill for any expense involved to:

Mr. William Safire
N.Y. Times Bureau
1000 Conn. Ave., NW
Washington, D.C. 20036
Thank you for so doing.

> *Yours truly*
> *Hamilton A. Long*
> *Philadelphia, Pennsylvania*

Copy: Mr. Safire

Robert Entenmann
Somerville, Massachusetts

Dear Mr. Safire:
  The only thing necessary for the triumph of evil is for good men to do nothing. You may quote me on that.

Sincerely yours,
Edmund Burke

---

quotation marks, *see* sneer words

---

real estate lingo, *see* propertese

---

reason why not

"Theirs not to reason why," wrote Lord Tennyson in his *The Charge of the Light Brigade,* "theirs but to do and die."

  The poets who work at the Bureau of Public Affairs of the State Department vaguely recalled Tennyson's words—or the title of Cecil Woodham-Smith's book *The Reason Why* about the ill-fated gallant 600. Although the reason for choosing a military disaster as their metaphor is unclear in this case, the State Department crew titled their publication giving the rationale for the strategic arms limitation treaty *SALT II: The Reasons Why.*

  "The reasons why" is a solecism. (A solecism is what grammatical softliners call "a violation of conventional usage" and what hard-liners call "a mistake in English.") In Tennyson's use, "reason" was a verb, and thus "to reason why" was correct, but when reason is a noun, "why" is not needed. The correct word to follow "reason" is "that," or "for." Not "why," and not "because." The reason why not is because it's redundant, and in this sentence redundant twice over.

  This cause is worth fighting because it makes sense to save words. The reason is that clarity beats clutter (not "the reason why is that clarity beats clutter," or "the reason is because clarity beats clutter").

  Mrs. Woodham-Smith, in dealing with the same subject as Tennyson, was within her rights to play on his phrase in the title of her book. But she confused a great many impressionable readers. As for the SALT-sellers at State—theirs not to make reply.

Dear Mr. Safire:

You reprove unknown State Department functionaries for choosing the title "SALT II: The Reasons Why." Why after the noun reason, *you find, is either a faulty allusion to Tennyson or a solecism. Yet the combination of* reason *with* why *is both well attested in English literature and in keeping with the grammar of English relative clauses.* Bartlett's Familiar Quotations *confirms my remembrance of the ballad*

> *"And shall Trelawney die?*
> *Here's twenty thousand Cornishmen*
> *Will know the reason why."*

written by Robert Stephen Hawker in 1825; as explained in a footnote, Trelawney was a 17th-century prisoner of conscience. Bartlett's index further reminds us of two famous epigrams:

> *If all be true that I do think,*
> *There are five reasons we should drink:*
> *Good wine—a friend—or being dry—*
> *Or lest we should be by and by—*
> *Or any other reason why.*
> *(Henry Aldrich 1647–1710, "Five Reasons for Drinking")*

> *I do not love thee, Doctor Fell.*
> *The reason why I cannot tell;*
> *But this alone I know full well,*
> *I do not love thee, Doctor Fell.*
> *(Tom Brown 1663–1704)*

In all these examples "the reason why" is conversational in style rather than elevated, but is nonetheless good English. . . . You do well to call for brevity in writing; yet not every construction which could be shortened is a solecism. Indeed "the reason why" tout court, as in Brown, Hawker, or the State Depart-

ment, is a fine example of our language's love of omitting words from complex constructions; a grammatically fuller version of Tom Brown's epigram would run

> *I do not love thee, Doctor Fell.*
> *The reason for which I do not love thee, I cannot tell.*

Yours faithfully,
E. W. Browne 3rd
Assistant Professor of Linguistics
Cornell University
Ithaca, New York

Dear Mr. Safire,

I cannot follow your obiter dictum on the idiom "the reason why." You give an example that I cannot quarrel with: "The reason is that clarity beats clutter (*not* 'the reason why is that clarity beats clutter')." No question there: the *why* is pleonastic. But how about: "I know no reason why he opposes me." (*I take that one from Webster's Unabridged, the Second Edition,* s.v. "*why.*") You might reply that it would be briefer to say, "I don't know why . . ."; but brevity, while the soul of wit, does not preclude the correct use of longer phraseology.

Let me conclude with a paragraph from Bergen and Cornelia Evans, *A Dictionary of Contemporary American Usage, page 557*:

> The word *reason is often followed by the word* why, as in I know the reason why he didn't stay. *This use of the word* why *is sometimes condemned as redundant or pleonastic, but the phrase* the reason why *is a standard English idiom, and has been for many centuries. Anyone who wants to can always omit words that are not strictly necessary to his meaning, but if this is done consistently the result is a stiff, unnatural English. As a rule, it is better to be natural than to be correct according to theories that other people have never heard of.*

Why don't you come back on this one?

Sincerely yours,
David S. Landes
Department of Economics
Harvard University
Cambridge, Massachusetts

Redundancy redounds

"Redundant"—with an "a," not "redundent"—is similar to "inundations," since both words are rooted in *unda,* the Latin for "wave." To be inundated is to be overwhelmed by a wave, and to be redundant is to be overflowing, unnecessarily wordy, tautologous, overabundant, excessive, or using too many synonyms in a single definition.

Be very careful in zapping redunders. My first foray was a snarl at the banks which proclaim "free gifts." Churlishly, I demanded: "What other kind of gifts are there?" The correct snarl would have been: "What other kind of gift is there?" Or: "What other kinds of gifts are there?" Verbalists may be disagreeable, but verbs may not.

The mail revealed the existence of The Redundancy Squad, which calls itself The Squad Squad—a group of single-minded citizens dedicated to the elimination of the superfluous.

"New record" infuriates Charles O'Neil of Jamaica, N.Y.: "If it's a record, it's got to be new; if it isn't, it isn't a record." Professor Robert Weigand of Chicago chides *The New York Times* for using a headline with the phrase "Past History." (The newspaper, to its stylistic credit, has dropped the phrase "investigative reporter," because editors felt that all reporters should be investigative.) Louis Wilson of Palo Alto, Calif., sends an advertisement from a furniture company touting "a most unique accent piece"—"unique" should stand alone, with no adjectives to give it a strange accent.

Sometimes redundancies are permissible. After an acronym, the last initialed word can be repeated: "SALT talks," "OPEC countries." ("OPEC" stands for "Organization of Petroleum Exporting Countries," which does not permit "OPEC nations.") And some redundant phrases have been joined together for so long that no grammarian may put them asunder: "bouquet of flowers," "false pretenses," "never before," and "joined together."

If somebody else's use of a redundancy puts a smile on your face, think about "smile on your face"—where else would you smile? Lose face.

Play it again, Sam

I dealt with redundancies—here we go again—in a piece recently, and referred to "Play it again, Sam." The allusion was to the line most old-movie fans remember Humphrey Bogart or Ingrid Bergman to have spoken to pianist "Sam," played by Dooley Wilson—a line that has become the touchstone for nostalgiacs. Rounding up the usual subject, John Wicklein of Long Island Public Television sends in the accurate quotation:

ILSA: Play it once, for old time's sake.
SAM: Play what, Ilse?
ILSA: Play it, Sam—"As Time Goes By."

That was it—no "again" in "Play it again, Sam." But I resist that correction: There is such a thing, in quotation, as "the editing of history." We know that Count Cambronne never said, "The Old Guard dies, but never surrenders"—indeed, the expletive he really used—*merde!*—is known in France as *"le mot Cambronne."* We know that Herbert Hoover never promised "a chicken in every pot" (that was France's Henry II); that F.D.R. never said "My fellow immigrants" to the Daughters of the American Revolution, and Richard Nixon never said "I have a secret plan to end the war." These are all should-be quotations—if the original lacked a sense of history, or was never even spoken, legend does for truth what fact can never do.

I stand uncorrected. Play it again, Sam. . . .

Dear Mr. Safire:
   The "mot de Cambronne"—"de" is obligatory—frequently appears in many French books and periodicals. In most of its uses it is not considered as vulgar or objectionable as its four-letter literate English translation. It is perhaps closer to the word "nuts," used in the Battle of the Bulge in similar circumstances but with quite a happier ending than Cambronne's about 132 years earlier. General McAuliffe must have studied the history of Waterloo.
                                    Sincerely
                                    J. Vuillequez
                                    New York, New York

Dear William Safire,
  Add redundancies: (subtract?)

> *end result*
> *pizza pie*
> *sum total*
> *close proximity*

Leah Harris
Valley Stream, New York

Dear Mr. Safire,
  I must disagree with your example of a redundancy: "Smile on your face."
What else are Irish eyes doing?—So please take that smile off your face. I
must admit mine is usually on when I read "On Language."

Helen Dondy
Larchmont, New York

Dear Mr. Safire:
  Re: today's redundancies—how about revert back *and* Prosciutto Ham *(I*
can't even spell it!). . . .

Wayne S. Goodall
(Ms. McChesney Goodall Jr.)
Chapel Hill, North Carolina

Dear Mr. Safire:
  Mr. John Wicklein of Long Island Public Television may be your regular
informer on film dialogue, but from now on, I suggest you consider his infor-
mation with some degree of suspicion. The correct quotation from Casablanca
is:

> *ILSA: Play it once, Sam, for old time's sake.*
> *SAM: Ah don't know what you mean, Miss Ilsa.*
> *ILSA: Play it, Sam. Play, "As Time Goes By."*

My authority? 21 viewings.

Very truly yours,
Lori Lutz
Boston, Massachusetts

Dear Mr. Safire,
  I disagree with your designation of redundancy in two instances.
  First, a bouquet is not always of flowers. A 'bouquet garni' is a term well
known to cooks. It usually consists of parsley, thyme and bay leaves, but cer-

tainly not petunias and roses. An alternate term is 'herb bouquet.' A wine has a bouquet but this has floral allusions.

Second, a 'new record' is a redundant term when the record is current. The prior record is the 'old record,' or there may be 'older records' or an 'oldest record.' If 'old record' has an opposite it would be the 'new record' soon after its establishment before it becomes well recognized and old hat.

> *Sincerely,*
> *John William Hare*
> *Boston, Massachusetts*

Dear Mr. Safire:
> *Are you full of amorous love today?*
> *Are you tickled by titillations?*
> *Has an osculatory kiss been passed your way,*
> *or the abstract essence of distillations?*
> *The dark-skinned Negro has died in his grave,*
> *the childish infant has sung her song;*
> *the Muscovite Russian is daringly brave,*
> *and the considerable extension of the road is long.*
> *The bantling brat is angrily wrangling,*
> *the worldly earth rolls by, revolving;*
> *you go fishing while I go angling,*
> *intelligent wisdom melting, dissolving.*
> *So wherefore swear these abjurations,*
> *speaking sounds to the Iberian Spaniard?*
> *Why endure the length of durations,*
> *resting the neck in the hooked rope lanyard?*
> *The putrid pear is rotten,*
> *the inebriate drunk besotten,*
> *and my prerogative right*
> *is to put out this luminous light.*

Besides, I seem to be getting redundant again.

> *Sincerely yours,*
> *an interested reader,*
> *Hester Jewell Dawson*
> *Dover, New Jersey*

---

rejection, *see* ostentatious rejection

---

rhetoric

Why has "rhetoric" become a dirty word?

Not so long ago, the predominant meaning was "the art of expressive speech" or "the science of persuasion"; now, the much-abused word, with a root related to "oratory," is laden with artificiality: Empty talk is "mere" rhetoric.

"To those who call for an end to racial rhetoric, I say amen," amened New York City Mayor Ed Koch recently (faintly echoing a line of eight years ago that went "The time may have come when the issue of race could benefit from a period of 'benign neglect' ").

But rhetoric, in its positive sense, fills a linguistic need: "The technique of articulate argument" is too much of a mouthful. If we mean "empty talk," or wish to deride the fulsome fulminations of a blowhard, we already have a large selection of sneering synonyms available: from the euphemism "bushwa" to the acronym "bomfog." ("ZIP," an acronym for "Zone Improvement Plan," is written in all caps; "bomfog," an acronym for "brotherhood of man, fatherhood of God," is not—because it relies on its similarity to two small words.)

The most effective way to rehabilitate "rhetoric," I think, is to offer a colorful, yet suitably pedantic, term to cover its pejorative meaning. The word I have in mind is *bloviation,* a noun back-formed from the verb *bloviate.* (A verb is useful, too—you can't say "rhetoricize," and "orate" does not have the specifically spurious connotation.)

Bloviation is most often associated with the statements of Warren Gamaliel Harding—"Gamalielese," H . L. Mencken called it—but the word has deep roots as an authentic Americanism. In their 1889 Dictionary of Slang, Jargon and Cant, Albert Barrère and Charles Leland placed bloviate's origin before 1850, and defined it as "verbosity, wandering from the subject, and idle or inflated oratory or blowing, by which word it was probably suggested, being partially influenced by 'deviate.' "

So if you mean "bloviating," get off "rhetoric's" back: We need "rhetoric" to do a job that no other word does as well.

For Shame!

Much of my mail these days begins "Shame on you!" and goes on to belabor me—a big-shot language maven—for making some foolish error. An example from Joseph B. Kruskal of Maplewood, N.J.:

"Shame on you! 'Bloviation, a noun back-formed from the verb bloviate,' indeed. As any linguist can plainly see, if the noun developed from the verb it was formed, not back-formed. On the other hand, if the verb developed from the noun, it was back-formed."

My mock-furious correspondent explains: "Addition of a suffix is formation. Removal of what appears to be a standard suffix to create a previously nonexisting form is back-formation." He gives the example of the development of "pea" from "pease"—the collective noun "pease" was the name of the mess of vegetables on a plate, which called for a singular noun for one part of it—hence, "pea." "Pease" is not the plural of "pea"; "pea" is the back-formation from "pease."

Therefore, I should have written that "bloviation" (meaning pompous oratory) was formed (not back-formed) from bloviate. Okay. But what I was trying to do when I used the word "back-formed" was to make a verb ("to back-form") out of a noun ("back-formation")—and lo! I back-formed the verb "to back-form." Very subtle.

Roman numerals, *see* Second, the

---

ru·ing the day

"Embassy of Romania," it says on the front door. Once a year, usually when the Chinese are putting out a feeler, I get an invitation to a reception from "The Ambassador of Romania."

So how come, in *The New York Times,* the country is spelled "Rumania"? If Bucharest's Government wants "Ro," and our State Department goes willingly along, why do we hang in there with "Ru"?

To cite the Columbia Lippincott Gazetteer and the Merriam-Webster Dictionary is not enough; there has to be a more rational rationale for "Ru," especially since the word is rooted in "Roman." Answer: The name is pronounced closer to "roo" than "ro," no matter how the Rumanians spell it; indeed, when they officially spell it in French, it is spelled "Roumanie," which is pronounced "oo," not "oh."

Although I sometimes secede from *Times* usage (preferring "Quebecker" to "Quebecer"), I will not cave in to Communist demands. When they start pronouncing it "Ro-mania," I'll spell it that way, and not until then. That, I think, would be the decision of Brutus, the noblest Ruman of them all.

William Safire
Re: Roh-may-nee-yah.

I rue every Romanian story from The New York Times News Service. I also 'Roh' every Rumanian story I see from The New York Times News Service.

As a copy and news editor for The *(Springfield, Mass.)* Morning Union *and* Springfield Sunday Republican *for 12 years, I have made more deletion marks and insertions—now computer keyboard strokes—changing 'U's' to 'O's' in Rumania than I would care to estimate.*

I was converted to 'Roh' while covering the respective visits of Premier Chou (let's not get into Pinyin) En-lai and then-General Secretary Leonid I. Brezhnev to Romania in the summer of 1966 for UPI.

The Romanians, when speaking Romanian, pronounce it 'roh.' A Russian-Romanian phrase book I picked up in Bucharest, Editura Stiintifica, Bucaresti 1964, confirms as much on Page 13.

It urges Russian learners of Romanian to pronounce the 'o' long, as in tot, vot, kto, etc., the Russian unaccented 'o.'

But you might advise your Romanian reformers that for the sake of consistency, they stop spelling Romanian as Rumanian, in Russian, with the Cyrillic Y, or oo РУММЫНСКИЙ.

Nevertheless, I shall remain steadfast with the Romanians, empathizing with any maverick so bold as to resist both the Soviet Union and The New York Times.

> *Cheers,*
> *Tom Crawford*
> *Wilbraham, Massachusetts*

William Safire:

My roots are Romanian/Rumanian/Roumanian. On my father's "Act De Nastere" (birth certificate) a stamp is affixed with the name "Romania." On the certificate proper appears "Romaniei." How can you expect the correct spelling when an official paper is inconsistent?

To add to the confusion, consider Dorothy Parker:

> *Oh life is a glorious cycle of song*
> *A medley of extemporanea*
> *And love is a thing that can never go wrong*
> *And I am Marie of* Rumania

Perhaps not Brutus, but I am the noblest Rouman of them all.

> *Lena Meyers Klein*
> *Fair Lawn, New Jersey*

Dear Mr. Safire:

You wonder why the Bucharest government refers to its country as Romania instead of Rumania. As proof of the validity of the latter spelling you cite the French term "Roumanie."

I am unable to follow your reasoning. The Academie Française monitors the French language, but I was not aware it had any authority in any other tongue. Although I was brought to the United States at too early an age to have learned the language I distinctly remember my father referring to his native land as "Romanie." My colleague, Dr. Marcel Sufrin, more recently arrived from Romania (Romanie to its inhabitants) assures me that there is no "oo" or "ou" sound whatever in the name of our mutual country of origin. The pronunciation was always the same, even before the Communist takeover.

Please accept my heartfelt apologies for contradicting you.

Sincerely,
Felix Feraru
Great Neck, New York

SALT sticks

Faced with the need to enliven a dreary subject, headline writers have sprinkled us with almost every possible play on SALT, the acronym for Strategic Arms Limitation Talks.

I have written my share: Eighteen months ago, I entitled a diatribe against the people who were promoting the treaty "The SALT Sellers." Another piece, on a less-than-top-level treaty, was labeled "Below the SALT" (a reference to the seating of an unimportant guest past the saltcellars, which once divided the big shots from the small potatoes). Recently, desperate to avoid the overworked acronym, I put forward a suggestion about the arms treaty under the heading "The Saline Solution."

Others have been more brazen. "Passing the SALT" is a favorite of newsmagazine headhunters, and a recent headline describing President Carter's difficulty in winning Senate approval was "The Pinch of SALT." Cartoonists have been picturing the President running after the Senate's Byrd seeking to put salt on his tail.

Before we put away our psalters, we can expect to be peppered with a series of extensions of the salt metaphor, along with the saline efforts of paronomasiacs.

The Senators who join the ranks of the treaty's nitze-pickers will be dubbed "SALT shakers"; politicians who lose their seats as a result of their

advise-and-consent vote will be said to have been sent "up SALT river," and the opponents who grab their salaries will be described as "shedding SALT tears"; those who taunt the President on this matter can be said to be "rubbing SALT in Carter's wounds." Mr. Carter's efforts to "buy" the treaty by spending billions on new weapons like the MX missile will be branded "SALT pork." And if Senator Pete Domenici, Republican of New Mexico, casts his vote in favor of the treaty, you can guess what his nickname will become.

In the midst of this furious play on the treaty that chemists call "NaCl," we should toss a salute to the Foreign Service officer who coined the acronym a decade ago: Robert Martin, who recalls that his superiors at the State Department at that time "did not view the acronym as sufficiently formal and serious." Now the word is accepted even in Russian. Mr. Martin, and those who pioneered the negotiations with him, are today referred to as "old SALTS."

Enough! We must strive to make our future news diet SALT-free.

Salutations

Today is the last day you can get away with "To Whom It May Concern." In a recent piece grumbling about "whom," I asked readers (who may have been concerned) to suggest alternatives to that stilted salutation, and present herewith a bunch.

"Dear Reader" was a heavy favorite among those who liked the "Dear" form, followed by "Dear Recipient" (sounds too much like "occupant" for my taste) and a grumpily asexual "Dear Person." ("Gentleperson" and "Gentle Reader" were also suggested by a pair of tough-minded correspondents.)

The "To" crowd—people who use memo pads on all occasions—went for "To the Interested," "To the Reader," "To Those Concerned" (a good straight translation of T.W.I.M.C.), and "To the Prospective Employer of—." The most effective salutation is the most personal: When writing Julius Caesar, nothing beats "Hail Caesar!" The second best, when addressing a crowd, is to evoke the association of occupation; Napoleon always greeted his men with "Soldiers!" But when taking pen to paper, and addressing some Uriah Heep in an admissions office, or a committee, or perhaps a computer, the need for a personal or an inspiring salutation withers.

A significant portion of the suggestions were for no salutation at all. "I'm sure a guy named Safire," began one letter, "would avoid the whole stilted structure and say, 'A guy named Zilch has asked me to put in a good word for him.' If you use this comment, just say that Zilch himself wrote to you."

That's a good way to avoid the awkwardness or formality or strained informality of a "To Whom" or a "Hi There!" or a "You Don't Know Me, But" on a letter pushing the attributes of one person you hardly know to another person you do not know at all. Begin simply with "This is to commend Josephine Zilch . . ." Or "Here's what I have to say about Josephine, who is looking for a job."

You say you need a heading? Here are a few:

- For your attention (military feeling).
- For your consideration.
- For you to heed (godfather version).
- Dear Admissions Officer (rifleshot approach).
- *Si cuius intersit* ("If it should be of concern to anyone").
- Dear Sir or Madam, as the case may be (from the Henry Morgan radio show of the 1940's).
- Greeting (General Lewis B. Hershey version).

Throughout the mail, the insistent note recurs: The best salutation to a disembodied entity is nothing at all. "Since the days we recognized that there were women as well as men at the end of 'Dear Sir' letters," writes psychology professor Mitchell Berkun of Quinnipiac College, "we have found that no salutation at all works perfectly well. . . . Plunging right in with the text has got as good a response as anything I have ever written and saves a lot of typing besides." He concludes: "With the customary, stilted sincerity."

Now that we've solved how to salute the unknown—how best to close?

"Yours truly" means nothing, "Sincerely" is overworked, "As ever" cautious, "Cordially" just a shade too hearty, "Affectionately" patronizing, "Love" actionable, and "See ya" forlorn. There hasn't been a really good sign-off written since "Your lordship's most humble, obedient servant," written by Samuel Johnson to Lord Chesterfield, a man he despised. Reader suggestions were culled and are reported in the section on "closings."

I was reading your column on salutations *and couldn't refrain from bringing to your attention the very sane way they're handled in Spanish. A letter addressed to either an important person one doesn't know, or an institution, carries the heading, "De mi consideración"; after a half hour of ruminating, I can only come up with a lame and very loose translation as "This is what I have to say," or "It is my considered opinion." When one wants to stress the importance of the addressee, one writes "De mi major consideración"; in essence, that means, "You're a highly respected person and I have something important to tell you." Or something to that effect.*

Traditional endings are also very reasonable: "Saluda a Ud. atentamente" means "(The undersigned) Greets you respectfully"; or simply, this is abbreviated to "Atentamente," or even "atte."

Perhaps in English we could try something along these lines: "For your consideration: You have billed me again for an item I have paid; please reset your computer. Thank you for your attention. With respectful greetings, John Doe."

My respectful greetings to you and thanks for a very informative column—what with English being my fourth language, I need it.

Annemarie Colbin
New York, New York

Sir—for I dare not say my dear Safire,

It is expedient that I should inform you that the undersigned is Crushed. Not only do I find, in a recently published literary production of yours entitled "Salutations," reference to a creature loathed by myself and countless others for more than a century, one I may speak of as a consummate Villain, Forger, and Cheat, a veritable HEEP of infamy, but I find, too, an unforgivable slight to an eminent ancestor. How dare you recklessly asseverate, thereby misleading your innocent readers, that the good Doctor Johnson was the last to commit "a really good sign off" to a letter. Patently untrue!

We have been, sir, an impecunious and wayward family in many respects and are doubtlessly deserving of any and all aspersions cast before us. But still I must affirm that to maliciously overlook the epistolary brilliance of my beloved forebear is NOT called for. Therefore, permit me to refer you and your readers to the correspondence between a misguided but honorable gentleman and the eponymous character—in short, the correspondence faithfully recorded in the Inimitable Boz's David Copperfield. *I am certain that after perusal of this immortal tome you will repent heartily of your statement about Doctor Johnson and that you will agree that the weight of neglect has now been added to the dust and ashes forever scattered*

On
The
Head
Of
Wilkins Micawber
And His Descendent,
Wilkins Micawber V

---

sanction, *see* **floutsmanship**

---

scam, *see* stings and scams

---

season's greetings, *see* yule

Second, the

The use of the Roman numeral "II" seems to have doubled recently, replacing "revisited" or "the return of" or—in stage reversion to its earliest use—"son of."

Jaws II has taken its second bite at the paperback racks, and *The Godfather, Part II* was better than the original movie. The device, which now means any recurrence of the original idea, was stretched to an extreme recently in a Sunday newspaper supplement which headlined Senator George McGovern's description of the genocide in Cambodia as "Holocaust II."

The two-timing was pioneered by the Ford Motor Company, which named its Continental line the Mark II in 1955; the fad for Roman numerals was given a swift kick forward by professional football, which uses the lofty enumeration to designate its Super Bowls.

Where did it all begin? The use of a Roman numeral after the name of a king dates back to ancient times, but the modern use after words rather than names began with the war that broke out in 1939.

That war did not come by its monicker overnight. According to an editor of Merriam-Webster, many publications were referring optimistically to "the war in Europe"; *Time* magazine gloomily began referring to the "second World War" in September 1939, and chose to write it as "World War II." President Franklin Roosevelt was not happy with the phrase: In 1942 he called for the public to make suggestions; after considering the anti-German "Teutonic Plague" and antidictator "Tyrants' War," he chose "The War for Survival." The phrase did not survive.

Finally, in 1945, with historians getting impatient, the *Federal Register* announced that—at the recommendation of Secretaries Henry Stimson and James Forrestal and with the approval of Harry Truman—the late unpleasantness would officially be known as "World War II," just as *Time* had told. The rest, as arch editors of *Playboy* like to say, was history.

It must be a comfort for many people to know that the nuclear holocaust we are now trying to avert is not what H. G. Wells dubbed "the war to end war," but the warmly familiar "World War III."

That numeral habit is infectious; if a follow-up on this subject appears in this space, a catchy subhead comes quickly to mind.

---

second to none, *see* standing busily by

---

self-addressed, *see* pet peeves

"Shame on you!"

Time to clean out the "Shame on you!" file.

In writing that *Hobson's choice* was no choice at all and should not be confused with a *dilemma,* I added, "from whence it became a proverb." Corrected Lisa Schwarzbaum of Cambridge, Mass.: "Whence comes from whence?" *Whence* means "from where," and is never used with "from," which makes it as redundant as "pie" with "pizza."

The salutation "Greetings," recalled as a salutation from a draft board, was misremembered: The Selective Service grabber was the singular "Greeting," which is the sort of thing only Richard Hanser of Mamaroneck, N.Y., would notice.

"It fell between the cracks," I wrote confidently. Wrong. Between the cracks is where the wood is, and nothing falls through that; the expression is "through the cracks," and should not be confused with "between two stools."

A handsome "Group Leader" of the R.A.F. was referred to here, in a piece on the way *group* was overtaking *committee* and *task force*;* my offense was rank. I had in mind a "Squadron Leader," who is usually dashing and doomed; the "Group Captain" is the stodgy one.

You might think that somebody writing about the use of "God" in expletives would spell "deity" correctly. The lion's share of corrections sent in by readers chewed me out for writing "diety," which is not even a word for a very thin god.

Some kindly readers have suggested that mistakes have been placed in this space deliberately to see if anybody is paying attention. Not so. The mistakes are genuine, with the exception of the "lion's share" in the preceding paragraph: The lion's share is not a majority, or the greater part. The lion's share is the whole thing.

* *See "working group."—W.S.*

Dear Mr. Safire:

"Diety, nondiety"? Even without the intervention of a deus ex machina, *you should, for offending the deity of spelling, confine yourself to a diet of worms.*

> *Very truly yours,*
> *Philip Winters*
> *New York, New York*

Mr. William Safire,

. . . There is a lovely construction in which "pie" with "pizza" is not *redundant: "As American as pizza pie." It's not only not redundant, it's absolutely essential, and I'm sure you'll agree.*

> *Arthur Adkins*
> *Associate Professor*
> *University of Maryland*
> *College Park, Maryland*

William Safire

You weren't quite tidy enough when you cleaned out your "Shame on you!" file.

"It fell through the cracks" still is incorrect grammatically, and, therefore, logically. "It" is a singular pronoun. "Cracks" is a plural noun. It just doesn't make sense that a single item is going to fall through multiple cracks.

Thus, the expression should be: "It fell through the crack (singular agreement) or "They fell through the cracks (plural agreement, but stilted and corrupting the original colloquialism).

> *Wallace Abel*
> *Scottsdale, Arizona*

Dear Mr. Safire,

Again I read that "from whence" is incorrect. The translators of the King James version of the Bible were evidently unaware of this grammatical nicety when they wrote, "I will lift up my eyes unto the hills from whence cometh my help. . . ."

Bertrand Russell once wrote that Americans make an inordinate fuss about correct grammar while he & other Englishmen believed that correct English was what good writers wrote. We haven't had many better than the King James translators—hence, I'll use "from whence"—(but probably not frequently).

> *Sincerely yours,*
> *Shirley Deeter*
> *Scottsdale, Arizona*

Shangri, La.

A postcard came in the other day from a man who signed himself " 'Hy' Lama of Shangri, Louisiana." The happy play on a name called to mind the sad passing of the humorist who did so much to satirize clichés by using them for names: S. J. Perelman of *The New Yorker* and Hollywood.

The late author's farm was called Rising Gorge; his brokers were White-lipt & Trembling; his lawyer was Newmown Hay of the firm of Ashen, Livid & Hay (which sometimes clashed with Null, Null & Void) and his architect was Urban Sprawl.

For the names of characters, he chose nouns and adjectives that quickly sketched their features: Prosper Gipf was president of the Absconders' and Defaulters' National Bank; Dewey Naïveté, his real-estate agent; Lowing Klein, his neighbor who raised cows.

Puns were mother's milk: Perelman's favorite street in Hollywood was Mammary Lane (near Plushnick Productions) where Blanche Almonds rescued him from a predatory starlet; for nose and throat problems, he turned to Dr. Lucas Membrane. His favorite "rusty dusty family hotel" was the San Culotte.

Fresh and piquant words would turn up in his work: Barnaby Chirp was the name of a "brilliant young publisher, writer, book reviewer, anthologist, columnist and *flâneur.*" That last word, from the verb *flâner,* "to stroll," means, in French, "one who strolls about aimlessly; an idler."

Perelman named a collection of his writing *The Most of S. J. Perelman,* and professed it to be a heavy tome; my copy was inscribed as "sent together with a small jar of antiphlogiston to rub on your deltoids should you read this compendium in bed."

Now—whether a client of Perlie & Gates, or a member of Beelzebub & Perelman—he has moved on, one hopes, to Green, Pastures, Elysian & Fields.

Dear Mr. Safire,
Flaner is not just a fresh and piquant Perelmanism; it is earthy French slang for 'cruising homosexual.' You missed some of Perelman's piquancy that time.
NB

Dear Mr. Safire:
I think you should reprimand yourself for using the euphemism "passing" when you referred to the death of Mr. S. J. Perelman.
Sincerely yours,
John Cauman
New York, New York

Dear Mr. Safire,

Perelman's marvelous Pun Game you wrote about so affectionately reminded me that I've been accumulating adjectives over the years and then giggling at the gaggle.

Surely Mr. Perelman's insurance agents were Rape, Pillage, Plunder & Burn (a subsidiary of Stagger, Topple & Fall). Nuance & Innuendo were his private investigators, Scylla & Charybdis his plumbers, and Flair, Panache, Duende & Charisma his interior designers.

Rhea Goodman
New York, New York

---

slippage

Two cometlike synonyms, one based in physics and the other in geology, re-enter the earth's political atmosphere every four years, permeate our vocabulary for about six months, and then vanish until four years later.

One term is *slippage,* which physicists know as the difference between the theoretical and the actual output of power. The other is *erosion,* which geologists know as destruction of the earth by such means as wearing-away by water or glacier, from the Latin *erodere,* to gnaw, as by a rodent—as the dictionaries say, "See more at RAT."

In politics, erosions and slippages are what happen to leads. Before conventions, and before elections, leads never grow, or lengthen, or widen; gaps do not merely narrow; instead, the distance between front-runner and the pack is said to suffer "erosion" and "slippage." Watch for these interchangeable pseudoscientific terms, which will begin re-entry in February. After Election Day, what happens to these terms? Does their usage suffer erosion or slippage? No. The words just disappear. See more at "anchor desk."

---

smoking gun, *see* straight arrow, smoking gun

---

sneer words

As the crisis began, those who took over the American Embassy in Teheran were described as Iranian students. After a while, the word "students" began

to appear in quotation marks, as if reporters were uncomfortable with the designation. Finally, former diplomat Henry E. Catto Jr. demanded: "What schools do these people attend? . . . What course are they taking, American Humiliation 101? The fact is that these young Iranians are political terrorists, blackmailers and kidnappers, and they should be so labeled. . . . They are 'students' to the gullible."

Since "students" is a word connoting youth and idealism, many reporters and commentators—to avoid the appearance of being manipulated by propagandists—took to placing quotation marks around the term, or to adding sneer words.

Sneer words are those adjectives that put some distance between the speaker and the subject by saying "I'm using this next word under protest." Examples of sneer words are "self-proclaimed," "self-styled," "would-be," "purported," and that Soviet favorite, "so-called." Thus, the terrorists at the embassy were referred to as "the so-called students"; if the commentator was on television, the listener could almost hear the quotation marks added: "The so-called students . . ." Reporters who were unhappy with quotation marks, but did not want to go so far as to call the occupiers "terrorists," chose the neutral "militants."

The use of quotation marks to say "their word, not mine" is growing. The editor of *American Speech*, John Algeo, says it was noted with disapproval by H. W. and F. G. Fowler in *The King's English*, in the 1931 edition, as a device used by writers who regarded "the reader's case as desperate"; World Book Dictionary editor Sol Steinmetz thinks that "disbelieving quotation marks" first became popular during the Nazi era, and then were given a boost in the Vietnam years, especially around the word "advisers." He cites

247

Time magazine, in 1964, as writing: "Sihanouk . . . claimed that American advisers had been in on the attack," and the same publication, in 1970, as writing: "Soviet 'advisers' serving with the Egyptian army. . . ."

Disdain now has its own punctuation. One reason is that quotation marks are being used more often to call attention to a special meaning: Henry L. Trewhitt of *The Baltimore Sun* calls these "cop-out quotation marks"— when a writer uses a bit of jargon or a colloquialism and encloses it in quotes to show he really knows better. Another reason for putting rabbit ears on a word is the growing popularity of skepticism: Those whose illusion is disillusionment revel in the use of the device that expresses disbelief and disavowal with four inverted commas, and trendy critics can even put quotation signs around a spoken word by wiggling two fingers of each hand.

I've been overworking the quotation-mark disdainer myself (and the hyphenated compound adjective, too) by knocking those self-appointed "guardians" of English "skills" or reviling the language slobs who "enrich" our discourse with quotation "marks." Consider, instead, the style of Charles de Gaulle. He needed no attention-getting ironic quotes to put down the United Nations. He called that organization *"les nations dites unies."*

Dear Mr. Safire:

Regarding "Sneer Words," I found a "beauty" [sic!] in the paper, clipping enclosed: "An avowed atheist." Did you ever notice that one is never simply an atheist! He is always referred to as an avowed atheist.

Sincerely yours,
Gary C. Furin
Atlanta, Georgia

Dear Mr. Safire:

I'm disappointed that your article on the overuse of quotation marks omitted one awful misuse that I encounter quite a bit. Small stores in Manhattan and Brooklyn often place quotation marks around the names of sale items on signs because the proprietors (evidently) think that the rabbit ears merely lend emphasis to a word. For example, billiard balls are not sold in sporting goods stores; "Billiard" balls are. I can't help but wonder if those orbs are not really billiard balls; perhaps they are . . . No, it's unspeakable.

As a high school teacher whose students use quotation marks around every third word, I tried an experiment. I drew two butcher shop signs on the blackboard. One said:

Chopped beef for sale. $1.50 per pound.

The other sign said:

Chopped "beef" for sale. $1.50 per pound.

When asked which store they would patronize, almost all of my students pointed to the second sign. "That one," they assured me, "is the one with the real beef."
I'm not making this up.

> Sincerely,
> Ed Wetschler
> New York, New York

Dear Mr. Safire:
One of Fowler's most charming barbs in The King's English *involves the use of quotation marks:*

EXAMPLE   *John Smith, Esq., 'Chatsworth,' 164 Melton Road, Leamington*

FOWLER'S COMMENT

> *The implication (of the quotation marks) seems to be: living in the house that sensible people call 164 Melton Road, but one fool likes to call Chatsworth.*

My other favorite foot-in-mouth use of quotation marks is that of the elderly lady in Chatham on Cape Cod who kept a rooming house. The sign out front read:

> *ROOMS TO RENT*
> *By day or week*
> —
> *Salesmen*
> *Vacationers*
> *Transients*
> *"Tourists"*

It was a lot funnier 30 years ago, and anyway you had to have been there. . . .

> Very cordially,
> John C. Dowd
> Framingham, Massachusetts

---

so-called, *see* **sneer words**

---

sophisticated, *see* euphemism

---

soundalikes, *see* Mondegreens: "I led the pigeons
to the flag"

---

spelling bee

Most of us are proud of two things we ought to be ashamed of: illegible
handwriting and poor spelling. If our scrawl makes no sense, we assert defiantly: "Einstein had terrible handwriting" (he did not); when we are
caught writing "miniscule" or "embarassing," we *congradulate* ourselves as
if busy writers have no time to be bothered with silly corrections to "minus-
cule," "embarrassing," and "congratulations."

Regular readers of this space ought to be burning with chagrin for flunk-
ing the hidden Spelling Bee cleverly embedded in these lines a few weeks
ago.

One test question identified a letter writer as a man working in the United
States Embassy in Columbia. Gordon Bock, on the city desk of United Press
International in New York, whose booming adjuration "Downhold mis-
takes!" sends shivers of inspiration through his colleagues, passed the test
and wrote: "One question: Is Everett Briggs employed in the U.S. Mission in
Columbia, S.C., or on the Columbia University campus?"

The South American country is, of course, non-U: Colombia, with an "o."
Another test passer, Liane Gutman of New York, wrote to explain: "There
is no English spelling for Colombia. Christobal Colon is the Spanish name
for Christopher Columbus, and I assume the South American republic is
named after him. The reason for the change from 'n' to 'm' before 'b'—i.e.,
Colombia and not Colonbia—is a phonetic one." (Colonbia is a vacation
spot for ulcer sufferers.)

The next question in the hidden Spelling Bee was my reference to Jim
Fisk's "corrupt Eire ring" in upper New York State.* "What were they
doing?" demands alert Charles A. O'Neil of New York, "selling watered
shamrocks to gullible shareholders?" "Eire" is the Gaelic name, and former
official name, of Ireland; "Erie" is the lake, and the canal, and the corrupt
ring.

* See "verbs from nouns."—W. S.

Am I getting away with this spelling-bee charade? I think not. Nor is it advisable for me to try to shift the blame to copy editors who have been putting together an extensive file of embarassments (embarrassments?) from which they have saved me, for blackmail purposes. Nor is "transmission error" a good alibi: The fast fist who usually sends this copy from the Washington bureau of *The New York Times* is an orthographic superstar who would retaliate by sending my stuff out warts and all.

The truth is that I have never been good at spelling, which most of my teachers and friends never knew, because they couldn't read my handwriting. But at least I'm not proud of either.

Mr. William Safire

In view of your confession that you never have been good at spelling, it will be no surprise to you that you did it again!

Christobal Colon is not *the correct Spanish name of Christopher Columbus!!!*

> *Yours truly,*
> *José de Vinck*
> *Allendale, New Jersey*

Hit Me

When the nation of Colombia was herein misspelled "Columbia," I ran a correction from Liane Gutman of New York, who wrote, "Cristobal Colon is the Spanish name for Christopher Columbus." However, I mistranscribed her letter to read "Christobal Colon," and Miss Gutman, who is proud of being the best speller on her block, was profoundly embarrassed (two r's, two s's) by the incorrect "h." Nothing else will ever appear in this space about Latin America.

Next, a woman White House aide was referred to here as a "honcha," a word mistakenly assumed to be the feminine form of "honcho," which is a term in vogue for "person in charge." That was not just a mistake, but a *filet*

251

de solecism: "Honcho" is a Japanese word for "squad leader," and a woman who is in charge is also a honcho.

Finally, in explaining the variety of slang meanings of the noun "hit," now best known as a "line," or dose, of cocaine, I suggested that poker players would say "Hit me." Card sharks from all over sniffed at my error: The phrase belongs to blackjack and occasionally to pinochle.

Spit of '76

Compulsive correctors like to take the old phrase "spit 'n' image" and prettify it to "spitting image." That's a mistake: "Spit" means "perfect likeness," and the "n" sound stands for "and" (as in "soup 'n' fish," which should not be corrected to "souping fish").

In a piece about soundalikes entitled "I led the pigeons to the flag"— which veteran readers mistakenly refer to as "I paid the legion for the flag"—I excoriated the snobbish changing of "spit 'n' " to "spitting." However, I was unable to come up with a decent etymology of "spit"—although its origin as a verb, meaning "to propel from the mouth," can be traced to the 10th century; its origin as a noun, meaning "likeness," is obscure.

Atlanta-born Jean Glick writes to suggest that "spit" should be written as "spi't"—that is, "spirit," or "ghost." "The child is the spirit and image [vocalized "spi't 'n' image"] of his father," she speculates, adding facetiously: "This eliminates the need for an expectorant parent."

She could be right; many old English forms are preserved in U.S. Southern regionalisms, and "spirit" seems to make more sense as a meaning for "counterpart" than the spewing action that signs in the subway prohibit.

Such folk etymology is seductive, but it is hard to dispute Eric Partridge, the Samuel Johnson of slang, who held that the phrase "spit 'n' image" came

from the notion of "speaking likeness." He cited uses in the early 17th century to make the point: "He's e'en as like thee as th' had'st spit him."

As a gun lobbyist would say: "Images don't spit—people do." Though others may summon spi'ts from the vasty deep, I will hang tough on the derivation from "spit," meaning "likeness," with an American redundancy—"and image"—tacked on later. Further correspondence on this matter will be unavailing.

Dear Mr. Safire,

Your speculation on "spit 'n image" reminded me of a literary device known as hendiadys whereby two nouns connected by and *express the idea of a noun and adjective. (E.g. we drink from* cups and gold, *for* golden cups.)

This device is used in the Bible, e.g. Genesis 47:29: hesed we'emet, kindness and truth *properly translated as steadfast loyalty. The hendiadys is used in Greek poetry as well as in English poetry.*

Is it possible that spit 'n image *is such a form, meaning* exact likeness?

Sincerely,
Menahem Meier, Ph.D.
Teaneck, New Jersey

Dear Sir:

When one polishes something made of brass, he first spits on it, and then rubs it vigorously with a cloth until he can see his own image reflected from it. From this practice came such expressions as: "spit 'n' polish," "spit-shined" and "spit 'n' image."

Respectfully yours,
Stephen P. Anthony
Concord, Massachusetts

Dear Mr. Safire,

Surely, "spit 'n image" is "spitten image" (spit, spat, spitten) and the spit refers not to expectoration, but to ejaculation. So, oyster 'spat.' Hence, one is always the "spitten image" of a father, never a mother nor other relative.

The antiquity of the phrase is indicated not only by the obsolete past participle, but by the mediaeval biology (theology?) involved: the belief that the child was contained intact in the father's semen, the "homunculus." A son who resembled his father grew up to look just like he was when spewn from his father's body: a spitten image.

Partridge, Origins, *records the archaic "spitten" but then gets wondrously naive about what it means. As he also is about oyster 'spat' ("o.o.o.," he says, "perhaps from spot") and about 'spawn' (from Latin* expandere, *he thinks), when they are surely the same word with the generalized meaning "spew" (itself related).*

At least he is not so naive as to suppose the English language would contain, for centuries, the clumsy redundancy "spit and image," meaning likeness and likeness, especially when the supposed meaning of likeness for "spit" is found only in the phrase. For shame, Mr. Safire!

> Sincerely,
> Robert R. McBride
> Pittsburgh, Pennsylvania

Dear Mr. Safire:

Don't be too sure that spitting image isn't correct. Down home in middle Tennessee there is an expression that I first heard at the knee of my maternal grandmother. Here is the scenario:

One lady might say to another, "Why look at that Parker boy, Ida! He sure does look like his daddy, doesn't he?"

And the other lady might answer: "I do declare. Mr. Parker can't deny that young un. He spit and he grew."

Just a thought that you might consider.

> Very truly yours,
> Willard Largent
> Cleveland, Ohio

---

spookspeak

"U.P.S."—to most of us not on downers—is initialese for United Parcel Service. To the guardians of the nation's secrets, however, U.P.S. stands for "uncontested physical searches," the newest euphemism for the break-ins formerly known as "black-bag jobs."

It's good to know that the spooks are coming up with new terms for temporarily unpopular activities, after their long linguistic freeze: The once-secret language of secrecy has become too widely known. To qualify as argot, a lingo must retain its sense of mystery—once in print, an argot is no-go.

Take "mole," which professional spies and readers of spy thrillers know means "an agent clandestinely placed within another power's intelligence agency." That word, insists former Director of Central Intelligence Richard Helms, was never used by the professionals—their term for that dread activity was "penetration." But today, as life follows art, C.I.A. men have adopted "mole," and intelligence historian Walter Pforzheimer even found

a 1622 citation in Francis Bacon's history of King Henry VII: "Hee was carefull and liberall to obtaine good Intelligence from all parts abroad. . . . He had such Moles perpetually working and casting to undermine him."

The language of classification is aging. The three main categories—"Top Secret," "Secret," and "Confidential"—are well known. ("Administratively Confidential," used often in the White House and the departments, is not a security classification, merely a way of stamping a document with "C'mon, you guys, let's not leak this until next week; it could embarrass us in New Hampshire.")

Along with each classification goes a distribution signal. Readers with security clearance (a "Q" clearance, the status symbol of a generation ago, applies to atomic secrets and is no longer anything to brag about) may see "LIMDIS," "EXDIS," or even "NODIS" atop a message. LIMDIS—limited distribution—means: "Hold this to about 50 people; we don't want it out right away." EXDIS adds a green cover sheet and makes the distribution "exclusive" to a dozen or so officials. NODIS comes closest to the facetious "Burn Before Reading" and is sometimes hyped with "Eyes Only." (Arnold Weber, a former budget official, who wanted his directives carefully chewed over during the era of price controls, stamped his memos "Teeth Only.")

Other distribution designations you are likely to see if leaked a classified document are "NOFORN," which is not a moral stricture but stands for "No Foreign Dissemination," a xenophobic "Americans Only," and "NO-CONTRACT," which means "Keep this inside the Defense Department and don't let those contractors working on the Norden bombsight glom on to it."

To answer the question "How do we know this—did we read it in the paper, or what?" spookspeakers include another acronym to identify the type of source. The much-mentioned "ELINT," which I once suspected referred to the bits of fluff or thread on the blue serge suits of undercover agents, turns out to be "electronic intelligence," or "electronic intercept"—stuff from bugs and the like—not to be confused with "COMINT," or "communications intelligence," from blabbermouthed satellites or radios, heard by "big ears." "WNINTEL," which means "Warning: Intelligence," is neither of the above, and gives the incognoscenti the impression of being a rueful self-criticism of the product.

Because such terminology has been around so long, and is so well known to foreign intelligence agencies, no thrill of leakage attaches to discussing it here. Specific "channels" of distribution do not affect national security, and current code names deserve continued privacy.

In his 1973 book *The Politics of Lying,* reporter David Wise revealed what happened when a code name slipped into a picture published in *The New York Times Magazine* in the mid-60's. The picture showed McGeorge Bundy, then national security adviser, conferring with President Johnson; in Bundy's hand was a partly obscured document headed "TOP SECRET DINAR"—"DINAR" was then a closely guarded Vietnam code word. After dropping by *The Times* to pick up the negative, which the newspaper willingly handed over, C.I.A. men spent some $250,000 retrieving all documents about DINAR around the world and restamping them "UMBRA."

Code names can also contribute to confusion. I was present at a conversation between Henry Kissinger and Defense Secretary Laird in 1970 as they argued over "toxin"; it later turned out one man was talking about ending our capacity for germ warfare while the other thought he meant "Operation TOCSIN," a wholly unrelated battle cry.

It is not always a good idea to kid around with spookspeak. When writing a Vietnam cease-fire speech for President Nixon, I was given a "point sheet" of items to be included from the Kissinger shop, each page carefully headed with a variety of secret designations. In my speech draft, I gaily festooned the cover page with a collection of labels that showed just how hush-hush and important my work could be: "TOP SECRET SENSITIVE NOFORN EYES ONLY."

A couple of days later, I asked Bob Haldeman to let me have the speech draft back, because it required more work. The staff chief shook his head: "Sorry, I can't give it back—you're not cleared for TOP SECRET SENSITIVE NOFORN EYES ONLY."

Dear Mr. Safire,

In "Spookspeak," you've made a couple of "boo-boos." Before I give them to you, I have to give you another acronym which you missed—SIGINT—signals intelligence. This is the term which encompasses both ELINT and COMINT. It is defined as "The intelligence derived from the interception and processing of electromagnetic radiations other than those caused by a nuclear detonation." (Presumably there is another kind of "INT" for the latter, but I don't know what it is.)

COMINT is that part of SIGINT derived from radiations that carry an in-

telligible language—radio, radio teletype, etc.—that can be processed into English. ELINT is the rest of it—radar signals, telemetry, guidance systems signals and the like.

By law, as well as by practice, SIGINT does not include intelligence obtained by wiretaps or from "bugs," unless the bug is a radio transmitter. . . .

Your second "boo-boo" concerned the codeword DINAR. Rather than a "Vietnam codeword," as you described it, DINAR, as well as its successor, simply identified the material as having been derived from signals intelligence. Presumably, (although I don't know for sure), other codewords exist to identify other sources of intelligence. Since different sources of intelligence have varying degrees of validity and reliability, such identifications are helpful to the decision-makers when two analyses conflict, and they have to decide on a course of action based on one of them. . . .

> *Sincerely,*
> *Dick Tubbs*
> *(Richard H. Tubbs)*
> *Kensington, Maryland*

---

standing busily by

Politicians of all stripes and ilks like to put on a grim look and warn the Soviet Union that the United States will not "stand idly by" if the Soviets seek to take advantage of the turmoil in Iran.

Bystanding, usually the occupation of the innocent, gains a connotation of cowardice when the term is combined with "idle"—to "stand idly by" is always presented as something one should not do, and is often used when it may not be wise to say what one may do.

At a time when United States foreign policy often counsels restraint, there is a need—not quite a crying need, but a need—for a phrase that puts restraint in positive terms.

To illustrate: Throughout the Presidential campaign of 1968, a favorite Nixon applause line was "America must remain number one"; came responsibility in the White House in 1969, some other locution was needed that could accommodate the need for nuclear parity between the superpowers. "Parity" sounded like a farm problem; "sufficiency" sounded weak. The solution was a line that seemed to satisfy the public's desire to be number one, but that actually only promised a tie: "America must be second to none!" (The idea came from the United States Army's Second Infantry Division motto, "Second to None.")

Similarly, advertisers whose product is neither better nor worse than their

competitors' can truthfully exult: "Unsurpassed in fighting tooth decay!" "Unsurpassed," on the sober second thought, is like "second to none"—as good as, but not better than.

How can "standing idly by" be given this creative lift? The history books offer some ideas:

When Woodrow Wilson did not want to be drawn into a war with Mexico in 1913, he told Congress: "We shall not, I believe, be obliged to alter our policy of watchful waiting." That was a catchy phrase, giving a delay a purposeful quality.

Other political figures have tried "let the dust settle," but that retains a vague "who-lost-China" connotation. The best man in the oxymoronic field of doing nothing with great energy and industriousness was Sir James Mackintosh (1765–1832), who espoused the theory of "disciplined inaction," and reached the acme of heated freezing with the classic phrase "masterly inactivity."

Those who practice "masterly inactivity" today like the slogan "Don't just do something—stand there!"

Dear Mr. Safire:

Concerning your recent column on what the U.S. does when it wishes to display watchful restraint in international affairs—the solution is obvious. We take a "wait-and-see-attitude." ...

> *Sincerely,*
> *Jerome Foster*
> *West Redding, Connecticut*

state of the art

"You an inventor, or what?" The news clerk (formerly copy boy) has been wondering why, in the mail he sorts, I have been getting so many letters from patent attorneys.

The reason is a query in this space a while ago about "state of the art," a fashionable phrase applied to everything from aircraft design to cheating at cards.

Robert Sanborn of Vineyard Haven, Mass., a retired patent attorney, directs us to the "art" part of the phrase in Article I, Section 8 of the United States Constitution: "The Congress shall have power . . . to promote the progress of science and useful arts. . . ." Patent law describes existing technology as "prior art." That's close to "state of the art," but no cigar.

A chemist was also helpful. "Back in antiquity," writes Robert Rabinowitz of Norwich, N.Y., "when physicians really wrote prescriptions in Latin, and pharmacists actually compounded them, there were two related directions in common use.

"One was *'Fiat secundum artis regulas,'* or, 'Let it be made according to the rules of the art,' and the other was the terse *'secundum artem,'* or, 'according to the art.' In this way, the pharmacist was directed to use his skill, knowledge and judgment to produce an elegant dosage in a manner reflecting the 'state of the art.'"

That comes closer than ever, but we still have no "first use" of the phrase "state of the art," and nobody will have to pay a psychic income tax.

We are rewarded with this bit of serendipity, however: Mr. Rabinowitz, who describes himself as "an explosive chemist," notes that a professional organization, the American Oil Chemists Society, is so named because of its interest in animal and vegetable oils, and has nothing to do with petroleum derivatives; its members were willing to risk confusion with petroleum chemists because they did not want to belong to an organization called "The American Fat Chemists Society."

Stengelese

Baseball manager Casey Stengel is immortalized in the Linguistic Hall of Fame because he delivered the kind of earnestly confused double-talk that spawned the word "Stengelese." In Stengelese, a familiar phrase is taken and given a twist that turns a truism into a puzzling falsism.

Casey once admiringly said of a lucky player: "He could fall in a hole and come up with a silver spoon."

When the House of Representatives recently went on live television for the first time, cameras caught the vigorous, cigar-smoking Millicent Fenwick (Rep.-N.J.) decrying a proposal to set up a committee to study other committees: "This is a half loaf," she declared, "because we're too greedy to take the other half."

---

stings and scams

"That cove is too fly," confided the English thief in his argot; "he's been stung before." In J. H. Vaux's Flash Dictionary, published in 1812, that language was translated as "That man is on his guard; he has already been trick'd."

An earlier slang lexicographer, Captain Frances Grose, defined a "stingbum" in 1788 as "a niggard," a miser. Late in the 19th century, the meaning of "sting," as both verb and noun, shifted to simple thievery when it traveled to the United States. George Henderson's 1924 *Keys to Crookdom* cited this example: "Sting him for his rocks—steal his diamonds."

Then the element of trickery took over. A "sting" became the name of a small but successful confidence game; among tramps, it was a nice case of defrauding while begging. The word was popularized outside the petty rackets by David Ward, a screenwriter who wrote the 1973 movie *The Sting*, starring Paul Newman and Robert Redford as a pair of con men in the 30's.

" 'Sting' is standard con-man lingo," Mr. Ward informs me. "It's when

the 'mark' hands over the money. The 'mark' is the stingee, the one who's stung."

However, the notion of a sting as a large-scale fraudulent enterprise—as depicted in the movie and, as life followed art, by the F.B.I. in 1976 and 1980—is disputed by an anonymous underworld source, who recently told slanguist Stuart Berg Flexner: "The operation in the movie was a big operation—too big to be a sting. The movie should have been called *Wire Game,* which is a big con game." The shifty source added: " 'Scam' and 'sting' are underworld slang for small-time illegal operations for very little money. Small con games."

"Scam" has a simpler history. The word was spawned at carnivals, where games of chance were rigged to fleece customers. Some say it may have come from "scamp's game"; others point to the word's possible origin as a variant of "shame," but that's all guesswork—no precarny citations have been found.

"Abscam" is the F.B.I. code name for "Arab Scam"*; the operation to catch corrupt officials was called a "sting," in its movie-usage sense of a large confidence game. Neither "sting" nor "scam" will ever be small potatoes anymore; the meaning is now fixed as a large-scale operation, complete with video recording.

Another word has been coined at the F.B.I. in connection with this headline-making endeavor: "pro-active" investigations. F.B.I. Director William Webster says he has been forced to choose between "reactive" law enforcement—responding after a bank has been robbed—and "pro-active" enforcement, in which his men are in on the planning stages of a crime. Others would use "provocative," rather than "pro-active," as a more accurate antonym to "reactive."

Lawyers for the "marks" will be using a few words and phrases that students of the sting-and-scam lexicon should become familiar with. "Entrapment," first used in 1597 to mean "catch by artifice," means in law the inducement by the police of an otherwise disinclined party to commit a crime concocted by the government. The key is whether the trapped person was "predisposed" to commit the crime.

Some civil libertarians will add that the ensnared and highly publicized "stingees," in screenwriter Ward's useful word, have been denied "due process." That's an example of a couple of lackluster words combining to form a majestic phrase—the barrier keeping kings and lawmen from arbitrarily snatching away the liberties of citizens.

"Due process" first appears in the United States Constitution in the Fifth Amendment, bottomed on the Virginia Declaration of Rights, which traces its heritage to the 1354 statute of King Edward III: "That no man of what estate or condition that he be, shall be put out of land or Tenement, nor

---

* *Assistant Attorney General Philip Heymann, sensitive to criticism about ethnic slurs, insists the word was a shortening of "Abdul Scam."—W. S.*

taken, nor imprisoned, nor disinherited, nor put to Death, without being brought to Answer by due Process of the Law." Since that great day, many coves have been too fly to get stung by the fuzz.

Dear Mr. Safire,
  About SCAM:
  It probably derives from French

> ESCAMOTAGE = *juggling, filching*
> ESCAMOTEUR—EUSE = *juggler, conjurer, fleecer, pickpocket.*

My guess is that it came here as a gypsy neologism.

> *Sincerely,*
> *Saul Steinberg*
> The New Yorker
> *New York, New York*

---

straight arrow, smoking gun

"A 'Straight Arrow' Quits the Pentagon" was a headline in *The New York Times Week in Review* about Stanley Resor, described as a " 'straight-arrow' public servant who simply got 'frozen out' by a bureaucracy whose power games he had no taste for."

As every aficionado of Watergate lingo knows, "straight arrow" (hyphenated when an adjective, but not when used as a noun) denotes a person of pristine probity: one who would never deviate from the straight and narrow, no matter how strait the gate.

Where did the term originate? In the 16th century, straight gained a meaning of honest, and an early citation in the Oxford English Dictionary offers the simile "straight as a shingle." In women, straight meant virtuous, and "straight as an arrow" was a natural variant of "shingle" to speakers not engaged in roofing.

In the 1940's and 50's, slanguist Stuart Berg Flexner informs me, musicians gave the word a connotation of square—conservative, establishment, not jazzy. In another context but in a related usage, "straight" became the opposite of "gay." Also, as used by drug addicts, the adjective "straight" was applied to a nonuser, in the same way as one who despises all conventions uses "conventional."

In 1967, Jann Wenner chose the name Straight Arrow for his publishing house, which prints *Rolling Stone* magazine and otherwise gathers little moss. Mr. Wenner says he took the name from the phrase "straight as an arrow" because it was a term meaning "honest" and "square dealing." He says he did not intend it to be ironic.

The phrase was snapped up by the counterculture of the late 60's, followed by the eager-to-be-with-it crowd in politics; however, "straight arrow" soon gained its connotation of "Boy Scout" or "jock," in the way that the meaning of "straight" was twisted from "honest" to "conventional."

There you have the origin of "straight arrow," with its current coloration; in a related etymological breakthrough, I have run across the roots of another Watergate favorite, "smoking pistol."

The smoking pistol, or gun, meant the crucial piece of evidence; the cover-up instructions on the White House tape of June 23, 1972, became the smoking pistol that caused Richard Nixon to resign.

A Baker Street Irregular, Peter Blau of Washington, D.C., has nailed down the phrase's first use in its guilt-proving sense (until someone else sends an earlier citation). In the Sherlock Holmes mystery *The Gloria Scott,* first published in *The Strand Magazine* in April 1893, author Arthur Conan Doyle has a character describe a mutiny on a convict ship: "Then we rushed on into the captain's cabin, but as we pushed open the door there was an explosion from within, and there he lay with his brains smeared over the chart of the Atlantic which was pinned upon the table, while the chaplain stood with a smoking pistol in his hand at his elbow."

Dear Mr. Safire,

Your exhaustive historical derivation of the term "straight arrow" suffers from a serious omission, or rather falls short of the mark. We refer to the popular radio drama figure of the 1950's, the redoubtable Straight Arrow.

Straight Arrow was an Indian who was transformed from the savagery of his native people to the civilized ways of the white man. He lived as a mild-mannered rancher, but whenever that white society spawned evil, he re-assumed his Indian personna, mounted his golden palomino, and through the agency of his vaunted golden arrows, righted the wrong.

The example of this Lone Ranger/Superman type red man, of "pristine probity" as you describe, avenging the evils of his adopted society, was not lost on the pre-TV generation. The program was beamed at dinner time, and so we took a steady diet of do-gooder adventurers with our evening meals, including Sky King, Lone Ranger, Green Hornet, Sargeant Preston and Yukon King, and others. But Straight Arrow made such a profound impression that he is now the archetypal principled man enshrined in today's language.

There is a perjorative sense to "straight arrow," and thus, he has been depersonalized into a lower case appellation. Kids saw Straight Arrow as someone who did no evil, a position most middle class youngsters were ready to embrace. During college days, however, this position seemed quite shallow, for it failed to include the subtle nuances of temptation, the pleasures and lusts of adult life, the mature realization that rules can be bent and broken. Straight Arrow would never acknowledge, much less wink at, the usual monkey business associated with everyday life, and hence, the ambivalence.

Nevertheless, if you were to poll the 36–45 year age group, you probably would confirm that eating a bowl of Nabisco Shredded Wheat, the radio show's sponsor, still evokes, in Pavlovian fashion, the sound of the hoof beats and the tom-tom rhythm of that incorruptible hero, Straight Arrow.

Sidney P. Kadish, M.D.
Richard P. Goldwater, M.D.
Saint Vincent Hospital
Worcester, Massachusetts

Dear Mr. Safire,

You seem to regard "Boy Scout" and "straight" as synonyms for "jock." You may be right, but I have the impression that the word "jocks" was first applied to college athletes because they wore jockstraps. Today it may even apply to college athletes and their associates.

Sincerely,
David L. Graham
Freeport, Maine

Dear Mr. Safire:

About Straight Arrow:

I suspect the users of the term in the 60s were influenced by the radio program of the late 40s.

"Straight Arrow" was broadcast on Mutual for three seasons beginning in 1948, first as a 30-minute evening program and later twice a week in the afternoon. It was a typical ("classic") kids thriller serial drama.

The hero was white but had been raised by Comanches. When aroused to fight the bad guys he wore his Indian costume and had a horse named Comanche.

The program was sponsored by Nabisco which used the character in other advertising.

As I recall the Nabisco was in three layers in the Shredded Wheat box, separated by cardboards about 4 × 6 inches. These contained stories about "Straight Arrow" in cartoon form that could be colored but also had Indian lore and things to make.

"Straight Arrow" was as pristine as all of the afternoon radio heros. I am sure many of us were influenced to use the term "straight arrow" to refer to one who was pure, clean, honest, moral . . . in part because of this program. As I

recall in Southern California we (in the late 50s) used it more often to refer to girls but that might be a regional or personal perspective.

> *Sincerely,*
> *Lawrence W. Lichty*
> *Falls Church, Virginia*

Dear William Safire:

Sometime in the late forties, probably about the time radio was losing out to television for child listeners—or at least late enough for me that I did not give it the attention I had earlier accorded Superman, Tom Mix, Captain Midnight and the rest of the pantheon—there was a radio program called "Straight Arrow."

I remember only its beginning. An announcer describes, in hushed tones, the appearance of an Indian on the edge of a clearing. He sights a distant target, puts arrow to bow, draws and waits for the right moment. He releases the bow; we hear the whizzing sound of an arrow in flight, then the solid thunk of the arrow sinking deep into its target. Then the announcer intones portentously, "STIR-RAI-AIGHT AA-RROW."

My recollection is that the hero had one of those dual identities which were so popular then—by day Clark Kent, Lamont Cranston or Britt Reid; by night Superman, the Shadow or the Green Hornet. That recollection may only be my imagination working on the character to make it conform to the mythos, but I am sure about the way the program opened, and I never hear anyone described as straight arrow without associating him with that model of righteous straight shooting.

> *Sincerely,*
> *Paul A. Lacey*
> *Richmond, Indiana*

---

students, *see* sneer words

---

subsume

The new vogue word that has co-opted co-opt is "subsume." No academic can hand in a paper without having pointed out how Idea A has subsumed Idea B, or why the policy of détente has been subsumed by the rush of events. The word is often misused to mean "gobbled up by," or "overtaken by," or "become subservient to," which is a confusion with "consumed."

"To subsume" means to include within a larger group: "The problem of inflation is subsumed by the overall issue of the economy." It means "to encompass," but does not mean—as the vogue users have garbled it to mean—"to dominate" or "to put down." (Sighted "subsume"; sank same.)

syn

The Federal bureaucracy, and its handmaiden, the Washington press corps, are pleased to announce the birth of a word: "synfuels," for "synthetic fuels," those delicious slices of pie in the energy sky.

On the analogy of "comsymp" (for "communist sympathizer") and "radic-lib" (for "radical liberal"), this fusion of a phrase into a word is a boon to headline writers and other proponents of tersetalk.

Fatherhood is attributed to President Carter's domestic adviser, Stuart Eizenstat, who does not claim coinage but who popularized the new word in his June 28, 1979, "the worst of times" memo to the President: ". . . a comprehensive interagency review now under way to examine the synfuels issue. . . ."

(In that same leaked memo, Mr. Eizenstat complained of "confusion and bureaucratic tangling now occurring"; this was a new twist to the cliché "bureaucratic wrangling." The change from a wrang-to-tang was not a result of a typist's monkeyshines: "I meant 'tangle,'" reports Mr. Eizenstat. "To get a pipeline built, for example, you have to cut through a withering variety of regulations to develop a fast-track procedure. That's a 'tangle.'")

Is "synfuels" a mere nonce word, to vanish with the gas lines, or is it viable—capable of survival and growth in Washington's linguistic bulrushes? Working against the word is its pronunciation: In the mouths of television commentators, the new coinage sounds dangerously close to an adjective that means "morally corrupt." Confusion could reign in a quickly read "the energy adviser is a synfuel man," and that report could be interpreted as a severe editorial judgment.

As fuels rush in, grammarians are likely to call any new "windfall" revenues raised to support their production "syntaxes," from the Greek *syn* (together) and *taxis* (to arrange). On second thought—maybe not.

synecdoche, *see* wiseguy problem

systematics

Certain words grab business namers by the throat. For a time, "organization" had a vogue—"The Lawrence Organization." Then the British "group" surfaced, giving the impression of a vast array of enterprises under one roof: "The Continental Group," "The Diebold Group." Recently, the pretentious "center" was examined here—"learning center" for school, or "vision center" for an eyeglasses shop.

Comes now "system." It all began, I think, when a gun manufacturer who liked complexity began calling his weapon a "weapons system," because it fit with other weapons, or wheels. Interconnection was the key: Teachers like "school systems" like astronomers like "solar systems."

"Driving along a New England road last weekend," writes Richard Schickel, essayist and reviewer for *Time* magazine, "I observed, in front of a most unprepossessing wooden structure, little more than a shack, a roadside sign offering "energy systems" within. Wondering how anything so grand could emerge from such humble surroundings, I allowed my eye to slide down the sign only to discover that what was really being sold were 'wood-burning stoves.' "

Mr. Schickel then became systemically attuned: He noticed that the corner flower shop had become a purveyor of "foliage systems," and the advertisers of razors and blades liked to combine the two into a salable "shaving system." This shook him: "It seems to me that we ought to reserve the term 'system' for things no less complex than ICBM's."

He's right; I never liked calling a pond an "ecosystem." The systematic vogue must soon peak; we can wrap it together with "package deal" and get it out of our systems. Before accepting the pompous word again, I promise to recall my grandmother's remark, made whenever she surveyed evidence of disorganization: "Is this a system?"

Dear Mr. Safire,

Methinks you protest too much about the overuse of the word "system." You raise stellar chauvinism to new heights by commenting that "astronomers like 'solar systems.' "

Astronomers may like (or study) stellar systems, but until some other star is named "Sol," there will continue to be only one solar system, whose third planet is populated by provincial bipeds with a tendency toward linguistic colonialism. I'm sure you would agree that such attitudes would impede normalization of relations with residents of other "Milky Ways."

Robert Knight
New York, New York

Dear Mr. Safire,
   Slander! Ignorance! Repent! Only a non-biologist could have the anthropocentric conceit to suggest that the ecosystem of a pond is less complex than an ICBM. Not only are the organic and inorganic systems of a pond vastly more complex than the Pentagon's play toys, but a single algal cell from a pond is orders of magnitude more complex than any "system" that man has ever built.

Angrily yours
Stephen Clark
Graduate Fellow
The Rockefeller University
New York, New York

Dear Mr. Safire:
   Referring to your comment that "I never liked calling a pond an 'ecosystem,' " it would appear that you haven't owned a pond, or perhaps even a garden.
   Other people have ponds and gardens. But when I put on old clothes and go out to work in my garden, that is different: I first observe the great variety of bugs that are feeding on my vegetables and, occasionally, on me. The bees are good, the aphids and borers are bad. Then I observe the praying mantis, bird or toad that is feeding on the bugs. I might see a snake looking for a toad. Below the surface, worms fertilize the soil and gophers consume whole tomato plants. I know—but don't see—bacteria are working like crazy in my compost pile and elsewhere, and though I seldom arise at dawn the work of rabbits and raccoons is evident. My defenses against these depredations are nominal (onions, garlic, marigolds), and I like to think that everyone and everything gets a proper share of the bounty.
   I believe a botanist would testify that my garden, or a pond, is much more complex than any I C B M, and therefore richly deserving of the title "ecosystem."

Cordially,
James J. Burke, II
New York, New York

P.S.   *At my first law firm, we used "Lighting Messenger Service," and the cry to a secretary was "Summon a bolt!"*

Dear Mr. Safire:

I've been wondering about the manufacturer who called his weapon a "weapons system" because "it fit *with other weapons."*

Ogden Nash maintained that the past tense of "fit" is "fitted" and not "fit"; in fact, Mr. Nash once wrote that the only time "fit" should be used as the past tense is when one sings "Joshua fit de battle ob Jericho." All other times, it's "fitted."

What do you think?

> *Sincerely, enjoying your column*
> *hugely and profiting by it,*
> *Frank B. Michael*
> *Dayton, Ohio*

I'm fitted to be tied.—W.S.

---

task force, *see* working group

---

tautology, *see* Redundancy redounds

"Thank you much"

An odd locution—"Thank you much"— has been spreading like tamefire. A query about it in this space a few weeks ago brought fierce replies from a legion of linguistic Inspector Javerts.

Is it new? "For this relief much thanks" occurs in *Hamlet* and is quoted in James Joyce's *Ulysses,* but that's off target. Some recollectors point to the 1920's, with the phrase then changing to "Thank you muchly" in the 40's, then coming back strong as "Thank you much" in the late 60's, with an explosion in usage in 1978.

Where from? Of the hundred or so letters offering information, most pointed to the Middle West—Michigan and Illinois especially—while a bunch held it was from the Southwest, a handful from the South, two from Vermont, and one person claimed she heard it in the Bronx when she dipped her Devil Dogs in chocolate milk. Some say it comes directly from *"merci beaucoup"* or *"muchas gracias"*—I doubt it.

The petri dish in which it grew? Most say the military, with a special emphasis on radio communications. "The Army," writes Frank Carlini of Trenton, N.J., "which has strict regulations governing radio procedures, does not permit thank-yous to be sent over the radio, especially during tactical situations. However, it seems that the Army could not completely eradicate politeness ... thus this brusque form.... 'Thank you much' sounds 'military' and does not tie up radio time."

CB radio enthusiasts picked it up and made it part of their brisk argot. It has a rural flavor: "I hear 'thank you much' from people in towns all over the country," writes Margery Glassman of Glens Falls, N.Y., "but it is never uttered by a city slicker." Several correspondents agree, citing it as a phrase used by people who also say "I sure don't," or "Come with."

The popularizer? Entertainer Ray Charles, who says it often to applauding audiences. This 60's usage was repeated in recent years by entertainer Richard Pryor, and was heard often on such instant disseminators of slang as TV's *Happy Days* and *Laverne and Shirley*.

Significant "carriers": airline people. The military background of many pilots and the use of the microphone by flight attendants (formerly stewardae) make this a natural for "airline-ese." "I first heard it in 1956 when I began employment at LaGuardia Field," writes Bert Weiner of Philadelphia. "Pilots have a unique relaxed drawl that is obvious in public-address announcements, but they also employ a speech shorthand that could have originated in monosyllabic radio contact."

My guess is that it is a Middle Western affectation. Former Minnesotan Carmen Elliot heard it there in the early 60's, "used mostly by the 'Young Marrieds' set and meant, I think, to impart an air of breezy sophistication, implying that one was Terribly Busy and preoccupied with Important Things. . . . It was uttered with an ever-so-slight note of condescension and that roller-coaster, drifting-off-into-oblivion inflection peculiar to Middle Westerners."

Not all respondents agree, and some share their thoughts with such frankness that I refuse to reveal their identity. "My mother-in-law has been using that expression for at least five years. She has also managed to pass it on to one of her sons—thank God, not my husband. I take it as a conversational cuteness of hers. She is fond of them. She has two sisters who live in Los Angeles with whom she is in constant contact. In your hunt for the elusive origin, you may find it's yet another export from the land of fruit and nuts."

To all those who have participated in this swaydoscientific endeavor: I'm grateful. I'm in your debt, my appreciation, that's kind of you. . . .

Dear Mr. Safire:
  It's all very well to discuss "thank you much" but the phrase itself is not very interesting. What is interesting as a sidelight on national character (if there is such a thing) is why almost all other western peoples say thank you a thousand (merci mille fois, tusind tak) or just viel dank, etc. Americans have to say thanks a million. Why a million? Is all this part of the passion for bigness, for exaggeration, or is it just an accident—or might it have come originally from a misunderstanding of "mille fois"?

Sincerely
Henry Commager
Amherst, Massachusetts

---

thicken

A verb that recently entered the lexicon of Middle East negotiation is, in Hebrew, *"ibui,"* translated in English as "thicken." When Israelis are sent to West Bank settlements to increase population density without increasing geographic size, that's called "thickening."

It's an ugly word: Plots thicken when conspiracies grow; midriffs thicken when diets are unsuccessful. Since it is hard enough to explain the entire settlements policy to the State Department, why did the Israeli translators choose such a word?

Put yourself in the translators' shoes. *"Ibui"* could be translated as "enrich"—that's no good. Or as "strengthen," as when a bouillon cube is added to soup stock—but that would connote additional military strength. "Broaden" and "widen" are not acccurate, and would give the impression that the settlements were spilling out into more land. "Deepen"? They're not burrowing underground.

If such a verb as "densify" existed, it would apply—but this is hardly the time to make up new verbs. "Concentrate" leaps to mind, and as quickly leaps out—"concentration" is not a welcome word for an Israeli camp. In a case like that, Israeli translators must have been tempted to fudge the entire construction: Instead of saying "thicken the settlements," they could have called it a plan "to send more people to live within existing settlement borders." But then Israel would have risked a general adoption of "strengthen," only partially accurate and certainly warlike.

Which takes us back to "thicken"; sometimes you have to make do with an ugly word.

This is what

"This" used to be a pronoun known mainly for standing for something closer than "that." Then usagists began to notice a new, colloquial form of "this," as in "There is this woman—they call her SX-342434—who gives me this funny feeling." In both uses of "this" in that sentence, the word is used to mean the particular but unspecified; it is the deliberately mysterious "this," a locution that points specifically at something it chooses not to identify.

Comes now a new use of "this," to heap scorn or bestow pride on the noun it emphasizes.

The scornful "this" was noted by Bob Woodward and Scott Armstrong in their book about the Supreme Court, *The Brethren.* Justice William O. Douglas, they assert, "was still bitter toward [Chief Justice Warren E.] Burger, whom he had taken to calling 'this Chief,' reserving 'The Chief' as an accolade fitting only for retired Chief Justice Earl Warren."

At the same time, a rash of prideful "thises" could be heard from White House aides and Administration spokesmen. Instead of referring to "the President," they speak of "this President"—as if to dissociate him from previous Presidents or other Presidents. When next you tune in to a panel in-

terview of a White House staffer, keep an ear cocked for instances of *"this* President believes" or "not *this* President."

In the scornful intent of Douglas, the "this" is used to give a sense of transience to the title, as if to say "the particular person who now sits in the place once held by better men." In the proud intent of White House staffers, the word is used to separate the present holder of the office from his derogated predecessors. The vogue usage is exclusively American; in England, no toast is phrased "Long live this Queen."

Dear Bill Safire,

Oh no, not again! First it was "redundancy," now it's "transience." Is this to be a hebdomadal occurrence? Or, perhaps it is a calculated demarche on your part; an intercalated gambit, so to speak, to open the postal floodgates to epistolary nitpickers like myself.

However, your cacophonic cacography is becoming a cacodemonic cacoethes and because of this mumpsimus, the cacology in "On Language" will foster a cacodoxical cacotechny and "Safirism" will be a caconym to reign forever in the infamy of cacoepic literature.

Trusting that the above sciolistic fustian bavardage will be taken lightheartedly and attempting to avoid peripeteia and the bathetic, I remain faithfully yours in jocundity and propadeutics;

> *Mes devoirs*
> *John Wright*
> *New York, New York*

Dear Mr. Safire:

Your item "This is what" was interesting and correct, in my view. It prompted me to write to you about another use of "this" that you alluded to in your opening sentence but did not pin down. This and that traditionally have meant, both spatially and temporally, the nearer and the farther off respec-

tively. Thus, in polite response to my previous sentence you would say, "That's right." No one would say "This is right." But now I have been hearing something like this: "Carter seems to change his mind every day." "This is what I've been telling you"—instead of "That's what I've been telling you." Way back in 1965 some colleagues of mine in the linguistics field in Columbia said, when I called this neo-phenomenon to their attention, that they had not been aware of it, but would thereafter listen for it. I, in the habit of grammar teachers, must have a theory to account for this—that. It is this (which I am about to tell you): this (which I have mentioned) misuse has its provenience in the great number of persons around here who are in one way or another influenced by Yiddish and hearers of Yiddish. Yiddish makes no distinction between this and that in the sense I am talking about. So this non-distinction is carried over into English. This is my theory, I mean that.

> *Sincerely,*
> *Bertram Lippman*
> *English for the Foreign Born*
> *Queens College*
> *Flushing, New York*

Dear Mr. Safire,

So the vogue usage of "this" is exclusively American, not English? This reader says you've goofed.

See Richard the Second, *Act II, Scene I, line 40.* Now, see this:

> *This royal throne of kings, this sceptred isle,*
> *This earth of majesty, this seat of Mars,*
> *This other Eden, demi-paradise,*
> *This fortress built by Nature for herself*
> *Against infection and the hand of war,*
> *This happy breed of men, this little world,*
> *This precious stone set in the silver sea,*
> *Which serves it in the office of a wall*
> *Or as a moat defensive to a house*
> *Against the envy of less happier lands,*
> *This blessed plot, this earth, this realm, this England,*
> *This nurse, this teeming womb of royal kings, . . .*
>
> *This land of such dear souls, this dear dear land, . . .*
>
> *That England, that was wont to conquer others,*
> *Hath made a shameful conquest of itself.*

I count seventeen "vogue" usages of "this" and one of "that." How about that?

> *Sincerely,*
> *Herbert Bengelsdorf, M.D.*
> *Hastings-on-Hudson, New York*

tilt: pinball diplomacy

As soon as Pakistan came back into the news, the verb "to tilt" became the favorite of headline writers. "Tilting Toward Pakistan?" asked the newsmagazines. "The Tilt in South Asia" was the title of a *New York Times* editorial that warned the United States "could not afford to tilt to Pakistan. . . ."

The word in this sense may be rooted in pinball: When a player monkeys with the machine, the "TILT" sign lights up in blazing accusation and the game is forfeited. Richard Nixon used "tilt toward" frequently, in lieu of "lean toward," and when Henry Kissinger passed along the President's instruction in a 1971 National Security Council meeting—in effect, to rebuke the neutralist Indians and reward the helpful Pakistanis—the policy was accurately reported by Jack Anderson to have been phrased "tilt toward Pakistan."

The verb is less pejorative than "slant toward"; it avoids confusion with "lean on," which means "bring pressure to bear on." The origin of "tilt" is in the Anglo-Saxon word for unsteadiness, which may come in turn from the military origin of the word—to joust. The loser in a joust was upturned, left tilted, at an angle, upset. An evocation of that earlier meaning—playing on Don Quixote's tilting at a windmill, mistaking it for an adversary—was in an article by William Simon in the Heritage Foundation's Policy Review: "Tilting at Windfall Profits."

However, in its modern headline usage, the verb is wedded to stories about Pakistan and means "to give preference to." In its noun and participle forms, the word reverts to the angular: Just about every modern hotel in the Italian city of Pisa is called "the tiltin' Hilton."

top up/top down, *see* **ups and downs**

trademarks, *see* **Generic: What's in a name**

transgression

Sometimes it takes a great press agent to come up with the perfect word. In Washington, Joe Laitin is one of the veteran press agents who work under various titles in different agencies as administrations come and go, always landing on his feet because he has that certain touch with words. When the astronauts, circling the moon on Christmas Eve, moved mankind with a reading from Genesis in the Bible—that was Joe, operating on the global scale.

In 1978, he worked for Treasury Secretary Mike Blumenthal. He had been urging his client to travel to China, where Blumenthal had spent eight years as a youth. "Shanghai is your log cabin," Joe told him. So Blumenthal recently made his sentimental journey, accompanied by a dozen reporters who dutifully reported the Secretary's trade negotiations at a most delicate moment in diplomacy.

The problem was that Blumenthal was in Peking, helping the Chinese launch their modernization drive, at a time when the United States was officially frowning on China's invasion of Vietnam. How to sound tough and disapproving—without being offensive?

The word chosen by Blumenthal in China to describe the Chinese move across its Vietnamese border was "transgression." I had not heard that word used since Negley Farson's *The Way of a Transgressor,* a memoir of a foreign correspondent first published in 1935.

"Transgression" means "movement across a line," whether actually moving across a border or figuratively stepping beyond the bounds. The more accurate word for the Chinese action is "aggression," which also has the meaning of stepping across a line (the "gress," or grade, means "step") but carries the connotation of attack. In international law, aggression is condemned, and the use of that word by Blumenthal would have been considered insulting.

When the perfect choice—"transgression"—came over the wires from China, I asked: "Who's with Blumenthal?" Answer: Joe Laiten. It figured. I shot a message to Joe in Peking about the word, and received this message back from him: "I accept brickbats but not bouquets. The word is Secretary Blumenthal's." Always a pleasure dealing with a pro.

triumph of evil, *see* **Quotation Demolishers, Inc.**

trivia question

The word "belittle"—a great Americanism—coined around 1780 by Thomas Jefferson, meaning "to make unimportant"—has been disparaged and may soon be altogether replaced.

"Belittle" is being slighted in favor of "made trivial" and "trivialize."

In putting down press coverage of the Pope's visit, President Carter said: "A beautiful and significant moment was kind of glossed over and made trivial."

While seeking to derogate the challenge of some Quebeckers advocating separation from Canada, Prime Minister Joe Clark admitted: "We should not diminish or trivialize the importance of this local or regional pride."

"Trivial" is a significant word, from the Latin *tri via*, "three streets," a busy crossroads where much takes place that is commonplace. I don't want to minimize the achievement of "trivial" in becoming a vogue verb—"trivialize" has overwhelmed Jefferson's "belittle"—but I have this question: Since "ize" is a much-decried construction, why do the same people who condemn a verb like "prioritize" as some sort of bureaucratic monstrosity rush to embrace "trivialize"?

We're making too much of "trivialize"; the underrated "belittle" will make a comeback.

Dear Mr. Safire:

Your column is trivial. The Seven Liberal Arts, in the Middle Ages, of which one became Bachelor or Master, were divided into the quadrivium, viz.: arithmetic, music, geometry and astronomy, and the trivium, i.e.: grammar, logic and rhetoric. The adjective formed from trivium is trivialis, and it has little to do with roads. Your column is, then, essentially trivial. Students majoring in the quadrivium would today be called scientists. Does the pejorative connotation of trivial stem from the scientists' desire to belittle the literary?

Very truly yours,
Thomas J. Gilheany
Nutley, New Jersey

Dear Mr. Safire:

My understanding of the origin of "trivia" is a bit different from the explanation you provide in your column.

The Medieval study of the seven liberal arts was divided into two parts: the

WILLIAM SAFIRE

trivium and the quadrivium. Less important of the two was the trivium (rhetoric, grammar and logic); its study led to the degree of Bachelor of Arts.

The higher degree Master of Arts was conferred upon those who mastered the four subjects of the quadrivium (astronomy, arithmetic, geometry and music). It was considered the more advanced—and hence more significant—course of study.

Both terms are Late Latin in origin, and obviously refer to the number of subjects grouped within each, rather than to any markets, shops or roads that have been trifurcated (quadrifurcated?) in anything more than a figurative sense.

Nice try, though.

Sincerely,
Stephen J. Walden
New York, New York

---

tubes, *see* down the tubes

---

turpitude

The first verbal gaffe of the 1980 Presidential campaign occurred in a Washington Press Club speech by Evan Dobelle, chairman of the Carter-Mondale Presidential Committee. Apparently confusing the word "turpitude" with "attitude" or "rectitude," Mr. Dobelle stated: "As far as Jimmy Carter the man, his integrity, his moral turpitude, his commitment to government, his commitment to family, it is unimpeachable."

"Turpitude"—from the Latin *turpis* ("ugly," "vile")—means "depravity," and the phrase "moral turpitude" in law means a crime of such baseness as to set it apart from what has come to be called a "technical violation."

Mr. Dobelle, who was Mr. Carter's former chief of protocol, will not be the last to suffer from what politicians call "foot-in-mouth disease" in this campaign, but his error was a compound classic: Moral turpitude, if caught out, makes any office holder most "impeachable."

Dear Mr. Safire:

I hope you will take aim against those newspaper writers who confuse pore with pour, horde with hoard, effect with affect, etc. I suspect that they are victims of the look-see method of teaching.

It is both laughable and shocking that the chairman of the Carter-Mondale Presidential Committee did not know the meaning of moral turpitude. Or, was this a Freudian slip?

It seems as if the huge amounts of money spent on public education are producing very poor results.

> *Sincerely yours,*
> *Marjorie S. Billia*
> *(Mrs. H. J. Billia)*
> *Bradenton, Florida*

two, *see* Second, the

two-way words

When a cannonball serve tips the net before falling into the opposite court, the net umpire shouts "Let!" Or "Let ball!" Many people think he is mispronouncing "net," which is what he says when the serve hits the net without tipping over to the other side.

"Let" is a noun meaning "obstacle," an archaic word that lawyers enjoy putting in deeds: "without let or hindrance." When the tennis ball has encountered an obstacle—the net—the umpire calls out the ancient term. (When someone tries to ace you with the etymology of "love" in tennis—from *l'oeuf*, French for "the egg," symbolizing "zero"—return it smartly with the etymology of a let ball.)

The purpose of this cannonball lead is to introduce the arcane subject of two-way words. "Let," as a verb, is ambidextrous—meaning both "allow, permit" and its opposite, "hinder, obstruct." Other two-way words make life miserable for the student of English:

A *seeded* rye (caraway to go) has seeds put in; *seeded* raisins have the seeds taken out. A *fast* horse runs; a *fast* color does not. When you *dust* crops, you sprinkle the dust on; when you *dust* furniture, you wipe the dust off. When you *scan* a page, you glance at it quickly—or you scrutinize it

carefully. (Same thing with *peruse*—it used to mean "to read closely," and now it also means its opposite, "to run your eye over it.")

"If you *think better of* a person," wrote Joseph Shipley, "you admire him more; if you *think better of* a project, you cast it aside." Similarly, a *handicap* helps a long-shot horse compete with the favorite, but a *handicap* is usually considered a drawback.

Sometimes a word is turned into the opposite of itself through sarcastic use: A *fine* condition is a far cry from a *fine* mess.

Collectors of two-way words (we are a small fraternity) insist on absolute contradiction: *Fearful* meaning "frightened" is not quite the opposite of the *fearful* that means "frightening." Etymological purity is also required: *To pit* means both "to put pits in" and its opposite, "to remove pits," but the first sense is rooted in making an indentation while the second is derived from the seeds out of a fruit. Nor will *to cleave* qualify; the sense that means "to split or separate" has a root different in form from its opposite sense, "to cling or adhere."

All this is by way of answering a provocative postcard that asked: "Do you sanction the use of sanctions?" As to asking readers to send in their favorite two-way words, the more I think of it the less I think of it.

Dear Mr. Safire,
    What about "sell-out"? It's a positive term when applied to things (concerts, T.V.s, etc.) but very negative when applied to people. How come?
           Sincerely,
           Mary Zwiebel
           Woodside, New York

William Safire

What a dummy!

The handicap in a horse race is applied (usually in extra weight carried) to the horses judged to have the better qualifications for winning.

The handicap *does, as you say, help the long-shot, but it helps because the handicap is applied to the favorite(s).*

For a two-way word which can really louse up a dinner party, try parboil.

ever,

Mrs. Anne W. Warren

Blairstown, New Jersey

Dear Mr. Safire:

The opening cannonball distinction between the two meanings of let *does not meet the stringent criterion of etymological purity used to disqualify* cleave. *Like the two meanings of* cleave, *the two meanings of* let *stem from different roots. OE* lǣtan *became* let *'allow,' while OE* lettan *became the verb* let *'hinder, prevent,' whence the noun* let *'hindrance.' See* The Oxford Dictionary of English Etymology.

With respect,

Gerald Richman

Mankato State University

Mankato, Minnesota

Dear Mr. Safire:

The logical step after considering words that go both ways in their meaning might be to try for words seemingly opposite in form that bear precisely the same meaning. I can only think of two such pairs: ravel *and* unravel, *flammable* and *inflammable. The second pair might be considered suspect, since* in- *is an intensive and thus makes* flammable/inflammable *equivalent to* radiate/irradiate, radicate/irradicate, *and numbers of others. The difference, arguably, is that "inflammable" is often taken to mean "unable to be flamed." Perhaps, then,* ravel/unravel *are a unique pair, since* un- *is clearly meant to reverse meaning; and they will remain unique until "irregardless" becomes (black day!) an accepted form.*

Sincerely,

Kit Konolige

Philadelphia, Pennsylvania

Dear Mr. Safire:

When a serve tips the net court, the net umpire shouts "net." Immediately the chair umpire calls a "let" only if the ball lands in the proper service court. The net umpire's act is to inform the chair umpire that the ball has touched the net.

A "let" call is not always called by the chair umpire; i.e. if a ball does not land in the proper service court then it is a fault.

When a ball hits the net whether on a service or during play without going over the other side no call is made. The ball is dead as soon as it bounces and assumed by everyone not to be in play.

Sincerely,
Frederick J. Roa
USTA Chair Umpire
Hackensack, New Jersey

Dear Mr. Safire:
. . . I agree totally with your comments on how "let" has changed. On "net" you haven't done so well. I've umpired dozens of matches and have seen many more umpired ones. If a serve lands in the net, failing to clear it, he doesn't say "net," but "Fault," or "Double-fault," as the case may be, followed by the score in the latter case. In a rally after a serve has been returned, he also doesn't say "net," but simply gives the score, on the theory that spectators have seen the ball fail to clear. . . .

Appreciatively,
Parke Cummings
Saugatuck, Connecticut

Up: Down with it

Words beginning with "up" sometimes come down quickly. "Uptight" had its origin in the music world, and meant "A-O.K.": Maureen Gillespie of New York City recalls singer Stevie Wonder's "Ev-ry-thing is al-right, up-tight and out of sight." Jazz musicians used it to mean "thoroughly known," presumably from "buttoned up tight"; earlier, it had meant "financially embarrassed."

Then "uptight" was upstaged by the obsessive "hung up," and came out meaning "nervous," "anxious," "tense." That is how it is usually used today, but the word has a quicksilver quality and may squirt off in another direction. ("Up" in slogans is equally confusing: "Up the [ethnic group]" is positive, while other short directives using the word are insulting.)

The most subversive "up" is in the voguish "upcoming," which destroys precision in meaning. Does it mean "up-and-coming"—that is, with a bright future? Or does it mean "forthcoming" (which used to mean "imminent, coming soon," but now is slopping over to mean "open, frank")?

Bernard Kilgore, former president of Dow Jones, which publishes *The Wall Street Journal,* had a good thought about the confusing "upcoming," which he posted on a newsroom bulletin board: "If I read 'upcoming' in *The Wall Street Journal* again, I will be downcoming and somebody will be outgoing."

For fifty years I have understood that "upcoming" was devised by accountants of U.S. newspapers to beat the cable tariff on the dispatches of their foreign correspondents.

Cable count was (and may still be) per word of ten letters or less. "Forthcoming" has eleven letters and counts as two words. "Coming up" is two words.

Later generations of journalists apparently think "upcoming" is a real word.

> *In appreciation,*
> *Harold A. Hagen*
> *Falls Church, Virginia*

---

uphill, *see* downhill

---

ups and downs

The Federal Government has serendipitously solved a great linguistic problem. With passenger safety in mind, regulators have banned the construction of convertible automobiles; in so doing, they have swept the confusion of convertible nomenclature.

When you wanted the top to open, so that your hair would blow in the breeze and the radio could be heard for miles around, you said: "Let's put the top down." Or, you said: "Let's put the top up."

Conversely, if it looked like rain, you said: "Better put the top down—we don't want to get wet." Or, you said: "Better put the top up—we don't want to get wet." In this situation, "up" and "down" meant both "open" and "closed"—an expression to make proud the heart of Humpty Dumpty. The words communicated nothing, meaning what the listener chose them to mean. (It's like saying "The alarm went off," when the alarm goes on.)

Except in foreign cars, the canvas convertible top is gone, and the up-down problem is solved. Today, the outdoorsy car or van may have a sliding "sun roof," which presents an open-and-shut case. But some old-timers, just to hark back to the breezy days of their youths, will say: "Put the sun roof up." Or down.

Dear Mr. Safire:

I was amused by "Ups and Downs." Having gone through more than my share of convertibles built during the '50s, I, too, have somewhat of a semantic problem with putting the top up or down, when I wanted the roof opened (closed).

But it didn't really matter, because I always knew, that when someone said, "let's lower (raise) the roof," my choices were limited. If the roof was, in fact, up, i.e. in a position over my head, then quite obviously they wanted it in a different position, i.e. lowered (or raised). So it really just didn't matter what people said; nor does it today, although there are no domestic convertibles being produced which is a different story, I'm sure.

> *Sincerely,*
> *Robert J. Trevorrow*
> *Philadelphia, Pennsylvania*

---

uptight, *see* gorilla

---

urgent, *see* ASAP's fables

---

verbs from nouns

Have you positioned yourself on the issue of verbification? Put another way: Have you taken a position yet on the issue of turning nouns, adjectives, and the like into verbs?

My revered colleague in columny, James J. Kilpatrick, author of the classic *The Foxes' Union* and a conservative before that persuasion became *de rigueur mortis,* was taking me to task recently for abandoning the ramparts on "hopefully." He added: "Linguistic surgery continues, in the fashion of a sex change, transforming nouns to verbs. Three times in the past ten days I have encountered 'to obsolete,' as in 'The B-1 bomber would have obsoleted the B-52.' If my brother Safire accepts that excrescence, all is lost save honor."

Let's chew that over. When the purpose of turning a thing into an act is trendy brevity, or chicspeak, the practice is bad style. A headline writer picks up a few picas when "plays host to" becomes "to host"; when a gushy host wants to show enthusiasm for a guest, he "enthuses." People who want

to pretend their speaking time is valuable use such headlinese as an affectation.

The verbifiers become more offensive when they turn a coinage into an instant cliché: as "to impact on," rather than "to have an impact"; or "to critique," for "write a critique" (or the more direct "criticize"). But at least the shorteners can claim the advantage of brevity: The abomination is the creation of a wholly unnecessary word. "To author" has replaced "to write" in the vocabulary of those who consider authors more important than writers. (At some opening night of a well-authored play, I intend to leap up, shouting: "Writer! Writer!")

Therefore, I would look askance at (I would "askan"?) pretentious or unnecessary noun-turnings. "To contracept" is shorter than "to control births" or "to practice contraception," but it should be quickly aborted; "to groundswell," used in politics recently, would give rise to a past tense of "groundswelled" and then to a distortion like "groundswollen"; that verb form is better contracepted.

To other-hand it (formerly "on the other hand"), some new verbs from nouns are blessings, enriching and enlivening our discourse and making meaning more precise. Stephen Potter's "one-upmanship" led to the verb "to one-up," nicely blending "to seize an advantage" with "to patronize." Nobody objects to using "pocketed" instead of "putting the money in his pocket"; in the same noun-to-verb way, we carpet the stairs and wallpaper the room. Adjectives can make good verbs, too: If we can sweeten our coffee and blacken a reputation, why can we not obsolete a bomber?

Well, there goes honor, too. That reference of my brother Kilpatrick's— "all is lost save honor"—is usually attributed to Napoleon after Waterloo. To show how whole phrases, and not just words, can be happily transmogrified, consider wheeler-dealer Jim Fisk's 1869 quip after a group of political reformers defeated his corrupt Eire* ring, but then generously paid the old pols off: "Nothing is lost save honor."

* To confuse Erie with Eire is eerie.—W. S.

Dear Mr. Safire:

   Authors may be writers, of course, but writers are not necessarily authors. I was astonished that you place yourself outside the category of "those who consider authors more important than writers." Surely there is a useful distinction to be preserved. The very word "author" connotes authority which is missing in the word "writer." By OED definition, an author is "a person who originates or gives existence to anything; an inventor or constructor or founder." Matthew, Mark and Luke were writers. Margaret Mitchell was an author. Whoever did the screenplay of GWTW was a writer, or perhaps a team of writers.

   I would not want to see the word "writer" downgraded either. Many authors are not first-rate writers (Theodore Dreiser, for example). Charles Darwin needed Thomas Huxley to defend his theory. Many finely honed writers, like yourself, are also authors, writing with unquestioned authority in fields of their choice.

   I could understand leaping up at a movie premier shouting "Writer! Writer!" but not at the opening night of an Arthur Miller or Tennessee Williams play.

Respectfully yours,
Kenneth Godfrey
Orient, New York

Dear Mr. Safire:

   On the matter of verbing generally, I wish you had distinguished between pure and altered forms of "nouns, adjectives and the like." For instance, can you explain why "warm" and "cool" may serve without alteration as verbs, but "hot" and "cold" may not?

   I support circumspect use of "host" and "enthuse" (your examples) as verbs. "Host," to my ears, connotes friendly, sincere entertaining and provisioning, whereas "play host to" has overtones of discomfort, of performing an assigned role. Similarly, "enthuse" sounds ebulliently supportive, but "show enthusiasm" shows the strain of demonstrating unfelt emotion. Perhaps the problem lies in the use of "play" and "show," words which bring to mind the shadowy side of the "appearance versus reality" theme preached by junior high school English teachers. Furthermore, nouns seem to adapt to verbal service more readily than do adjectives, although certainly there are exceptions on both sides: Leslie White unconvincingly attempted to coax a verb out of "science" in The Science of Culture, *and "sweeten" (your example) has gained popular acceptance.*

   Finally, let us avoid "blacken a reputation" because it is arguably a racist expression. A few years ago, black students objected to Professor Weinstein's choice of those words in his lectures on "Evidence" at Columbia Law School. "What should I say?" asked Weinstein, a federal judge in New York's Eastern

District. "Whiten," suggested a black student. Personally, I prefer "besmirch," "tarnish," or "sully" to "blacken," "darken," or "whiten."

> *Sincerely,*
> *David Bersohn*
> *Brooklyn, New York*

Dear Mr. Safire:

After having read and enjoyed your comments on unnecessary noun-turnings in to-day's New York Times Magazine *I found myself through fortuitous but unfortunate circumstances come face to face with a door on 56th St. in Manhattan bearing an impressive sign which read:*

> *"This door is alarmed 24 hours a day."*

Evidently, New York City living takes its toll on doors too.

> *Sincerely yours,*
> *S. E. Liverhant*
> *New York, New York*

Dear Mr. Safire:

You might be interested in knowing that some of the back-formations you cite have been around for quite a long time. Usages cited for some of them by the Oxford English Dictionary are: pocket, 1589; sweeten, 1550; blacken, 1300; host, 1485; critique, 1751; enthuse ("an ignorant back-formation"), 1859; author (OED says obsolete, but obviously wrong), 1596; and carpet, 1626.

> *Best wishes,*
> *Josiah F. Hill*
> *Hanover, New Hampshire*

---

viable

Six years ago, in my first appearance as a newspaper columnist, I vowed never to offend readers with any of the words then rampantly in vogue: *relevant, meaningful, knowledgeable, hopefully, viable, input, exacerbate, dichotomy,* and the ambivalent use of verbs as *program, implement,* and *structure.*

Since then, I have adopted *hopefully,* because no other word better substitutes for the awkward "it is to be hoped that"; contrariwise, I am pleased that most academics have responded to a general ridicule of the "relevant meaningfuls." I remain of two minds about *ambivalent.*

Viable, however, cannot be killed. Of all the clichés of the 60's, this adjective alone seems capable of survival and growth. The root of the word is, of course, "life," though the term is most often used in its nonscientific sense—as a hot possibility, or a good bet for success.

Last month, in an article about the popularity of self-destruction, *The* (Toronto) *Globe and Mail* quoted a doctor in a usage that carries the still-voguish adjective to the point of parody. Said Dr. Diane Syer, head of the crisis-intervention unit at Toronto East General Hospital: "If someone is confronted with certain knowledge that he or she is going to die a painful, undignified death through terminal illness [sick], then suicide can be a viable option."

Dear Mr. Safire,

Your quote that "suicide can be a viable option" reminded me of a remark I heard the other day that "Lebanon is western-oriented." In both cases words come to mean their opposites! Life (viable) is death and east (orient) is west. I am also reminded of the Greek "pharmakon" which can mean both poison *and* cure. *But that's not quite the same. In the first two cases the words come to mean their opposites through ignorance on the part of the speaker. There must be other examples. We should start a collection!*

Yours sincerely,
LeRoy C. Breunig
Professor of French
Barnard College
New York, New York

---

vogue words

Now hear this: It is time for the Vogue Word Watch.

In the closely guarded Citation Room of Webster's New World Dictionary in Cleveland, lexicographer David Guralnik is watching the file thicken on the locution *do a number on.* Is it an evanescent nonce phrase, or will it work its way into dictionaries?

"The phrase 'do a number on' first appeared in our files in the late 1960's," says Mr. Guralnik, "with a steady growth to more than 100 citations. Although in its earliest uses it always seemed to mean 'to deceive,' it has been extended, and softened in meaning so that it now often means no more than 'to affect,' but generally in some devious way: 'She stumbled into the bathroom and did a masochistic number on her teeth with an electric toothbrush. . . .' "

Meanwhile, in his clipping-cluttered rooms in San Francisco, Peter Tamony, who watches words for the Oxford Dictionary, is also eyeballing "doing a number on." "To do one's number," word-watcher Tamony suggests, "was to do one's act, one's specialty in the old vaudeville days, taken from the numbered sequence of acts on the bill or program. The meaning evolved from an act, to a general pretense, to a deception."

Sic transit terrific

Some words streak across our discourse and soon fade. Last year's *terrific* is this year's *incredible!;* last year's *right?* is this year's wrong; yesterday's *way to go* is gone; *whatsisname* has changed to *whatsisface.* Where do the vogue words come from? In the past, jazz musicians led the way. Black English has also been the source of vogue words, and today, a perfume advertiser who sloganeers "It's ba-a-ad—and that's good!" is using the reverse-twist of black lingo employed to confuse outsiders. Another source has been "Needle Park," land of the narcotics junkies, that lingers on with *It's the pits,* a common derogation, taken from the addict's resort to the armpits when other blood vessels have collapsed from too frequent injection of dope.

Spitballing

But other sources of vogue words are taking over. Games and sports, for one: *Square one,* a games term, is what we reluctantly go back to; a basketball phrase, *one-to-one,* is used now to describe any direct confrontation, tête-à-tête or match-up; football has contributed *cheap shot* (a tackle after the whistle, or late hit) and *blind-side,* a verb for dealing an unexpected blow. Because an old-time baseball pitcher never knew which way his spitball would break, the verb *to spitball* now means "to speculate."

The advertising-publishing-news world, which can no longer be called Madison Avenue, is another powerful source. *Media event,* a variant of Daniel Boorstin's "pseudoevent," connotes staginess and manipulation. Publishers looking for a *good read* lean weakly on books they advertise as *page-turners.* To appeal to nostalgia or to associate with newly fashionable Southernism, copywriters use the adjective *down-home* to sweep the countryside—as in "real down-home taste" for a cigarette, or "that down-home quality" of a political figure.

Up the down-home

The down-home Carter Administration will surely make its linguistic contributions. *Compatibility* is enshrined and *disharmoniousness* abhorred, and *zero-based* is the bottom line of the future (a management term taken from technology's "zero error," sociology's "zero population growth," and a 1969 White House usage, "zero mistakes").

"He's *behind the power curve* on this," said a Carter aide of a colleague who was unaware of the latest top-level decisions. Lexicographer Anne Soukhanov shows a mid-60's use of "power curve" based on a statistics-graph test for alternatives, which has since come to evoke a keening arc of fast decision-making.

Political trendsetters have replaced the term for permanent power center that Henry Fairlie named "the Establishment." *Community* has taken its place—as in defense community, intelligence community. It has a friendly air. When attacked as the "power structure," "new-boy network," or one of the "complexes" (military-industrial, academic-media), the group allies itself with *The System,* always capitalized, as in "The System works."

Women's-movement politics provides new terms. The flip "lib" has long been set aside, and the exaggerated substitution of "person" for "man" has been ridiculed. However, *queen bee* is a useful characterization of one who benefits from, but contributes little to, the struggle for women's rights. The use of *upfront* is growing, lately as one word, but with Merriam-Webster citations also in hyphenated form and as two words, to mean forthright and disdainful of deviousness. (The word may be rooted in the exploitation of women by antiwar demonstrators of the 60's in the saying "Chicks up front.") Even the meaning of *multiple* is changing; formerly taken to mean the price-earnings ratio of a share of stock, the dull old word is now assumed to refer to a highly desirable form of orgasm.

New vogues

Here's the point: A sound lexicographic case can be made for the theory that our traditional sources of vogue lingo—the argot of musicians, the cant of the underworld, and the inventive richness of black English—are being replaced by the political and communications worlds, acting not merely as disseminators but as originators as well. (Adman Leo Greenland calls this kind of thinking *breaking new snow,* the ski-based vogue term for originality.) How will this change of wellsprings affect the future of American slang?

The first effect will be—get this—"stretched-out words." A word lengthened by a redundancy may be an offense to the sharp eye, but it can be an aid to the less attentive ear. That accounts for the vogue of *early on,* a Britishism, with American television commentators; it adds emphasis to the simple "early," and cachet to the indeterminate long ago: "Early on, God created Heaven and Earth."

Similarly, nobody is selected to "head" an agency, but to *head up* the agency, which adds an intensifier desired by a speaker as in "eat up your cereal," or "write down your name." (Or "stretch out" the word.) "At this point in time" was well derided, but the meaningless intensifiers are increasing: "That's *flat-out* wrong," said Press Secretary Jody Powell, using an auto-racing word meaning to drive with the accelerator flat against the floorboard, and, by extension, to act without restraint. In Mr. Powell's usage, the word-stretching for emphasis introduces error, or is flat wrong.

The mediamania for verbal stretch-out can be seen in the high price of the *prix-fixe* "co-." "Congress will be a *co-equal* branch," says Speaker "Tip" O'Neill. How is co-equal more equal than equal? For the same reason a *judgment call* is more judgmental than a mere judgment, or a *match-up* more evenly matched than a match: With Orwellian evenhandedness, the "co-" stretch gives "equal" a more equal ring, and the sound is more important than the sight.

Here it comes

The second effect of the rise of gray-flannel English as a new main well-spring for colloquial speech is—are you ready?—the telegraphed punchline. In written English, the writer may add emphasis by underlining, *italicizing*, or punctuating (!!!) (?).

Or paragraphing.

In spoken English, however, to add emphasis the speaker must shout, glower, or gesticulate. Since none of these methods is permissible on television, the question is: How can the speaker cue a listener to pay attention, or remind a sleepy cameraman to roll film?

The answer is: with a waker-upper, some oral telegram that the punch is coming. That familiar device has been implanted throughout this piece, unnoticed because its force is in show-news business, not on the printed page.

The answer is *The answer is*. Or *Here's the point*. Or *Get this*. Or *ta-dahh!* Or *Would you believe?* Or—and this'll killya, as comedians used to say to dead audiences—*Are you ready?*

That verbal jab-in-the-ribs, that telegraphed punchline of co-host hype, is destined to be the voguish speech pattern of the immediate future. That is, unless readers and writers band together to keep the ill-spoken word from— are you ready?—doing a number on the English language.

---

vulnerable

"I am very vulnerable woman," Bianca Jagger told an interviewer in Munich. "I am not strong, tough Bianca everyone imagines. I am little girl."

The article-dropping Mrs. Jagger is not the only one to temper toughness with a desirable weakness. "No-nonsense tough one minute," wrote *Washington Star* profilist Lynn Rosellini about *Washington Post* publisher Katharine Graham, "and unexpectedly vulnerable the next."

"Vulnerable" is what every celebrated or successful woman now wants to be. The new vogue word is replacing "sensitive," which used to be the char-

acteristic sought after to balance such attributes as "drive," "brilliance," or "glamour." (Similarly, "very private person" replaced "publicity-shy," which replaced "reclusive," which replaced "hermit.")

"Vulnerable" means "woundable," "exposed to attack"; its antonym is "impregnable." Why should so many achievers want to assert their susceptibility to injury? The old "I've got feelings, too" ploy is making a strong comeback. Now that "macho" (formerly "machismo") is frowned upon, powerful men are joining successful women in demanding recognition of their Achilles' heels, especially to interviewers. Burt Reynolds is vulnerable, too.

In the vocabulary of image projections, to be "tough," "shrewd," "sassy," "with it," "upfront," and "power-oriented" is okay—but to be "vulnerable" is to be invincible.

---

wait on/wait for, *see* on line/in line

---

watersheds

Senator Edward Kennedy's favorite locution seems to have become "mindful." In a single interview in *The New York Times* he said that he was "extremely mindful that as we move into the 80's we have to come to grips with the different realities of this period"; that we had been "unmindful in many instances that [programs] were administered by those who never believed in them," and—regarding his refusal to "rule out" a Presidential race—"I was very mindful when I made this decision, what its implications were going to be and where it leads."

While pursuing the life of the mindful, the newly unruled-out candidate used such favorite words of the 60's as "decency" and "compassion," adding: "We have to move away from labels, slogans, clichés . . ." which he found unacceptable.

Then, in another interview, he was reported to have used a word that I thought had been stamped out in recent years: "watershed." This is a watershed era, we're coming to a watershed, the early 60's were a watershed, etc.

As a service to the Senator, let me wave him off "watershed." I had something to do with its brief vogue, and know that it is a word that can get a politician sandbagged.

The year was 1968, and I was writing speeches for Richard Nixon. Looking for some metaphor to picture a turning point, or dividing line, I turned to "watershed," which had been used in that sense in the mid-60's by such pundits as Theodore White and C. L. Sulzberger. The dictionaries still had the meaning as "drainage area of a river system," or "strip of high land dividing drainage areas" (taken about 1800 from the German *Wasserscheide*), which meant the metaphor was still fresh. So I used it in the title and text of a speech.

Other political writers snorted the word up, and it blew their minds. The election of 1968 was to be one of those "watershed elections," everyone agreed, following which a flood of watershed usages inundated the political landscape.

In time, a raft of rationality appeared. Meg Greenfield, editorial writer for *The Washington Post,* blew the shed out of the water in 1969: "I have become an incurable, even obsessive collector of printed watersheds, of which I believe I now have the best collection in town—watersheds perching on escalation ladders, watersheds embedded in arms spirals, watersheds wrapped (like chicken livers, perhaps) in an enigma. It is not, however, an expression that I would dare to use myself. I came to that drainage basin two years ago and paddled left, into the sunset."

After this suppressing fire, Br'er Watershed, he lay low. Then Henry Kissinger revived the term; then an unwary editorialist went on to hail a space shot as "a watershed in space history"; gloomily, Miss Greenfield wrote, "I would be less than candid if I did not report that, at the present time, there is no light at the end of the watershed."

But she was gloriously wrong. Thanks to her sustained scorn, to the transient nature of trendiness, and to efforts to assuage my conscience by expunging the word from Presidential speech, "watershed" soon sank from view. The fashion had passed; the vogue was over. The 60's definition found

its way into dictionaries, which now supply us with both its literal, catchment meaning and its modern, dividing-line sense, but the flood of usage receded.

These lessons of hard experience are offered to Senator Kennedy in the hope that he will be mindful—or at least not unmindful—of the need for original labels, fresh slogans and clichés attuned to the 80's.

Dear Mr. Safire:

". . . [A] flood of watershed usages inundated the political landscape"?

Substituting "flooded" for "inundated," which would be perfectly legitimate, your construction would read aweful. How about simply "Watershed usages flooded (or inundated) the landscape."

I have a hunch you are going to be inundated with protests of this nature. Will you kneel and repent over this assault on the beauty of the English language or are you going to use some contrived escape from the expected deluge of angry letters from readers like me. Whichever response you choose, the best!

> *Vipin Chandra*
> *Assistant Professor of History*
> *Wheaton College*
> *Norton, Massachusetts*

welfare

When words die, they deserve a decent burial, or at least a respectful obituary. One noun bit the dust recently, at least in government usage, and it is herein bid adieu.

The noun is "welfare," as in "Department of Health, Education and Welfare." This fine old word was born before 1303, the offspring of the Middle English *wel,* meaning "wish" or "will," and *faren,* meaning "to go on a journey."

In its youth, the word enjoyed a period on the stage: "Study for the people's welfare," Warwick advised Henry VI in Shakespeare's play. In middle age, the word was used in the same sense but with more of a governmental connotation, beginning in a 1904 *Century* magazine article about "the welfare manager . . . a recognized intermediary between employers and employees." About that time, *The Westminster Gazette* was pinpointing its sociological birthplace: "The home of the 'welfare policy' is the city of Dayton, Ohio." According to the etymologist Sir Ernest Weekly, *"Welfare,* as in 'child welfare,' 'welfare center' and so forth, was first used in this sense in Ohio in 1904."

White House-ese

Argot used by White House aides soon percolates through government, then—perhaps on a trickle-down theory—reaches the people.

A few years ago, "impacted" was very big, as an affected synonym for "affected"—"How does supplemental assistance impact on our constituency?" Similarly, "targeted" became voguish, replacing "tailored" on pressing concerns. These verbs will probably go the way of "spearhead" and "pinpoint" into the jargon graveyard.

But some terms are colorful and descriptive. "A White House aide," wrote Steven Weisman in *The New York Times,* "also said that Stuart Eizenstat was still 'bent out of shape' by the Governor's comment." The picture of the angular Domestic Council aide twisted like a pretzel after a blast from Hugh Carey is vivid and a good use of language.

The jury is still out on "We'll close that loop later." The "loop" bandied about in the White House is not a short form of "loophole," but an electronic loop that keeps a tape playing forever. To say "I'm not in that loop" is to say "That's not my area of responsibility" in an excitingly trendy way. We'll keep an eye on that figure of speech. Word-watchers are in that loop.

Dear Mr. Safire:

With some trepidation I submit that your account of the derivation of the term "loop" may be in error. I suspect rather than originating in "an electronic loop which keeps a tape playing forever" (by the way, I am unaware of such a device) the more probable origin of the term may be found in the language of computer programmers, who would define a loop as an operation or series of operations which are repeated infinitely or until such time as the condition or conditions required for the cessation are fulfilled. Thus, for example, a program might continue to add a series of figures until the sum of one thousand had been reached or until a negative number was encountered. Once the criteria for ending the loop are encountered, the loop is "exited" and the program continues.

> Sincerely,
> John Walter Putre
> North Pownal, Vermont

Dear Mr. Safire,

You give a derivation of "closing the loop" which I believe to be incorrect. The term, I believe, comes from control theory, a branch of engineering.

A closed-loop control system is one in which the "output," the quantity to be controlled, is compared with the "input," the desired quantity. The difference, or "error," is then used to control the system. Thus, the output is "fed back" to the input to form a "feedback loop."

An example is a home heating system. The heater raises the temperature; this is compared with the temperature setting of the thermostat, and the difference turns the heater on or off. Another example is the steering of a car. The driver watches the position of the car on the road, and corrects any errors by turning the wheel. Without the driver, the car would be "open-loop." The driver is literally in the loop; he may be said to close the loop.

The colloquial use of the term appears to be a proper one—to be part of the decision-making process is equivalent to being in the loop of a control process.

> *Sincerely,*
> *Herbert Winter*
> *Snyder, New York*

Dear Mr. Safire:

... Take it from an engineer that "closing the loop" is the most important concept extant, possibly excepting "mushroom cloud." One can mention Norbert Wiener as father of control theory, wherein systems have the effects of their power controlled by "closing the loop." This control is effected by comparing the actual ouptut of a system to the desired output, and "feeding back" the result of this comparison to be mixed with the input. For a system having the ability to amplify or "snowball" its input into a large output, injecting our "feedback" control signal into the input, where the system is sensitive to small changes, controls the amplification. Such systems include Wiener's radar antennae, my hi-fi, seed money, the prime interest rate, and letters to The Times.

> *Thomas Spettel*
> *Milford, New Hampshire*

---

wholesale

In a grave near "welfare," the adjective "wholesale" has been interred. The "Wholesale Price Index" is no more; the Bureau of Labor Statistics changed the name last year to the "Producer Price Index." The "Wholesale Price Index" (born 1902, died 1978) began to rise too fast to suit wholesalers. The attention focused on the index by inflation was beginning to give the profession a bad name.

"The wholesalers' association wanted a change," says John Early, chief of the bureau's Division of Industrial Prices and Price Indexes, "but so did just about everybody." Names that were considered included "Sellers' Price Index," "Primary Market Price Index," "Industrial Price Index," but it was "Producer Price Index"—in sharp contrast to "Consumer Price Index"—that was finally chosen by then-Commissioner Julius Shiskin.

The vice chairman of the board of the National Association of Wholesalers, William McCamant, stoutly denies that any derogation has attached to the word "wholesaler," but the name of the organization was changed in 1970 to "National Association of Wholesaler-Distributors." (The word "jobber" mainly denotes a small-scale wholesaler, and "middleman" is considered a fighting word.)

"The index is not our price, it's our cost," says N.A.W. chief McCamant, to dissociate his group from the idea of "middleman's profit." Wheat is a "raw" product; flour is a "semifinished" product; bread is a "finished" product, and the Producer Price Index for "finished goods," which is the one you see quoted most often, measures the change in the price of the bread sold by the baker to the distributor. The recent price jumps, then, are not primarily the middleman's fault, which is why he is happy no longer to be fingered in the index.

---

whom, *see* salutations

---

whorehouse

What determines when a "dirty word" is acceptable and when it is not? The answer usually depends on whether the word is being used in public or private, in conversation or in print, or in what used to be called "mixed company." But not in the case of "whorehouse": There, context determines whether the word is obscene or acceptable.

As part of the title of a current musical play, *The Best Little Whorehouse in Texas,* the word has been appearing regularly in all New York newspapers and many magazines. Advertising-acceptability departments reported no complaints from readers; perhaps the public's readiness to accept the word in theater advertisements stems from the occasional revival of *'Tis Pity She's a Whore,* a play about incest by John Ford first performed about 1630, as well as from the 46 times the word "whore" was used in the plays of Shakespeare.

Since nobody had objected to the name of the play in advertising, the producers of the musical took a step further: "Have Fun at 'The Whorehouse' " was the message displayed on 80 New York City Transit Authority buses. Single quotation marks, like little fig leaves, were draped around the words "The Whorehouse," as if to preserve modesty by oblique reference to a title of a performance in the legitimate theater.

But that new context, introducing a double meaning, overstepped the bounds of propriety; buses emblazoned "Have Fun at 'The Whorehouse' " offended many New Yorkers, including a representative of Terence Cardinal Cooke. The double meaning was obviously deliberate, intended to cover both the spectator sport of watching a dramatic performance and the dramatic sport available at a sporting house.

The Transit Authority decided the controversy was no fun at all. It ordered the signs removed from the buses, thereby providing a laboratory case of the "dirtiness" of a word: It ain't what you say, it's the context in which you say it.

As part of a title of a work of art, or as the subject of a beard-pulling inquiry such as this, "whorehouse" raises no eyebrows because it is once removed from reality. But blaring its invitation on the side of a bus, and playing on the more direct meaning, "whorehouse" holds fast to its taboo.

Dear Mr. Safire,

Your remarks about the context respectability of Whorehouse *reminded me that in 1967 our Performing Arts Company at Michigan State University produced Ford's* Tis Pity She's A Whore. *Our practice was to print a brochure containing the titles of all our plays for the season and mail it to students. The university editors objected to a university sponsored brochure appearing in the homes of students' parents containing the word* whore. *Likewise the university newspaper which now freely advertizes porno films objected to the word* whore *in print.*

Consequently, we advertized the play as Tis Pity She's A ———. *This concession to print morality was exceedingly profitable since the reader could respond with whatever perversions his or her imagination could conjure: lesbian, fucker, deviant, etc. This leeway in filling in the blank produced a large and enthusiastic audience for this antique and relatively unknown play.*

Sincerely,
Frank C. Rutledge
Chairman, Department of Theatre
Michigan State University
East Lansing, Michigan

who/whom

A mistake in tiny type can trouble you for days, but a gaffe in a headline can haunt you for years. Especially when it is more than a typographical error.

The most egregious big-type blunder in recent months was the creation of a hapless headline writer on *The New York Post:* A banner head that shouted: "CAREY TO UNIONS—TOW THE LINE OR ELSE." Evidently Governor Hugh Carey had called for union leaders to "toe the line," a metaphor taken from placing one's foot at the starting line at the beginning of a race, which was mistaken for towing a line like a tugboat.

In the same way, a right-wing columnist who should have known better headlined an essay about which side to take on local wars in these words: "Who to Root For." A legion of who-dinis (or a strikeover of correctors) took exception to the use of "who" as an object; a virtual "Whom's Whom" of protesters made their views known. Sorry about that; but "Whom to Root For" looked *too* right, as if the writer was straining to show he knew when to use "whom." Safire's New Law of Who/Whom: In Headlines, When "Whom" Is Correct, Use Some Other Formulation.

Dear Mr. Safire,

In Two Years Before the Mast *Dana records an example in which the phrase "toe the mark" is used (chapter 27—3 pages in). To "toe the mark" is to maintain your honor as a man among men. Given the assertive characteristic carried in "toeing the line" I think the shipboard robustness of Dana's era is more likely father of the orphaned phrase in question.*

> *Roy W. Penny*
> *New York, New York*

Dear Mr. Safire:

"as if the writer was straining to show . . ." Doesn't this call for the subjunctive "were"?

> *Mrs. B. G. Rosenwasser*
> *Rego Park, New York*

Yes, but if I were to correct my own articles before reprinting them, the point would hardly be made. —W.S.

Mr. Safire,

As regards your recent statement that you are "down on whom," even in instances where its use would be correct, I beg you to remember what happens when one asks 'For Who the Bell Tolls.'

It tolls for he.

> *yours faithfully,*
> *William Paul Wittman*
> *New York, New York*

windfall, *see* **June bugs**

wiseguy problem

Everyone who cares about the use of language is faced sooner or later with this problem: When the person you are talking to makes a mistake in grammar, or pronounces a word mistakenly, do you interrupt with a correction? Or would such a correction be seen as a put-down, the action of a wiseguy? Or would failure to correct be taken as agreement with the mistake?

The wiseguy problem especially afflicts interviewers of public figures. I had the problem a few months ago in a talk with Governor Jerry Brown of California.

The Governor, who likes to use unfamiliar words to clothe fresh ideas, was talking about space-age projects in California "as a synecdoche for the world's future space interest." He used the word "synecdoche" correctly, as part to be taken for the whole—as one speaks of "head" for cattle.

But he pronounced it wrong. He said "SY-neck-doash," when the Greek-rooted word should be pronounced "sin-EK-doe-key," roughly rhyming with "Schenectady." The problem in interviewing etiquette: Do you say "Hey, Guv, you tripped over your booklarnin'," or do you quietly ignore the error? I started to ignore it, but my conscience nagged—what if he made that mistake during a televised Presidential debate? Would my failure to correct him cost him the Oval Office?

I compromised by handling it obliquely: Later in the interview, I asked a question using the word as if repeating his own use, but pronouncing it correctly. That was intended to show him how to use the word correctly without requiring an overt correction, thus keeping faith with grammarians while not being a wiseguy. "If the pen is mightier than the sword—to use a couple of synecdoches, Governor, as you did before . . ."

I dribbled off onto another subject, but the Governor stopped me: "Is that how you pronounce it? I'd seen the word in print, but I never heard anybody pronounce it before." That was direct and disarming: My fancy footwork was for naught.

But not all speakers are so willing to learn. (I had been pronouncing "chimera" as "shimmera" for years, until some wiseguy little kid insisted rightly it was "ky-MEER-a.") To get the etiquette from the expert, I wrote to Letitia Baldrige, editor of the latest edition of *The Amy Vanderbilt Complete Book of Etiquette.* Her answer:

"If the Mary Joneses correct the John Smiths of this world, I think it hurts. I think the following people have the right to correct the 'one they

love' or 'the one they respect,' and the person who stands corrected should consider it quite natural:

"Parents correcting children; teachers correcting children; employers correcting employees; married people and lovers correcting each other to help the other person out."

That makes sense. Correcting a stranger's English is impolite at best, cruel at worst. It's being a wiseguy, who is the sort of linguistic show-off who has to tell you that "wiseguy" and "wisenheimer" were preceded by "wiseacre," derived from the Dutch word *"wijssegger,"* or "soothsayer." As for the person taking pen in hand at this moment to point out that Webster's New World Dictionary writes "wiseguy" as two words—you know what you are.

Dear Mr. Safire:

As a professional language nut myself, I enjoyed "The Wiseguy Problem." However, the phrasing of your lead disturbs me. How can "the person you are talking to" make a mistake in grammar or pronunciation?

It seems the resident wiseguys on the copy desk let you down. One of them should have suggested, at least, that the phrase read: "the person talking to you."

> *Cordially,*
> *John Artopoeus*
> *Editorial Director*
> *Burson-Marsteller*
> *New York, New York*

Dear Mr. Safire,

I brought your article "The Wiseguy Problem" to my English Composition class and discussed with them the meaning of synecdoche and your example (as given to Governor Brown). Now, sir, we had a bad split in the class....

*We find (at least some of us do) that "The pen is mightier than the sword"
gives examples of* metonymy *rather than synecdoche—that is, the expressions
"pen" and "sword" stand for a closely related idea more than they represent a
part of a whole.*

> Sincerely,
> Charles R. Lefcourt
> English Dept.
> SUC Buffalo
> Buffalo, New York

Dear William Safire:

*Word from another wiseguy to add to the heap of response from your item
on the problem of interrupting.*

*The way to have handled your difficulty with Jerry Brown would have been
to interrupt. Promptly.*

*"I'm sorry, Governor. Is that the way to pronounce the word? I always heard
people say "sin-EK-doe-key"; it sounds really Greek!"*

*His learnability, as you later discovered, would have opened up a pleasant
discussion (maybe better than space-age projects). And I'm sure there must
have been a pronouncing dictionary within reach, which would have settled the
matter for both of you.*

*This is the gee-but-I'm-dumb technique. Best application I have ever re-
corded involved the red-necked, oil-rich, multimillionaire who had bulled,
bribed and threatened his way into membership of the very, very, very exclusive
club. When his habit of spitting on the carpet in the main lounge was protested
by members, the House Committee turned the problem over to his sponsor, a
banker whose commercial viability leaned on the oil-man's wealth. He met the
oil-man for drinks in the lounge, lit a cigar, ostentatiously spit on the carpet
himself then quickly said, "Migawd, Herb. I forgot. We've got to quit spitting
on the carpet or we'll get tossed out. The members are complaining."*

> Regards,
> Colin Haworth
> Montreal, Quebec

Dear Mr. Safire,

*Regarding your "synecdoche" anecdote, the last line reads, "My fancy foot-
work was for naught." Haven't you left out a* not?

> Sincerely,
> Barbara Bernstein
> Rockville Centre, New York

No—W.S.

working group

"Appoint a committee" used to be the political answer to charges of confusion and inaction. When the word "committee" became synonymous with "delay" in an impatient public's mind, a new, active-sounding phrase was employed: The politician would crisply and authoritatively "designate a task force," which had the connotation of aircraft carriers churning resolutely toward Midway Island and a rendezvous with destiny.

Government task forces proliferated in the 1960's, if only to accomplish the mission of task forcing. Members of these task forces occasionally verbified their own favorite noun by saying "We've been tasked to . . ."

When the task forces were recognized as the same old committees wearing gold braid and epaulets, a new term was sought to convey action rather than consultation. The preferred new word comes from British military aviation, which has since been adopted by British business executives: the Group. (In late-night television movies, the Group Leader is the handsome one who usually crashes.)

Accordingly, when a bunch of guys get together in the White House Situation Room to figure out how to shape an image or sell a treaty, they now call themselves a Group. In the case of SALT (Strategic Arms Limitation Talks), the Group has added a refinement: Since the way to justify time taken for a long midday meal is to call it a "working lunch," and since the way to get a few weeks in the sun is to take a "working vacation," the name of the most modern committee is a "Working Group." Presumably, "the SALT Working Group," as it is officially designated, can thus be distinguished from, say, "the SALT Playing Group," or "the SALT Lollygagging Group."

One day soon, someone will appoint a committee to designate a task force to assemble a working group to pick a new name for a committee.

In your zeal to equate "Task force" with "committee," I think that you have overlooked an important distinction between the words.

For example, it is possible for a group of people to be designated by an authority to gather information on a controversial subject that will not favor one side or the other. This group reports back with or without a recommendation of its own. This to me is what a "committee" should do.

In contrast to this idea, is that of the "task force" a group also designated by an authority but charged with marshalling material favorable to a stated objective, ignoring other pertinent matters. For example, William Safire is an individual self-appointed task force dedicated to denigrating President Carter.*

Another example showing the difference between a committee and a task force is Mr. Nixon's Committee to Reelect the President (CREEP). In this case I think the word "committee" is erroneously used and that the group was really a "Task force." The "committee" members were not interested in whether the president should be reelected, but used every device, legal and illegal to complete their task.

A committee should be an open-eyed and open minded group while a task force is more or less mindless and acts with blinders.

> *Sincerely,*
> *George F. Adams*
> *Bridgewater, New Jersey*

* P.S. Referring to paragraph 3, it is only fair to point out that you are also a committee of one to arbitrate the usage of words.

---

yule

Why do carolers grimly insist that " 'tis the season to be jolly"?

Because it is yuletide, when the yule log is burned. To the cheery "Merry Christmas," aging hipsters reply "Have one cool yule."

Whence "yule"? From the Old English "geohol," a name for a month slopping into January, corresponding to the Old Norse "jol," a heathen feast taking place about the winter solstice—and "jol" is the source of "jolly," which 'tis the season to be.

I would send "season's greetings," except that I think it should be "seasonal greetings."

Dear Sir:

"Season's greetings" is one of many seasonal greetings used in the United States. Others are "Happy Easter," "Happy Independence Day," "Happy Thanksgiving," etc. There are many seasonal greetings. There is only one "Season's greetings." The latter applies only to the Christmas-New Year period.

Sincerely
Richard Patrick Wilson
Mobile, Alabama

ZIP codes

Nobody resents language change that comes about naturally; for example, people who once said of their mental state, "I'm hurting," now say, "I'm in pain," and we accept this as a normal turnover of vogue terms. But resentment and resistance set in when language change is dictated or promoted by government.

For example, *The New York Times* recently adopted the Pinyin system of converting Chinese characters into the Roman alphabet. Mao Tse-tung became Mao Zedong, and Teng Hsiao-ping became Deng Xiaoping (Teng, we hardly know ye), because the Government in Peking decided that its new spelling more faithfully represents the pronunciation of the language, and the United States and United Nations agreed.

But *The Times* dug in its heels at four names: Peking will not become "Beijing" in its pages, nor will Canton become "Guangzhou"; nor Inner Mongolia, "Nei Monggol," and Tibet will certainly not be written Xizang (land of pizazz).

In a more subdued manner, the United States Postal Service has been pushing through a change in the way we abbreviate our states. No more three- or four-letter abbreviations: Two letters is all you're allowed. Thus, "Mass." becomes "MA," to go with Pennsylvania's "PA," and Mississippi goes along with a feminist trend from "Miss." to "MS." Alaskans are labeled, or libeled, "AK." Familiar two-letter abbreviations stay the same, without the periods—"DC" and "NJ" and "NY" and "KY," for example—but traditionalists find jarring such designations as "CT" for "Conn." and "IN" for "Ind." Letters to Kansas are to be sealed with a "KS."

Under a zippy headline of "OH, but WY, ME?" columnist Neal Peirce objected: "The two-letter abbreviations are designed for confusion. . . . How

are we to remember that AK stands for Alaska rather than Arkansas, that MI means Michigan, not Mississippi or Minnesota, that CO stands for Colorado rather than Connecticut, and NE is for Nebraska and not Nevada?"

A Postal Service spokesman, dedicated to the swift completion of his appointed state names, informs me that the abbreviations, which the postal people have been gently promoting since 1963, "are provided for use on addressing equipment that will not accommodate unusually long city and state names *and* the ZIP code."

In other words, the new abbreviations are a convenience to addressing machines. It saves money if the address is on fewer lines, so the Postal Service—desperate to get companies to use the really necessary ZIP codes—gave back a little space on the state names.

I am not interested in making life easier for machines in general, or for junk mailers in particular, and will continue to write the whole "Iowa" rather than "IA," and the sunny "Calif." rather than the cold "CA."

In fairness to the mailman, we should recognize that he does not insist on the new system. It's entirely voluntary. If you use the old abbreviations, or even if you laboriously write out the whole state name (at the cost of God knows how much trouble and ink), the mail will go through.

And here's the beauty part: *As long as you use the right ZIP code, you do not have to write in the state or city at all.* That is not generally known, even to addressing machines, and it is not a tip I would put to the test, but it's true.

Resistance to change by bureaucratic fiat—fighting the Chinese mailman—can be successful. A few years ago, the House Foreign Affairs Committee—jealous of the Senate Foreign Relations Committee and vaguely embarrassed at the double meaning of "affairs"—changed its name to the more modern, stately, august "House International Relations Committee." Recently, the committee members officially changed it back to the old name: "It just didn't catch on," says Benjamin Rosenthal, D.-N.Y. (or Dem., N.Y.). "One of the members said that after 4 o'clock in the afternoon, he had a hard time remembering the name of the committee, so we said the hell with it and went back to House Foreign Affairs."

Acknowledgments

"Shame on you!" "You, of all people!" That's how a great deal of my mail begins, and how a great many of my columns originate. Contrary to the belief of conspiracy-theorists, I do not deliberately make mistakes, although I will occasionally take the chance on a bit of usage or speculate on some etymology to see what corrections will come in.

At *The New York Times,* my cap is reverently doffed to Executive Editor A. M. Rosenthal, whose idea it was to thrust me into the language dodge on a weekly basis.

New York Times Magazine editor Edward Klein guided me away from turgidity and calmed my queasiness about breeziness. My op-ed political columny is blessed by two of the most careful, sagacious, and skilful copy readers known to pundits: Robert Barzilay and Betty Pomerantz. My Sunday language column is examined by the eagle eyes of Sherwin Smith and Phyllis Shapiro, who have saved me from hundreds—yes, hundreds, that's no hype—of shame-on-yous. ("Hype" is from hypodermic needle, a drug culture shortening of "hyped up" meaning "to get high," later applied to any exaggeration, such as "media hype." My children think it comes from "hyperbole" or "hypocrisy," but what do kids know?)

At the Washington bureau of the *Times,* where shame-on-you letters should be sent (1000 Connecticut Avenue, Washington, D.C. 20036), I am assisted in research by Margaret Miller ("Peggy—how come people are using 'as far as' when they mean 'as for'? And why can't I use 'how come'?"). Kathie Wellde, cookbook author and my secretary, also lends a hand on locutions. At Times Books, production editor Pamela Lyons, copy editor John Carter, and proofreader Sharon Kapnick made a bunch of last-minute saves.

Professional lexicographers and linguists never fail to respond to a query. The wordniks I turn to most often are David Guralnik, editor of Simon & Schuster's New World Dictionary; Fred Mish, editorial director of Merriam-Webster; Anne Soukhanov, associate editor of Houghton Mifflin's American Heritage; Sol Steinmetz, editor of the Second Barnhart Dictionary of New English, and Laurence Urdang, editor of *Verbatim,* the language quarterly. On usage, the most helpful usagarian, or usagist, has been Jacques Barzun, editor of Wilson Follett's *Modern American Usage.*

The driving force behind *The New York Times Manual of Style and Usage*—News Editor Allan M. Siegal—is a winner who tolerates sinners, and has been an unfailing source of good advice even if he refuses to put a "k" in Quebecer.

For Americanisms, my resources include Professor Frederic Cassidy at the University of Wisconsin, now at work on the Dictionary of American

Regional English, often identified herein as "the man from DARE"; Stuart Berg Flexner, author of *I Hear America Talking* and chief lexicographer of the Oxford American Dictionary; Peter Tamony, whose apartment in San Francisco is jampacked with citations of the most arcane slang (he's remarkable on "hot-dog"); and Professor Emeritus I. Willis Russell, of the University of Alabama, who oversees the "Among the New Words" section of *American Speech* magazine.

Inspiration's acknowledgment is due to William Cobbett, an early nineteenth-century English polemicist and vituperator who taught himself to write and later wrote an influential grammar. He is the "Peter Porcupine" to whom this book is dedicated.

The most fervent (either "fervent" or "fervid" will do) thanks go to the Lexicographic Irregulars. These are the people who care about clarity and who take the time to write about their pets, invariably named Peeve. They respond to queries, too, turning up material that few researchers could assemble. Their comments, suggestions, and emendations make up the best part of this book and brighten my days.

Index

Index

Index

Index

Index

Index